The Yoga of Love

Dance of Divine Love: The Wondrous Circle of the Rāsa Maṇḍala

Painting by Kim Waters commissioned by the author.

The Yoga of Love

Krishna and the Rāsa Līlā from the Bhāgavata Purāṇa

GRAHAM M. SCHWEIG

OXFORD
UNIVERSITY PRESS

Oxford University Press is a department of the University of Oxford.
It furthers the University's objective of excellence in research, scholarship,
and education by publishing worldwide. Oxford is a registered trade mark of
Oxford University Press in the UK and certain other countries.

Adapted from Dance of Divine Love: India's Sacred Love Story:
The Rasa Lila of Krishna by Graham M. Schweig.

Published in the United States of America by Oxford University Press
198 Madison Avenue, New York, NY 10016, United States of America.

Library of Congress Cataloging-in-Publication Data
Names: Schweig, Graham M., 1953- author.
Title: The yoga of love : Krishna and the Rāsa Līlā from the
Bhāgavata Purāṇa / Graham M. Schweig.
Description: 1. | New York, NY : Oxford University Press, [2025] |
Includes bibliographical references and index. |
Identifiers: LCCN 2025002475 (print) | LCCN 2025002476 (ebook) |
ISBN 9780197768433 (paperback) | ISBN 9780197768426 (hardback) |
ISBN 9780197818619 | ISBN 9780197768457 (epub)
Subjects: LCSH: Puranas. Bhāgavatapurāṇa—Criticism, interpretation, etc. |
Rāsa līlā (Dance) | Krishna (Hindu deity) | Radha (Hindu deity)
Classification: LCC BL1140.4.B436 S39 2025 (print) | LCC BL1140.4.B436
(ebook) | DDC 294.5/925—dc23/eng/20250128
LC record available at https://lccn.loc.gov/2025002475
LC ebook record available at https://lccn.loc.gov/2025002476

DOI: 10.1093/oso/9780197768426.001.0001

Paperback printed by Marquis Book Printing, Canada
Hardback printed by Bridgeport National Bindery, Inc., United States of America

The manufacturer's authorised representative in the EU for product safety is Oxford University Press España S.A. of El Parque Empresarial San Fernando de Henares, Avenida de Castilla, 2 – 28830 Madrid (www.oup.es/en or product.safety@oup.com). OUP España S.A. also acts as importer into Spain of products made by the manufacturer.

Overjoyed by
the touch of Krishna,
the whole universe
became filled
with their song.

Rāsa Līlā 5.9

Contents

PART III DANCE OF DIVINE LOVE | THE RĀSA LĪLĀ

PART IV BACKGROUND OF THE TEXT

PART V MESSAGES OF THE TEXT

PART VI THE SANSKRIT TEXTS

About the Paintings

COVER

Love Call of the Divine: Krishna's Intense Yearning
The picture on the front cover is a digital reproduction of an original work painted for this book, depicting the beginning scene of the Rāsa Līlā dramatic poem. The painting illustrates the Bhāgavata Purāṇa, Book 10, Chapter 29, Verses 1 through 4 (or Rāsa Līlā, Act One, Scene 1, specifically verse 3).

FRONTISPIECE

Dance of Divine Love: The Wondrous Circle of the Rāsa Maṇḍala
This painting illustrates the ultimate scene of the Rāsa Līlā drama, Krishna's eternal dance of divine love with the Vraja Gopikās, or cowherd maidens, described in the first scene of twenty verses within the final chapter or act of the dramatic poem. Bhāgavata Purāṇa, Book 10, Chapter 33, Verses 1 through 20 (or Rāsa Līlā, Act Five, Scene 1, specifically verse 20).

The five paintings reproduced in this book were executed by fine artist Kim Waters of Bethesda, Maryland, in her own unique style of painting, inspired by traditional Indian as well as western forms of art. The book's author worked closely with the artist to determine the general composition of the paintings and many of their details. The medium: pen and ink, with opaque watercolor, acrylic gouache, and pastel on archival cold press illustration board (39" x 31"). The paintings were commissioned by the author and funded by generous gifts from David R. Petree of Dallas, Texas.

Figures and Tables

Figures

Tables

Preface

This Edition

The contents of this book are derived from my original work, *Dance of Divine Love: India's Classic Sacred Love Story, The Rāsa Līlā of Krishna from the Bhāgavata Purāṇa*, published by Princeton University Press in 2005. This softcover printing is an abridged edition of the original, reducing the 448-page hardcover book to almost half the length. It leaves out most of the content found within the Notes and Comments section. It also eliminates the critical apparatuses found in its appendices.

However, the contents preserved here have been edited to suit a wider readership, and my essay-chapters have also been rearranged from the original for a somewhat different focus—thus, the new title for this work. In effect, framing the heart of the work, namely, the translated passages of the Rāsa Līlā drama and poetry, are the sixteen chapters—the first eight prior to the translated text, and the second eight following the translated portions.

Despite the abridgement of the original work, some new material has been added to several of the chapters as well as several newly commissioned paintings. Also, there are just a few small improvements in the translation itself. I have also provided full English transliterations of the original Sanskrit text for both the Song of the Flute and the Song of the Black Bee sections, as well as for the Dance of Divine Love, The Rāsa Līlā.

Academic Background

My focus on the subject matter of this book, and the original work from which it is derived, arose many years ago during my doctoral studies in the field of the comparative study of religion at Harvard University. Back then, for quite some time while pursuing graduate school, my intention for a dissertation was a comparative theological focus on Catholic Christian and Vaishnava Hindu mysticisms of divine love. However, my doctoral mentor, Professor John B. Carman, guided me to focus exclusively on the highest vision of the Vaishnava side of the comparison, which is, for the Chaitanya school of Vaishnavism, the Rāsa Līlā—the famous five-chapter poem in the Bhāgavata Purāṇa—the story of Krishna with the cowherd maidens of Vraja that leads up to the climactic event of Krishna's great circle dance of divine love with his eternal beloveds. Thus, I was directed to focus on the Rāsa Līlā and its interpretation since it had received far less scholarly treatment than its Christian counterparts. In doing so, I was preparing the highest vision of the Vaishnava tradition for more comparative work in the future.

Even early on during my graduate studies, I was inspired by Professor Daniel H. H. Ingalls, my teacher of Sanskrit, whose strong words claim that "the *Bhāgavata* remains, especially in its tenth book, the most enchanting poem ever written."[1] Indeed, I had attended several readings from the tenth book that Professor Ingalls offered occasionally to students in his home at the time, when he focused upon the traditionally most treasured early chapters of the tenth book. I was struck by how these stories clearly moved Ingalls when he focused on the stories of Krishna in the village of Vrindāvana as beautiful poetry. For example, Ingalls expresses eloquently his appreciation of Krishna's divine realm in the following words: "the world appears as a magic land where every object, if

[1] Foreword in *Krishna: Myths, Rites, and Attitudes*, edited by Milton Singer (Chicago: University of Chicago Press, 1966), p. vi.

only it is rightly seen, is a key to truth and to eternity."[2] Additionally, during a semester's course on these precious portions of the Bhāgavata that was taught by Professor Sheldon Pollock, who at that time was a visiting scholar at Harvard, I encountered yet again the power and beauty of the text.

[2] Ibid., p. vii.

Acknowledgments

First, I would like to acknowledge A. C. Bhaktivedanta Swami Prabhupāda, the inaugural world-teacher of Krishna *bhakti*, who introduced to the West, and then to the major cultures around the globe, the tradition from sacred India that most treasures the vision of the Rāsa Līlā. He claimed that "the greatest benediction" for humans is to be lifted up into Krishna's highest heaven and "dance there with Krishna in the Rāsa Līlā."[3] For it was the Swami who introduced to the world, starting back in the 1960s, the rich teachings of Vaishnava philosophy and theology, and specifically the philosophical depths of the Chaitanya tradition in which the Rāsa Līlā as its ultimate vision is celebrated.

My gratitude naturally goes to Professor John B. Carman, my academic mentor during my doctoral studies at Harvard, for his direction that ultimately led to the writing of the dissertation, the very foundational work from which ultimately this volume comes. I would also like to recognize Professor Norvin Hein, formerly a professor at Yale University, for the many enlightening visits to his home in Bethany, Connecticut, where we would ponder together the text of the Bhāgavata's Rāsa Pañcādhyāyī, or the five chapters on the Rāsa dance.

I am grateful to Cynthia Read, the former long-time, executive senior editor of religion at Oxford University Press, with whom I had worked on previous projects, for her encouragement and her efforts in negotiating with Princeton University Press to be licensed to publish this book. I am also grateful to the current editor

[3] Recorded conversation with John Lennon, Yoko Ono, and George Harrison.

at Oxford, Thomas Perridge, and his capable staff, who have seen this work through production and to completion as a book.

I would like to thank my dear friend and colleague, Miranda Shaw, professor *emerita* at the University of Richmond, who constructed the book's index. Her own excellent scholarship makes her indexing especially sensitive to and valuable for this work. And then my gratitude goes to fine artist Kim Waters, who is also a dear friend, whose newly created five commissioned paintings have contributed much to the illumination of the drama and poetry of my translated text. The five paintings for this book are richly endowed with color in their original form, as can be seen with the color reproduction of her painting adorning the front cover. However, these colorful renditions also reproduce beautifully here in this work in a greyscale presentation.

Financial support from various sources has been essential for the preparation of this work. The creation of these paintings was made possible by the generosity of my dear friend and supporter of my work, David R. Petree of Dallas, Texas. Art is the soul of a culture, and private donors such as David, who is a great lover of the arts, ensure that the arts remain at the heart of cultural life. I am also very grateful for the grant I received from the Uberoi Foundation for Religious Studies, which allowed me to conduct research in which I was able to develop further some important parts of this work. Finally, the subvention funds grant I received from the Provost's Office at Christopher Newport University was very helpful for completing different aspects of the book, preparing it for publication.

The process of turning my original work into the present abridged form is fully credited to the hard work of Catherine, my best friend, my wife, my beloved partner in everything. As a writer and a poet in her own right, she adds a reader-friendly dimension to the whole work that was not there in the original book. In some places, she even embellishes and appropriately adds to the text eloquently. Catherine is my best critic, my constant source of inspiration, and my rigorous content editor. But it will always be the case that Catherine will never know how much she energizes me in all my writing and teaching.

Graham M. Schweig
Śrī Krishna Janmāṣṭami Mahotsava
August 26, 2024

Abbreviations

Translations from foreign language texts presented throughout this work are the author's unless otherwise credited to others.

BG	Bhagavad Gītā
BhP	Bhāgavata Purāṇa
CC	Krishnadāsa Kavirāja Gosvāmī, *Caitanya Caritāmṛta* (Gauḍīya Mission ed.)
KK	Līlaśuka Bilvamaṅgala, *Kṛṣṇa Karnāmṛta*
MW	*Sanskṛit-English Dictionary* by Sir M. Monier-Williams
NBS	*Nārada Bhakti Sūtra*
PrS	Jīva Gosvāmī, *Prīti Sandarbha* (in *Bhāgavata Sandarbha*)
RL	Rāsa Līlā
RLP	Rāsa Līlā Pañcādhyāyī (The Five Chapters of the Rāsa Līlā) from the Bhāgavata Purāṇa
SD	Viśvanātha Cakravartin, *Sārārtha Darśinī*
TS	Jīva Gosvāmī, *Tattva Sandarbha* (in *Bhāgavata Sandarbha*)
VA	*The Practical Sanskrit-English Dictionary* by Vaman Shivaram Apte
WEB	*Webster's Third New International Dictionary*
YS	Yoga Sūtra of Patañjali

Introduction

When Divinity Calls Our Souls to Dance

A Revelation of the Innermost Heart

The Yoga of Love is about an ultimate calling of souls—a calling to unite with the highest, the All—a love-call that comes from the sound of the flute played by Krishna as depicted on the front cover of this book. This union into which this love-call invites souls takes the form of an eternal dance of divine love that is described in the beautiful flowing poetic verses from the Sanskrit, the translations of which are presented herein.

Ancient sages describe the heart as the seat of the soul, and, therefore, the realm in which the soul and divinity come together forever. As such, the heart is also known as the dwelling-place of the divine and the sacred source of the highest knowledge. When the soul lovingly embraces the divine within the heart, it ultimately manifests as a joyful dance, constituting the perfection of all meditation and all yoga practices:

> Total ecstatic absorption, *samādhi*,
> and the perfection of this very state,
> is achieved because one's relationship
> with the divine core of all reality, *īśvara*,
> has been established by moving deeply
> into the space within the heart.[1]

[1] The Yoga Sūtra, Sādhana Pāda 45: *samādhi-siddhir īśvara-praṇidhānāt.* All translated aphorisms in this work are from my book, *The Yoga Sūtra: Patañjali's Concise Teachings on Perfect Union*, forthcoming from Yale University Press. All translations in this book are my own unless otherwise indicated.

The Yoga of Love. Graham M. Schweig, Oxford University Press. © Oxford University Press 2025.
DOI: 10.1093/oso/9780197768426.003.0001

A powerful example of this most elevated state in yoga is India's classical sacred love story, presented here in this book, known for its very fine poetic verse.

This poem can be read as great literature and the exquisite poetry for which it is known. Or, it can be read as a revelation of the heart, and its practice known as *bhakti*—the offering of all one's heart to the divine in perfect love. Indeed, *the sacred story in poetry presented herein reveals a dramatization of the inner workings of the heart.* These inner workings involve four stages through which the heart must go to ultimately attain the full perfection or the yoga of love:

(1) *The worldly conditioning of the heart*
The world, most fundamentally, suffers from an impoverishment of the heart, and yet the universe, in the end, is a most loving place. In the drama presented herein, the human condition is symbolized by the female protagonists, the cowherd maidens, Vraja Gopikās (or simply Gopīs), who find themselves in their homes performing their motherly and wifely duties. Indeed, their hearts were in many ways lovingly absorbed in domestic activities, but the eternally perfect fulfillment of the whole heart had yet to be achieved.[2]

(2) *An awakening and opening of the heart*
The divine most ardently sends out a love-call for each soul to hear for entering into the ultimate loving state of the divine.

[2] The beginnings of several of the great sacred writings of India contrast with the start of western sacred texts, such as the Hebrew Bible, the New Testament, and the Qur'ān. While western sacred books immediately reveal the identity of God, divine attributes and acts, and sacred nomenclature, the major sacred texts of India focused on the divinity of Krishna launch with some expression of the human condition: the Rāmāyana's prologue begins with the cruel hunter's senseless killing of a male crane in a tree with his lover; the Bhāgavata begins with a cursed king who seeks a sage to prepare for death; the Bhagavad Gītā begins with Arjuna's breakdown precipitated by the irresolvable ethical dilemma as to whether he should engage in warfare with loved ones on the opposing side of the battlefield. Each of these texts begins with some aspect of the human condition while only gradually introducing the divine reality in all its grand and intimate splendor.

This stage is symbolized by the scenes in which the Vraja Gopikās are suddenly awakened from their worldly situations by the love-call in the form of flute music coming from Krishna. They either ran out to the forest to be with Krishna, or they went deep into meditation to be with Krishna in their hearts. Either way, the Vraja Gopikās open their hearts to Krishna, which symbolizes how the heart becomes more and more open to the source of love.[3]

(3) *The purification and deepening of the heart*

True teachers and sacred writings reveal that all of Reality, or the divine, lovingly embraces souls. The hearts of the Vraja Gopikās become more and more purified from even the slightest tinges of conditioning as their love for Krishna becomes evermore deepened. This stage symbolizes how the heart becomes completely transparent so that it can reach a perfect and eternal love.[4]

As powerful as the human condition is, as expressed by the tradition, the *bhakti* school of Chaitanya Vaishnavism (which will be introduced below in this Introduction) asserts that all conditioned beings have pure love, or *premā*, lying dormant within their hearts. And according to this tradition's analysis of the stages of achieving pure love, *premā*, and also the stages of deepening within pure love, faith, or *śraddhā*, is the first. The tradition draws from the Bhagavad Gītā's seventeenth chapter, in which *śraddhā*, or "where one places one's heart," is present in everyone. In the conditioned state, the soul places the heart on worldly things.

[3] The soul's movement from the first stage, "the worldly conditioning of the heart," to the second stage, "an awakening and opening of the heart," can be understood as the tradition's term, *sambandha*, or the "coming together into a relationship" with the divine. At this stage, a soul has placed the heart on the divine, *śraddhā*, the soul has come together with persons whose hearts have been purified and absorbed in divine love, *sādhu-saṅga*, and has now engaged in a sacred life of loving actions and connected to a holy lineage, *bhajana-kriyā*.

[4] The movement from the second stage to the third can be identified by the tradition's term of *abhidheya*, or "the application of practices." At this third stage of greater and greater levels of the heart's purification, such a soul discovers that all the meaningless things in life are now ineffectual, *anartha-nivṛtti*, one becomes very established in the practice of *bhakti* yoga, *niṣṭhā*, one acquires a natural taste for *bhakti* practices, *ruci*, and one eventually develops intense attachment to such practices, *āsakti*, to the point that

(4) *The free flowing and overflowing of the heart*
At this final perfect stage, souls return the embrace of the divine and attain the realm of eternal love. Such liberated souls can now turn to the world to nourish starving hearts. In the climactic scene of this drama, the Vraja Gopikās collectively enter the eternal dance of divine love in which they each have the exclusive attention of Krishna, the divinity. This stage symbolizes the heart's capacity to become full, freely overflowing in its abundance of loving energy that draws from and reciprocates with the divine source of all love. And such abundant, pure love also spills over into the hearts of all.[5]

The drama's final concluding verse declares that its poetry is meant to purify the heart. Once achieving a pure heart, its innermost workings can be realized—the human heart and the divine heart enter into a shared experience of boundless affection.

The greatest teachings of yoga call humans to achieve entrance into this joyful dance through the practice of meditation. The meaning of yoga is "union"—a uniting of the soul with the highest vision of an eternal beloved (or the divine) by taking a meditational pilgrimage within. This inner journey of the heart deepens the capacity to love, to be connected to the hearts of others, and to be in harmony with all of Reality.

one's heart is filled with affection for the divine, *bhāva*, the penultimate phase prior to achieving *premā* itself.

[5] The movement from the third stage to the final fourth stage can be identified by the tradition's term of *prayojana*, or "the attainment of perfection," that is, the attainment of purest love, or *premā*. After reached, *premā* also has seven stages of greater intensity: a tenderness in pure love, *sneha*; honor or pride in pure love, *māna*; affection in pure love, *praṇaya*; feelings of passion in pure love, *rāga*; a further intensification of passionate feelings in pure love, *anurāga*; a heart overflowing with uncontainable feelings of love, *bhāva*; and finally, such uncontainable feelings as they connect with the supremely overflowing love coming directly from the heart of the divine, *mahābhāva*, a loving energy that especially spills over into the hearts of those who have achieved the highest realms of *premā*, and also a loving energy that embraces all worlds and all beings.

The sacred story presented here and illuminated in these pages is known as the Rāsa Līlā.[6] I have loosely translated these two Sanskrit words as "dance of divine love." This dramatic poem reveals the ways divine love forever dances between hearts, and the ways in which one can experience how everything is ultimately embraced within and without by divine love. It is about how the deepest practice of yoga involves an experience of returning the embrace of the divine.

The Heart's Dance of Divine Love

What we love, and what we most love, is where we have placed our hearts—this is unquestionably the highest human value. Whether religiously oriented, or spiritually, even secularly or humanistically, all humans are most essentially beings at their core, who constantly, and ultimately, place their hearts on something. The Bhagavad Gītā boldly asserts that all humans are made of this energy of the heart, *śraddhā*: literally "where one's heart (*śrad-*) is placed (*-dhā*)."[7] Indeed, it is virtually inarguable that *it is love that is the most powerful striving in humans.* When the loving energy of one's heart flows to the hearts of others—especially to the heart of the divine—this is called *bhakti.*

At the core of all religion, genuine spirituality, and true humanistic or secularistic pursuits, naturally, therefore, is some form of

[6] The four-syllable phrase Rāsa Līlā (sometimes abbreviated as "RL" in this book) consists of two Sanskrit words pronounced phonetically "RAH—suh LEE—LAH" ("AH" as "a" in *father*, "uh" as "u" in *sun*, and "EE" as in *see*). In addition, definitions of key Sanskrit terms are listed in the Glossary. In Hindi, the second short syllable is dropped, pronounced as the three syllable phrase "RAH-s LEE—LAH." In Bengali, the second syllable is also dropped but is pronounced "RAW-sh LEE—LAH." The specific sacred text known as "Rāsa Līlā" is to be distinguished from the name used for the pilgrimage dramas of Vraja, known in Hindi as "*rās līlā.*" Note that the distinction is made clear in this work through the presentation of the latter term in lower case italic letters, with the Hindi spelling. For proper pronunciation of transliterated words from the Sanskrit language used throughout this book, please see Pronunciation of Sanskrit starting on page 268.

[7] The Sanskrit word *śraddhā* is most often translated simply by the English word "faith." When looking at the two parts of the word *śraddhā* and their meanings, we discover the meaning of the word "faith."

love, some cultivation of the heart. If we accept this premise, then it should be the case that every sacred or secular tradition—drawing upon its deepest expressions and practices—points to something universal, something that can speak to the hearts of all, something that rings true to all humans in every corner of the earth.

Yoga challenges humans in a most personal way: to discover that very place or highest thing on which one can place one's heart, the very highest thing one can love for a perfect union:

> Because of one's deep
> contemplation on the self
> and intensive sacred study,
> in this practice known as *svādhyāya*,
> one longs for what is most beloved
> in a form of divinity with whom
> one can come together in a perfect union.[8]

However, in this pilgrimage, or this contemplation into the deepest recesses of the heart, one must move out from one's own heart in order to totally absorb the self in the heart of another, ultimately the supreme other.

It is natural that humans should long for a union with the greatest source of all love, because all love originates in a divine source that most ardently loves and longs for them. This divine love for humans is most sweetly expressed by Krishna in the great conversation of the Bhagavad Gītā:

> The greatest secret of all,
> once more please hear again,
> for it is my supreme message:
> "You are so much loved by me!"[9]

[8] The Yoga Sūtra, Sādhana Pāda 44.

[9] Bhagavad Gītā, Chapter 18, verse 64abc. All translated verses from the Bhagavad Gītā are from my *Bhagavad Gītā: The Beloved Lord's Secret Love Song* (Harper Collins Publishers, 2010).

Thus, divinity longs for human hearts, embracing humans from without and from within, and from all around. In the Yoga Sūtra, Patañjali eloquently expresses how the liberated person embraces that divine reality which already embraces souls:

> The liberated person
> embraces the divine in everything,
> and is simultaneously embraced
> in every way by the divine—
> thus, the most profound discernment
> of otherness and indivisibility,
> as eternally co-existent aspects
> of all reality. can become known.[10]

Indeed, it is the rare soul who can rejoice with the following words, as Krishna states in his teachings:

> The divine is my all, my everything![11]

And in the perfection of yoga, humans return the embrace of the divine, as Krishna so eloquently and lovingly expresses in these words:

> One who sees me everywhere,
> and sees all things in me,
> To such a person I am never lost,
> nor is such a person ever lost to me.[12]

Patañjali explains that when humans are moved by a calling from the divine, they must attain a state of selflessness, a pure state

[10] The Yoga Sūtra, Vibhūti Pāda 54.
[11] Bhagavad Gītā, Chapter 7, verse 19c.
[12] Bhagavad Gītā, Chapter 6, verse 30.

without even the slightest tinge of selfishness, self-centeredness, or pride:

> If from the realm of the divine
> there should be a calling to enter there,
> then, when coming together with divinity,
> there should be the absence of pride,
> because it would be a contrary,
> undesirable impediment for achieving
> a greater closeness with the divine.[13]

The female protagonists in the sacred drama presented herein, known as the cowherd maidens, or the Vraja Gopikās, were inexorably drawn by a calling to enter the paradisal forest of Vraja. The sounds emanating from his flute were experienced as the most powerful calling, so much so, that there is another chapter prior to the presentation of the Rāsa Līlā five chapters that is entirely devoted to describing and expressing the exquisite beauty and power of Krishna's love-call. The translation of this chapter follows my presentation of the five Rāsa Līlā chapters or acts, as the "Song of the Flute."

When divinity calls souls to dance, they must be rid of even the slightest tinge of self-centeredness or the subtlest modicum of pride. Krishna disappears when the cowherd maidens appear to be even slightly self-absorbed, even when expressing gratefulness for Krishna's presence, because it distracted them from their loving connection with Krishna:

> Keśava [Krishna] could see how they
>   had become intoxicated
>   with their good fortune;
> Bestowing upon them his grace,
>   in order to quell their pride,
>   suddenly, right before them,
>   he disappeared.[14]

[13] The Yoga Sūtra, Vibhūti Pāda 51.
[14] Bhāgavata Purāṇa, Tenth Book, Chapter 29, verse 48 / Rāsa Līlā, Act One, verse 48.

As the reader will learn when reading this drama, teachings on the nature of egoistic pride and pure love are offered so that the heart may attain an overflowing state. Such a state is full with pure affection for the divine beloved, without any interruption or obstruction. Indeed, Patañjali describes how such turnings within one's heart will blossom forth as one enters the meditative state of total ecstatic absorption, *samādhi*:

> When the conditioned mental
> impressions are entirely uprooted
> and can no longer emerge—
> because all of one's heart is filled
> with the pure mental impressions
> coming from the divine that have
> taken root and flowered—
> this is the seedless stage
> within the perfect state of
> total ecstatic absorption, *samādhi*.[15]

Indeed, Patañjali speaks about the pure, continuous flowing forth of the heart, *cittānvaya*,[16] which culminates in the state of *kaivalya*, the all-embracing divine Reality. This pure turning forth within the all-embracing divine reality that takes root in the heart is expressed in the drama with the following words:

> The Rāsa dance and its festival
> fully blossomed with
> the perfect turning forth
> of cowherd girls in a circular
> movement so beautifully adorned.[17]

What is read in the Rāsa Līlā's final chapter or act as the culmination of the whole drama—the performance of the great circle

[15] The Yoga Sūtra, Samādhi Pāda 51. These words are the concluding aphorism of the Sūtra's Part One on Samādhi: Total Ecstatic Absorption.
[16] The Yoga Sūtra, Vibhūti Pāda, 9.
[17] Bhāgavata Purāṇa, Tenth Book, Chapter 33, verse 3ab / Rāsa Līlā, Act Five, verse 3ab.

dance—is also the culmination of what occurs within the heart of the practitioner of yoga: the pure turning movements in the circle dance of the Rāsa is the perfect turning forth in the lotus of the heart. This occurs when the heart overflows with affection for the all-embracing divine Reality (*kaivalya*), which forever blossoms forth like the whorl of a lotus flower. In this state, meditation has reached its ultimate perfection: the love-call fulfilled.

The Divine Embodiment of Perfect Love—Krishna

In the sacred drama presented herein, it is Krishna who is the ultimate object of love for the hearts of the feminine protagonists. Krishna in a paradisal natural setting is always with his beloveds, be they male or female companions, or affectionate cows. Contemplation on the divine acts, or *līlās*, of Krishna are meant to stimulate in readers the perfect union in yoga and the purest experience of *bhakti*, or the offering of one's whole heart to the divine. Indeed, the poetic expressions of these *līlās* represent the irresistible sweetness, an unsurpassable beauty that is intended to soothe the soul, attract the heart, and ignite a sacred passion for the divine.

These dramas, or *līlās*, are meant to be meditations, or windows into a beatific world imbued with perfect love. The soul's yearning for divine love is palpable through the richly endowed poems of the drama as they paint the colorful, detailed descriptions and exquisite natural landscapes, which irresistibly draw the meditator more and more into the heart of the divine.

Krishna is the special deity. Krishna is known to be the supremely beautiful, supremely playful, and supremely joyful divinity. Among the multifarious representations and forms of the personal divinity in India, Krishna holds a special place, a rare closeness, and unexcelled popularity. Krishna is well known for his teachings and his affectionate relationship with his friend Arjuna in the Bhagavad Gītā, one of the most celebrated sacred texts in the world. But devotees especially delight in the more intimate acts of Krishna within the divine realm of Vraja as told in the Bhāgavata Purāṇa.

Krishna in his supreme yet intimate realm is most celebrated among Vaishnavas and considered the highest perfection attainable. Many Hindus consider Krishna to be an "incarnation" or more accurately an *avatāra* ("divine descent") of the cosmic divinity of Vishnu. Vaishnavas see the Krishna who comes to this world to display his divine acts, or *līlās*, as a divine descent *through* Vishnu. But Vaishnavas understand that it is from the intimate and ultimate Krishna of the divine realm of Vraja that Vishnu himself comes, along with Brahmā, the divinity of cosmic creation, and Śiva, the divinity of cosmic dissolution. Thus, the Krishna who comes to this world comes through the cosmic Vishnu as the Krishna from his highest heaven, an eternally divine and ultimate realm in which his divine acts are being enacted forever.

Here in the divinity of Krishna is a fullness of affections in his more intimate relations with souls. The special feature for which Krishna is most known is how he is often depicted as holding a flute to his mouth. The sounding of his flute represents a divine yearning for souls to come to him. When Krishna is with those he loves and yet still sounds his flute, he is yearning for more of his beloveds to come to him. When Krishna is seen as merely holding the flute away from his mouth down by his side or even when the flute is absent in depictions, his divine yearning is satisfied on some level—he is united with his beloveds.

As you enter the pages of this book, according to tradition, you will be on a pilgrimage into the very heart of the divine. And, according to tradition, what takes place there, what is enacted there, reflects what can take place within one's own heart. We will read how the cowherd women of Vraja, the Gopīs, leave their worldly lives and run off to the paradisal forest to be with their divine beloved, Krishna. So in meditation, we are to leave behind our everyday lives and experiences in order to fully reach what is ultimately beloved within our hearts.

Perfect Love According to Chaitanya Vaishnavism

There is one major tradition from within the Hindu complex of religion that especially treasures the Rāsa Līlā passage in the Bhāgavata Purāṇa—the Chaitanya Vaishnava tradition.[18] This important tradition has developed a very sophisticated theology based on the Rāsa Līlā as its center-point. In sacred India, seeing, hearing about, and contemplating the supremely beautiful, playful, and joyful acts of Krishna unites humans with the divine. Practitioners within Hindu traditions believe that the poetry, the art, and the dramas are forms of revelation that display the divine acts of Krishna disclosing the innermost and most intimate dimensions of divinity celebrated in the person of Krishna.

Love between the soul and the deity has taken a variety of forms, which have been articulated in great depth by the charismatic figure known as Krishna Chaitanya (1486–1533 C.E.). The Chaitanya Vaishnava tradition first arose in the eastern province of Bengal, and then spread throughout regions of Bengal, Orissa, and northern areas of India, such as Rajasthan and Uttar Pradesh.

Chaitanya left no written works, with the exception of his famed *Śikṣāṣṭakam*, or "Eight Instructive Verses."[19] He instead chose to inaugurate his devotional movement through direct instruction to key disciples known as the Six Gosvāmīs of Vrindāvana,[20]

[18] The Vaishnava *bhakti* school begun by Chaitanya has been referred to as "Bengal Vaishnavism," "Gauḍīya Vaishnavism," or "Chaitanya Vaishnavism." In this work, this tradition will be identified by the name of its founder Chaitanya, as other schools of Vaishnavism are identified, e.g., Nimbarka school, Rāmānuja school, and so on.

[19] These verses are woven into Krishnadāsa Kavirāja's CC. See CC 3.20.

[20] The Six Gosvāmīs were six monks famous for having assisted Chaitanya in his mission. Their names were Rūpa, Sanātana, Jīva, Gopāla Bhaṭṭa, Raghunātha, and Raghunātha Bhaṭṭa.

along with others, who established the doctrine of the school, built temples, and formed communities of worship in Vrindāvana.

Chaitanya's school was developed in part by his own exemplary and ecstatic behavior in *bhakti*, observed and recorded by these early writers of the school. Of these recordings, the most famous and loved text is the *Chaitanya Charitāmṛta* of Krishnadāsa Kavirāja Gosvāmī. This extensive work, considered to be an unequalled theological synthesis of the school's thought, presents a comprehensive blend of Chaitanya's theology and hagiography.[21] Written a half century after the passing away of Chaitanya in 1533, the author describes the mystic leader as imparting essential teachings of the school to the two leading Gosvāmīs, Rūpa and Sanātana. Of these two, Rūpa is perhaps the more important, as it was he who developed, under the direct guidance of Chaitanya, the articulated and formulated theology of *bhakti-rasa*—"the soul's particular relationship with the divinity in devotional love," within the realm of *līlā* or "divine play."

This ecstatic mystic and devotional revivalist of the sixteenth century, along with his close disciples, established a theological school of thought and religious practice centered upon devotion, or *bhakti*, to the supreme Lord Krishna. The late scholar Klaus Klostermaier states that, among the plethora of religious traditions in India, "perhaps the most subtle and detailed system of gradual ascent to God by means of love has been developed in the Chaitanya school of Vaishnavism."[22] Thus, throughout this work, I draw from the philosophical thinking of this tradition for illuminating the verses of the Rāsa Līlā.

In the Chaitanya Vaishnava tradition of yoga, "ascent to God" begins with a deep dive into one's own heart. This inner pilgrimage,

[21] S. K. De states that the CC is "by far the most authoritative biography of Chaitanya," and that it "at once took its place among the most authoritative texts of the sect. . . . It is a remarkable mediaeval document of mature theological scholarship." For a discussion on the significance of this text, see De, *Vaishnava Faith and Movement*, pp. 53–57.

[22] Klaus Klostermaier, "*Hṛdayavidyā*: A Sketch of a Hindu-Christian Theology of Love," *Journal of Ecumenical Studies* (1972): 765.

as illuminated by Rūpa Gosvāmī, culminates in being drawn to dance with the divine. In the ancient love story that follows, the Vraja Gopikās become our guides to the exquisite landscapes decorating the path taken to the eternal dance within the heart. When, as a result of their yoga practice, souls hear divinity calling them to dance, and yoga practice itself, the great circle dance, and the love exchanged between the dancers, all unite as one—the lotus of the heart. This is "the Yoga of Love," as revealed in the translated passages from sacred Sanskrit texts presented here in this book.

PART I

THE TEXT AND ITS CONTEXT

1

India's Classic Sacred Love Story

The Rāsa Līlā is India's classical sacred love story. It is a dramatic poem that focuses on the young cowherd maidens, the Gopīs, who seek and achieve union with their divine beloved, Krishna, the supreme masculine divinity, as they come together in the wondrous "circle dance," known as the Rāsa. Indeed, its five chapters of only 173 verses contain the ultimate revelational message and vision of one of India's most treasured scriptures, the Bhāgavata Purāṇa.[1]

This story is considered the greatest of all "divine acts," or *līlā*, for several reasons. First, Krishna is known as the divinity who is moved to call souls to his own heart by sending forth music from his flute. Also, in the Bhagavad Gītā, Krishna is clearly preoccupied throughout his famous discourse and conversation with Arjuna with his ardently expressed desire and yearning for souls to come to him, expressed many times throughout 575 verses he speaks. But it is here in the Rāsa Līlā that his love call has reached an ultimate pitch, a unique instance and also a certain level of fulfillment at the start of the drama.

Second, the Gopīs themselves are seen as the perfect exemplars of *bhakti*, or the soul's "offering of the whole heart" unto the supreme deity. The Gopīs are also extolled in this sacred story as the most elevated practitioners of yoga, as they are absorbed in the

[1] The words Bhāgavata Purāṇa mean "the timeless stories (Purāṇa) related to the divine (Bhāgavata)." The title for this most popular sacred text of India has two variations: Śrīmad Bhāgavatam and Bhāgavata Mahāpurāṇam. It is often called, simply, the Bhāgavata. Among the eighteen famous *purāṇas*, it is considered the most important, as shall be discussed further below.

The Yoga of Love. Graham M. Schweig, Oxford University Press. © Oxford University Press 2025.
DOI: 10.1093/oso/9780197768426.003.0002

yogic state described by Patañjali in the Yoga Sūtra as "the divine center of all reality (*īśvara*) that is realized by moving deeply within the space of the heart (*praṇidhāna*)."

And finally, this *līlā* constitutes the inner workings and the innermost dynamics of the highest attainable state of yoga. In this state, there is not even the slightest residue of self-interest or self-consciousness, only the purity of the self in connection with the divine self. Here, souls are lifted up into a purely godly realm. Thus, this *līlā* of divinity represents how "the play" of divine love conquers even God and subsumes him along with his beloveds in the interplay, or *rasa*, of love. As we shall see, Krishna takes full refuge in "the uniting force of divine Yoga and its creative power," or Yogamāyā. Within this power, all things are possible between devotee and divinity.

The narrator of this drama tells us that the greatest love for the divine is cultivated and attained when hearing or reciting the Rāsa Līlā. The poetry presented here is thus specifically *bhakti* poetry, precisely because it cultivates in its audience an intense yearning to be intimately united with the divine in love. Undeniably, its charming poetic imagery, combined with deeply resonating devotional motifs, expresses to any reader much about the nature of love. Narrated in eloquently rich and flowing Sanskrit verse, it has been recognized as one of the most beautiful love poems ever written.

The nature of this most elevated state of union and the various inner dynamics of this transcendent state are revealed in the Sanskrit poetry and dramatic story presented in this book. Cherished as the greatest vision of supreme love in India—and recognized the world over—the Rāsa Līlā is a dramatic poem about young cowherd maidens joining with their ideal beloved to perform the wondrous "circle dance of love," or *rāsa*, and the events leading up to its formation all constitute this "divine drama," or *līlā*.

The poetic presentation of the Rāsa dance is exquisite, and its ethical and theological messages profound. Moreover, *bhakti*, or the offering of one's heart fully to the divine in everything one feels, thinks, and does, is modeled in this passage as the highest. This sacred offering of the hearts of these young cowherd maidens constitutes a powerful sacred vision that has been an endless source of meditative inspiration for the devout worshiper, and thus has been celebrated in Indian art, poetry, and drama throughout the centuries.

Certain *bhakti* traditions within the Hindu complex of traditions have extolled the Rāsa Līlā as the essence of all *līlās*, venerating the *rāsa* dance itself as the great and central symbolic focal point of their worship and innermost meditations. Moreover, it is specifically the Rāsa dance itself within the Rāsa Līlā chapters that becomes the great vision, the great icon, and the ultimate symbol of boundless love that occurs between divinity and devotee. Similarly, as the Cross is for Christians, as Mecca is for Muslims, as the Ark of the Covenant is for Jews, as the image of the meditating Buddha is for Buddhists, so the Rāsa Līlā delivers the great symbol of divine love to countless numbers of persons in sacred India and worldwide.

The Rāsa dance consists of a circular formation, known as the Rāsa *maṇḍala*, in which the supreme feminine divinity in the *bhakti* traditions, personified as Rādhā, and her young friends, the cowherd maidens of Vraja, or the Gopīs, dance with Krishna, the supreme masculine divinity. Today, this ancient dance is mirrored in an archetypal fashion in many of the beautiful circle dances that are enacted in cultures around the world.

The word *rāsa* in the phrase Rāsa Līlā comes from the ancient South Asian form of this dance performed during the harvest season. Though, typically, many female dancers interlock hands or arms with one another in a chain-like manner, around whose necks the arms of their male dance partners are placed, in the Rāsa dance Krishna becomes the sole male partner for each and every one of the Gopīs. He does so by duplicating himself multiple times by virtue of his "divine power" (*-māyā*) of "greater union" (*yoga-*), or Yogamāyā, while remaining at the center of the Rāsa *maṇḍala* or "circle of the Rāsa dance." These multiplications of himself symbolize the dance that the divine heart shares with each and every individual human heart. Through reading *The Yoga of Love*, humans participate in this eternal dance.

In artistic depictions of the Rāsa dance, it is very common to have Krishna standing at the center with his most favored Gopī, understood to be his supreme consort, the Goddess Rādhā. As the Gopīs move in circular formation, each experiences the exclusive attention of Krishna while all sing songs of joy in harmony with Krishna. These songs are accompanied by the percussive sounds of the bells on their ankles and belts, while their bracelets clang to the rhythmic movements of their forms, and celestial beings shower flowers down, joining in with their voices and drumming from the heavens.

This harvest dance takes on special significance in the *bhakti* tradition's main text from which it emerged, the Bhāgavata Purāṇa. The enactment of the *rāsa* dance itself within the Rāsa Līlā chapters of the Bhāgavata Purāṇa becomes the climactic event that occurs in the final fifth chapter (or fifth act) of its story. For the Rāsa Līlā dance harvests the fruits of divine love, loveliness, and playfulness between souls in this world and divinity. Performed under autumn's full moon, Krishna's dance with the Gopīs unfolds in the paradisal forest of Vraja, where the lotus flowers, full fruit trees, and honeybees come alive with love. To this day, in Vraja's countryside about 80 miles south of the modern capital city of Delhi (see Figure 1)—and around the world—practitioners of *bhakti*, or the Yoga of Love, especially celebrate the *rāsa* dance on the autumnal full moon, inviting all souls to join them.

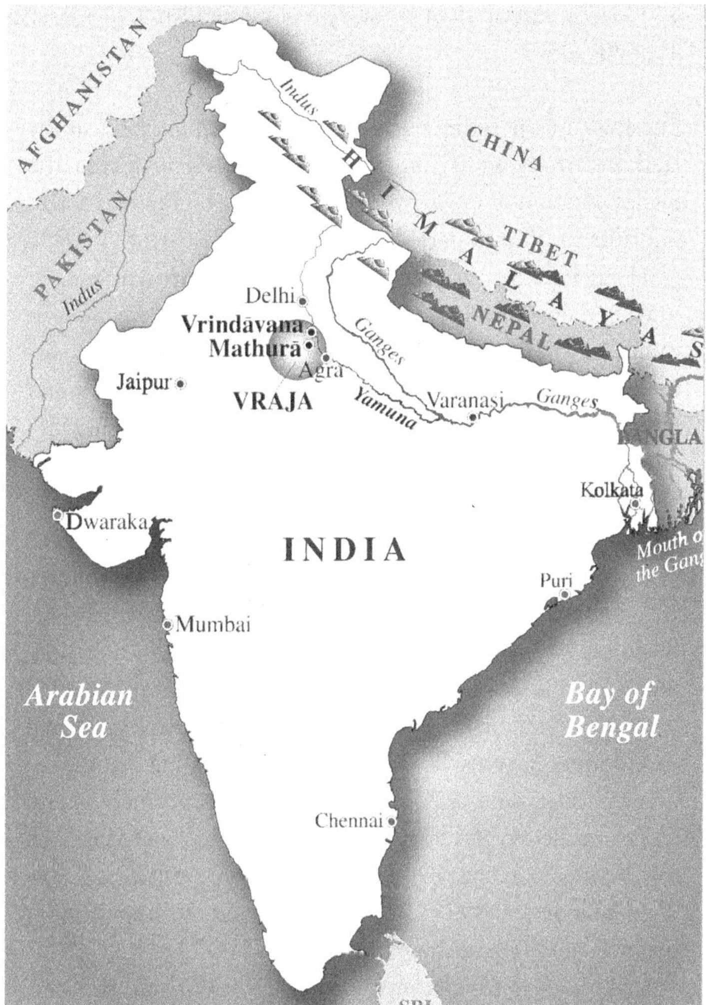

Figure 1. Location of the Vraja region in India.

Summary and Analysis of the Drama

The five-chapter story possesses the distinct structure of a drama. It is necessary, however, to provide a summary of the Rāsa Līlā story here before we analyze its dramatic and theological dimensions.

The following summary of the story is also intended to give a sense of its poetic tone:

> The Rāsa Līlā is set in a sacred realm of enchantment in the land known as Vraja, far beyond the universe, within the highest domain of the heavenly world. This sacred realm also imprints itself onto part of our world as the earthly Vraja, a rural area known as Vraja Maṇḍala ("the circular area of Vraja") in northern India, about 80 miles south of the modern capital city of Delhi. Vraja is described as a land of idyllic natural beauty, filled with abundant foliage heavy with fruit and bloom, roaming cows, and brightly colored birds singing melodiously. The Rāsa Līlā takes place in the earthly Vraja during the bountiful autumn season, when evenings abound with soothing scents and gentle river breezes.
>
> One special evening, the rising moon reached its fullness with a resplendent glow. Its reddish rays lit up the forest as night-blooming lotus flowers began to unfold. The forest during those nights was decorated profusely with delicate starlike jasmine flowers, resembling the flowing dark hair of goddesses adorned with flower blossoms. So rapturous was this setting that the supreme Lord himself, as Krishna, the eternally youthful cowherd, was compelled to play captivating music on his flute. Moved by this beauteous scene, Krishna was inspired toward love. The opening four verses of exquisite poetry paint the scene and set the tone for the whole drama.[2]
>
> Upon hearing the alluring flute music, the cowherd maidens, known as the Gopīs, who were already in love with Krishna, abruptly left their homes, families, and domestic duties. They ran off to join him in the moonlit forest. Krishna and the Gopīs met and played on the banks of the Yamunā River. When the maidens

[2] BhP 10.29.1–4.

became proud of his loving attention, however, their beloved Lord suddenly vanished from their sight. The Gopīs searched everywhere for Krishna. Discovering that he had run off with one special maiden, they soon found that she too had been deserted by him. As darkness engulfed the forest, the cowherd maidens gave up their search, singing sweet songs of hope and despair, longing for his return. Then Krishna cleverly reappeared and spoke to them on the nature of love.[3]

In the final verse of this passage, we witness the power of love and how this power melts the heart of God. Here Krishna explains to the Gopīs that the purity of their love is its own reward, beyond anything that even he as the supreme can reciprocate. The tradition then expresses how love is ultimately boundless, in that it is more powerful than even God. It is to love that God submits, and further, it is love by which God himself is intimately known and conquered. The great message here is that it is in the very act of love itself, or the purity of love that constitutes an offering of one's whole heart to the divine, that we find the greatest reward. The reward is not how our love or whether or not our love is reciprocated—the reward is found simply in the endlessness or boundlessness of the love itself.

The story culminates in the great celebration of this pure love in the performance of the Rāsa dance. The Gopīs link arms together, forming a great circle.[4] By divine arrangement, Krishna dances with every cowherd maiden at once, yet each one thinks she is dancing with him alone. Supreme love has now reached its perfect fulfillment and expression through joyous dancing and singing long into the night, in the divine circle of the Rāsa dance. Retiring from the vigorous dancing, Krishna and the Gopīs refresh themselves by bathing in the river. Then, reluctantly, the cowherd maidens return to their homes.

[3] BhP 10.32.16–22.
[4] BhP 10.33.3.

The five chapters of the Rāsa Līlā fall neatly into the structure of a five-act drama, and within them, thirteen subdivisions of scenes are discernable. Let us briefly review here the dramatic elements and structure of the passage. As we have noted, the hero of the drama is Krishna, the supreme divinity, and the heroines are the group of cowherd maidens from the village region of Vraja, known as the Vraja Gopikās, or simply "the Gopīs." The story is narrated by the sage Śuka to the king Parīkṣit (see Figure 2). While the reader hears the narrator's voice throughout the acts, two short catechismal dialogues between the sage and king, only once toward the beginning and another instance toward the end of the story, ensue, offering theological discourse on the proper way to understand the *līlā*. But it is the voices of the hero and the heroines that dominate the text, not only within their dialogue scenes and a middle act consisting completely of the heroines' nineteen verses of monologue, but also their voices will appear within narrative verses by inserting quoted words and phrases spoken by the hero or heroines.

Each of the five chapters constitutes an "act" of the total drama or play, respectively, within which there are observable subdivisions that function as distinctive "scenes," totaling thirteen scenes of the drama. These divisions of the text that form scenes are indicated by natural shifts both in the text's voice and in the discernably distinct events within the story line. Furthermore, a study of the poetic meter of the verses seen in conjunction with these naturally observed shifts in the story line finds that they provide further support of such chapter subdivisions or scenes within the acts.

Although the chapters of the Bhāgavata are technically untitled, I provide, however, in the outline presented (see outline on page 26), descriptive titles for each of the five acts, the dominant type of text (e.g., narrative, dialogue, etc.), with brief summary descriptions for each of the thirteen scenes to give a sense

Figure 2. Temple wall painting of the sage Śuka narrating the Bhāgavata's Rāsa Līlā to the king, sages, and worldly persons. From Gopīnāthjī Temple, Jaipur, Rajasthan, India.
Photograph by author.

of the movement of the story line, along with the inclusive verse numbers. The purpose of such an outline is to highlight the cohesiveness of the story, a story that has a beginning and an end, a story that has a climactic event in the end toward which the whole drama very effectively moves with its various building of narratively embellished scenes, enhanced by a dramatic momentum and rhythm. The thirteen scenes throughout the five chapters

THE BHĀGAVATA RĀSA LĪLĀ CHAPTERS STRUCTURED AS A DRAMA

ACT ONE: KRISHNA ATTRACTS THE GOPĪS AND DISAPPEARS (10.29.1–48)

Scene 1: NARRATIVE: Krishna makes flute music and the Gopīs come running to the forest (vss. 1–11).
Scene 2: DISCOURSE: On the Gopīs' passionate love for Krishna surpassing knowledge of divinity (vss. 12–16).
Scene 3: DIALOGUE: Krishna urges the Gopīs to return home and the Gopīs plead to stay in the forest (vss. 17–41).
Scene 4: NARRATIVE: Krishna plays with the Gopīs in the forest and suddenly disappears (vss. 42–48).

ACT TWO: THE GOPĪS SEARCH FOR KRISHNA (10.30.1–44)

Scene 1: NARRATIVE: The Gopīs imitate Krishna and inquire from inhabitants of the forest (vss. 1–23).
Scene 2: NARRATIVE: The Gopīs track footprints and discover a special Gopī who has been deserted by Krishna (vss. 24–44).

ACT THREE: SONG OF THE GOPĪS (10.31.1–19)

Scene: MONOLOGUE: The Gopīs express with a collective voice a variety of emotions and reactions to Krishna's absence in prayerful soliloquy (vss. 1–19).

ACT FOUR: KRISHNA REAPPEARS AND SPEAKS OF LOVE (10.32.1–22)

Scene 1: NARRATIVE: Krishna suddenly reappears and the Gopīs react in various emotional ways (vss. 1–14).
Scene 2: DIALOGUE: Krishna describes three types of love in response to the Gopīs' inquiry; Krishna is grateful for the Gopīs' love (vss. 15–22).

ACT FIVE: KRISHNA AND THE GOPĪS UNITE IN THE RĀSA (10.33.1–40)

Scene 1: NARRATIVE: The Gopīs form circle for Rāsa dance and Krishna dances with each Gopī simultaneously (vss. 1–20).
Scene 2: NARRATIVE: Krishna and the Gopīs play after Rāsa dance (vss. 21–26).
Scene 3: DISCOURSE: On the ethical question of Krishna's dancing with other men's wives (vss. 27–35).
Scene 4: NARRATIVE: The special nature of Krishna's divine play is presented; the Gopīs return to their homes; hearing Rāsa Līlā story bestows greatest benediction (vss. 36–40).

can be viewed as a symmetry that perhaps frames the songs of the Gopīs that express their deep sense of loss and loneliness from Krishna found in the middle chapter: four scenes for the first chapter; two for the second; one for the third; two for the fourth;

and, finally, again there are four scenes for the fifth. Although the climactic event of the Rāsa dance occurs in the fifth and final chapter, there is also a different kind of climactic plateau in the way feelings of intense loss and longing in separation from the divine beloved is reached in the middle chapter.

2
Framing Passages of the Rāsa Līlā

The tenth book of the Bhāgavata, significant not only because of its length, but also because of the *līlās* it presents, contains stories of Krishna's birth, his childhood, and his youth, including his friendships with village boys and cowherd girls. Also described are his later activities in which he assumes the role of royalty in distant places. The first nine books leading up to the tenth, along with the eleventh and twelfth books that follow, are filled with narrations, stories, discourses, prayers, and poetry about the powerful manifestations of God and souls who are devoted to him. The literary content of these chapters acts as a frame around the more intimate stories of the tenth book.

The Rāsa Līlā drama is colorfully anticipated as early as the *Bhāgavata's* third book, in the final verse of the second chapter. The first two lines of the verse invoke imagery drawn from the opening verse of the story, and the second two allude to the climactic event of the Rāsa dance in the final act:

> Regarding the mood of those nights
> brightened by the rays of the autumn moon,
> He enjoyed singing sweet songs
> as the ornament in the circle of women.[1]

This verse reveals essential themes of the Rāsa Līlā, not again referred to until the tenth book in which, approximately one third of the way through, the five chapters of the story are presented.

[1] BhP 3.2.34.

The Yoga of Love. Graham M. Schweig, Oxford University Press. © Oxford University Press 2025.
DOI: 10.1093/oso/9780197768426.003.0003

Preceding the Rāsa Līlā chapters (BhP 10.29–33), as well as following them are short references within verses, whole verses, sections of chapters, and even complete chapters concerning the Gopīs. The overall effect created by these surrounding passages is a complex composition that supports the innermost focal point of the Bhāgavata, the story of the Rāsa Līlā. Moreover, the episodes relating to the Gopīs, along with other intimate or *mādhurya līlās* from within the tenth book, contain elements of amorous devotion to God, making the text of the Rāsa Līlā inseparable from and continuous with the whole of the tenth book. Thus, the related surrounding passages effectively provide a rich frame within which the Rāsa Līlā is established as the most honored *līlā* among all the divine dramas of Krishna.[2]

Chapters 21 and 22 from the tenth book constitute the two major "Gopī" chapters prior to the presentation of the Rāsa Līlā. In Chapter 21, the Gopīs sing praises of the power of Krishna's flute music and how it affects all the residents of Vraja, even all of creation. The first six verses of Chapter 21 constitute a narrative description of the cowherd maidens who, inspired by the sounds of Krishna's flute, have achieved a state of constantly remembering him.

The narrator explains that when the Gopīs hear Krishna's flute music from afar, they converse about his acts and become overwhelmed with intense love, to the point of becoming speechless. Thus stunned and quieted by their love for Krishna, they again are able to hear his flute, which causes them to again react to the divine music, further perpetuating a blissful unending cycle

[2] The first partial-verse presentation of the Gopīs within the tenth book prior to the RL story is BhP 10.15.7–8. The first full verse presentation is BhP 10.19.16: "The greatest bliss for the Gopīs was the vision of Govinda. Each moment without him became like hundreds of ages." In Chapter 20, two verses express how the Gopīs cannot be relieved of the scorching late afternoon heat, due to the intense heat arising from love's separation (BhP 10.20.42, 45). The more significant passages following the RL, in addition to Chapters 35 and 47, are the twelve verses of a chapter in which the Gopīs speak prayerful words of separation (BhP 10.39.19–30). There are many other dispersed Gopī-related verses following the RL, up to a verse in the final chapter of the tenth book, expressing how Krishna's smiling face increases the passion of the Gopīs (BhP 10.90.48).

of remembrance for the cowherd maidens.[3] Chapter 21 clearly prepares the reader for the Gopīs' irresistible attraction to the sounds of Krishna's flute, to which they are helplessly drawn at the beginning of the Rāsa Līlā. This powerful force of the divine flute is also anticipated in earlier passages of the tenth book.

The Gopīs' attraction to Krishna becomes heightened to such a point, in Chapter 22, that each one desperately prays to the Goddess to make a conjugal arrangement for her:

> O Kātyāyanī,
> whose power
> is very great (*mahā-māyā*),
> O great *yoginī*,
> supremely controlling Goddess,
> O Devī, I offer my respects unto you.
> Please make the cowherd son of Nanda my husband![4]

The Goddess is one, though her names are many. The Gopīs take refuge in the Goddess as Devī, also called Kātyāyanī and "great *yoginī*," in order to be united with Krishna, who himself also takes refuge in the Goddess as Yogamāyā to arrange for his rendezvous with the Gopīs.[5] The significance of the role of the Goddess and her colorful nomenclature will be explored below.

The Gopīs' union with Krishna is anticipated through this prayer to the Goddess. Fulfilling their deepest desire, Krishna appears before them and playfully steals their garments while they are bathing in the Yamunā River, then carries their clothing as he climbs up a nearby tree. In order to retrieve their clothes, the cowherd maidens are convinced by Krishna to get out of the water. Their nakedness before him is taken as an expression of full self-surrender of love to

[3] See BhP 10.21.6 in the Veṇu Gīta, the translation of which is provided in this work.
[4] BhP 10.22.4.
[5] RL 1.1.

the supreme Beloved. The Gopīs experience great joy in Krishna's presence, for their desire to serve him as their husband has now been fulfilled. He then promises, "With me you will enjoy the coming nights,"[6] alluding to the nights that inspire Krishna toward love on the special evening of the Rāsa dance.

At least two chapters that follow the Rāsa Līlā drama depict almost exclusively the behavior of the Gopīs in Krishna's absence. In Chapter 35, they sing songs about Krishna's *līlās* whenever he goes into the forest with his cowherd boyfriends. The Gopīs once again describe Krishna's flute playing and the effect it has on Vraja's cows, rivers, trees and vines, lake-dwelling birds, heavenly beings, and others, and finally on themselves. They also tell of his glorious return from the forest and how he is greeted by various gods on the way.

Chapter 47 is particularly important because it focuses on the theme of Krishna's prolonged separation from the Gopīs while he resides in Mathurā. In order to appease the Gopīs, Krishna sends his messenger, Uddhava, who is amazed as he witnesses the intense devotional love of the cowherd maidens. Especially well known is the passage popularly named the Bhramara Gīta, "Song of the Black Bee," in which one Gopī, identified as Krishna's favorite, Rādhā, speaks in loving madness to a black bee, the translation of which is provided in this volume. Acknowledging the passionate devotion of the Gopīs, Uddhava desires to honor their superlative worship of Krishna, or "love of the whole heart" (*sarvātma-bhāva*). In verses 23–28, Uddhava's words praise the cowherd maidens for such exemplary devotion.

Uddhava then relates to the Gopīs a message coming from Krishna containing several essential points, his first point being: "You were never apart from me, for I am the Soul of all."[7] In verses 34 and 35, however, he appears to be more sensitive to

[6] BhP 10.22.27.
[7] BhP 10.47.29.

the Gopīs' despair and carefully addresses the intention behind his separation from them:

> I, who am indeed
> dear to your sight,
> am now far away from you.
> However, for the purpose of
> intensely attracting your minds,
> this [departure] was my desire
> in order to increase your meditation on me.
>
> The minds of women are not as fully absorbed
> in their beloved when he is present before their eyes,
> For he is not as much in their thoughts
> as when he is far away.[8]

The Rāsa Līlā is decorated by many such passages, prior to and following its story, that illuminate the prized devotion of the Gopīs and indicate the special status of the drama within the Bhāgavata.

[8] BhP 10.47.34–35.

3

The Poetry and Drama of Divine Love

What sets about the language and tone of the Rāsa Līlā apart from most of the Bhāgavata text is the pronounced presence of poetic and dramatic elements, reflecting the highly developed classical schools of Indian poetics (*kāvya*) and dramaturgy (*nāṭya*). I will attempt to highlight some of these features that contribute to the aesthetic achievement of this dramatic poem.

Good Sanskrit drama typically consists of no fewer than five and no more than ten acts, and the Rāsa Līlā appears to meet this requirement. The five consecutive chapters of the Rāsa Līlā are not arbitrary divisions; rather, each chapter functions as a principal act (*aṅka*) within the dramatic story line. Thus, in my translation, I have designated each chapter of the Rāsa Līlā as an "act": Act One corresponds to Chapter 29 of the Bhāgavata, Act Two to Chapter 30, and so on. For purposes of clarity and comprehensibility I have provided titles for each act, even though the chapters are untitled and only numbered in the original. Titles of the acts are worded to communicate the basic movement of the plot:

Act One: Krishna Attracts the Gopīs and Disappears
Act Two: The Gopīs Search for Krishna
Act Three: Song of the Gopīs: The Gopī Gīta
Act Four: Krishna Reappears and Speaks of Love
Act Five: Krishna Joins the Gopīs in the Rāsa Dance

The Yoga of Love. Graham M. Schweig, Oxford University Press. © Oxford University Press 2025.
DOI: 10.1093/oso/9780197768426.003.0004

These five acts represent a complete drama that can be appreciated in and of itself. Nevertheless, the deeper meanings of a text of this kind are fully understood only in relation to its greater literary and traditional contexts.

An act, in Sanskrit drama, generally consists of one or more "scene" (*sandhi*) subdivisions. In the Rāsa Līlā text, transitions from one scene to another naturally occur when there is a change in the situation of the drama, especially indicated by a shift in voice or activity. Furthermore, the subdivisions are often reinforced by visible changes in versification. Because these scenes are not determined in the original text, I have indicated scene changes with titles, along with sequential numbering. Although the story line is straightforward, titles for each scene are offered in order to provide the reader with general symbolic themes suggested in the various scenes.

There are essentially four types of voices in the Rāsa Līlā, simply described as narration, discourse, dialogue, and monologue. One of these types dominates each scene, although other types may also be present.[1] The majority of verses utilize the voice of narration—words of the narrator describing actions taking place within the story. In fact, there are eight distinctive narratives out of a total of thirteen scenes. The voice of discourse is employed twice, in the second and penultimate scenes. It consists of a didactic dialogue between the narrator Śuka and his audience, the king, guiding the listener's understanding of the drama. Scenes that engage the voice of dialogue also appear twice, once each in the first and fourth acts; they involve Krishna, the hero, and the Gopīs, the heroines. The middle act consists of only one scene in which the monologue voice appears. Here, the Gopīs offer passionate and prayerful songs to Krishna in his absence.

[1] For example, one can observe some monologue within the narration in scene 1 of Act 2. Also, one observes dialogue within the narration of scene 2 of Act 5, and some discourse-like verses in the dialogue of Act 4. There is also some narration woven into the two dialogue scenes in Acts 1 and 4.

THE THIRTEEN SCENES OF THE RĀSA LĪLĀ DRAMA

ACT ONE	ACT TWO	ACT THREE	ACT FOUR	ACT FIVE
Scene 1 Narrative 1 (vss. 1-11)	*Scene 1* Narrative 3 (vss. 1-23)	*Scene 1* Monologue (vss. 1-19)	*Scene 1* Narrative 5 (vss. 1-14)	*Scene 1* Narrative 6 (vss. 1-20)
Scene 2 Discourse 1 (vss. 12-16)	*Scene 2* Narrative 4 (vss. 24-44)		*Scene 2* Dialogue 2 (vss. 15-22)	*Scene 2* Narrative 7 (vss. 21-26)
Scene 3 Dialogue 1 (vss. 17-41)				*Scene 3* Discourse 2 (vss. 27-36)
Scene 4 Narrative 2 (vss. 42-48)				*Scene 4* Narrative 8 (vss. 37-40)

Table 1. The thirteen scene subdivisions among the five acts or chapters from the Bhāgavata Purāṇa's Rāsa Līlā drama.

In Table 1, the primary voice associated with each scene within the five acts is displayed diagrammatically. A natural symmetry is immediately observable in the arrangement of scenes within the various acts of the drama. Theorists of classical Sanskrit dramaturgy explain that five types of scenes are employed in a drama, each one moving the action of the story forward to build toward its climactic event. These scene types are to be found throughout the Rāsa Līlā drama, and are as follows: the opening scene, progressive scene, developmental scene, pausing scene, and culmination scene.

The opening narrative verse of the Rāsa Līlā presents a vivifying entrance into its drama. This simple metered verse paints an unexpectedly condensed picture of the drama as a whole:

Even the Beloved Lord, seeing those nights	*bhagavān api tā rātrīḥ*
in autumn filled with blooming jasmine flowers,	*śāradotphulla-mallikāḥ*
Turned his mind toward love's delights,	*vīkṣya rantuṁ manaś cakre*
fully taking refuge in Yogamāyā's illusive powers.	*yoga-māyām upāśritaḥ*

Much of Sanskrit drama focuses on the theme of romantic love (*śṛṅgāra-rasa*). Here, the romantic tone is created by the words "love's delights." Remarkably, all four constituent principals of the drama are introduced in the first verse: first, the leading male figure or divine hero, "the Beloved Lord," Krishna; second, the collective leading female figures or heroines, the young women of Vraja or the Gopīs, subtly revealed by way of a complex metaphor that is found in the following principal; third, the idyllic natural scenery of Vraja, described here as "nights in autumn filled with blooming jasmine flowers"; and fourth, the divine feminine power of loving union, Yogamāyā. The very "seed" or *bīja* of the plot, represented by the simple subject and predicate of the verse, is also sown, presenting the Beloved Lord who is inspired toward love by the beauty of the scene. The divine potency of Yogamāyā arranges for the seed of the plot to grow into the full drama of love.

Consideration of the ways in which the four principals participate in the Rāsa Līlā, can enhance appreciation of the literary and theological expression of this work. Of these principals, we shall address the Gopīs last, as their role is the most complex.

PART II

THE PRINCIPALS OF THE DRAMA

4
Vraja: Pastoral Paradise

The setting of the Rāsa Līlā is wondrous! Situated in this world—but not exactly *of* this world—Vraja is a sacred place of pastoral beauty that inspires divine love. There, every personality, including all plants, trees, and animals, participate in and fully experience the love between Krishna and the cowherd maidens. This is the vision of the devout practitioner, in which the divine realm of Vraja manifest in this world and known as Gokula, is identical with its divine counterpart, the "heavenly Vraja," known as Goloka.[1]

The natural Vraja of this world is the geographic region of central northern India, in which the pilgrimage town of Vrindāvana—depicted in the Rāsa Līlā as a small agricultural village—is situated. The name Vrindāvana means "the forest of Vṛndā or *tulasī*" (Krishna's favorite plant and the Goddess who embodies it).

The spiritual realm of Vraja is described as a place that clearly contrasts with the world as we know it. It is a mystical world of beauty; the ground is covered with devotional jewels named *cintāmaṇi*, each "a fabulous gem supposed to yield to its possessor all desires." Even the trees are not ordinary and are called *kalpa-taru*, or "wishing trees." Vraja is of extraordinary abundance: the trees produce fruit during every season, cows give milk unlimitedly, and the water is nectar. Here, all walking is dancing and all talking is singing, and time is only an eternal present within which unlimited varieties of divine events occur.[2]

The world of Vraja is devotionally alive as every object and soul exists only for the sake of the Beloved Lord. Every being and everything in this spiritual setting is full of knowledge and bliss, and

[1] CC 1.5.21.
[2] These verbal images of Vraja are taken from the *Brahma Saṁhitā* and the CC.

The Yoga of Love. Graham M. Schweig, Oxford University Press.
DOI: 10.1093/oso/9780197768426.003.0005

gives off a splendor like the various luminaries of the sky. "Glorious is Vraja, surpassing all," the Gopīs extol.

So wondrous is Vraja that the author of the Bhāgavata has devoted a full chapter to an elaborate description of its rainy and autumn seasons, often cleverly drawing parallels between characteristics of nature and the behavior of the spiritual aspirant (BhP 10.20.1–49). This relationship between the devotee and the world in which they find themselves is so exquisitely emphasized in the Rāsa Līlā that Vraja as a setting becomes one of the constituent principals of the drama.

The reader becomes acquainted with the landscape of the Rāsa Līlā in the first three verses, and it continues to play an indispensable role in the various phases of the story. In the second verse, the moon casts a reddish light above the horizon, contributing to the beauteous scene that inspires Krishna toward love. The light of the decorative stars and glowing full moon illuminate the sky and forest at night. Indeed, the narrator compares the beauty of Krishna and the Gopīs to the moon among the many stars.

Images of the bountiful forest and plant life are described by both the narrator and the hero or heroines. Flowers in general are mentioned, with special attention given to night-blooming varieties. The Gopīs, when separated from Krishna, talk to an array of forest plant life: from trees of all kinds to plants, vines, and other botanicals. Krishna also runs through the forest with the Gopīs. Enticed by its beauty early in the story, he shares his appreciation with the maidens:

> You have seen the forest
>   filled with flowers,
>   glowing with the rays
>   of the full moon;
> Made beautiful by leaves of trees,
>   playfully shimmering
>   from the gentle breeze
>   off the river Yamunā.[3]

[3] RL 1.21.

The Yamunā River, with its shores of cooling sands, is the place where Krishna and the Gopīs retreat in the first and final acts, in order to either play or refresh themselves after dancing. Gentle autumn breezes carve ripples in the waters of the Yamunā. In the second act, the wind becomes a messenger carrying news of which direction Krishna has gone, by sending scents from his garland to the Gopīs.

As the Gopīs are lured by the scent of Krishna's garland,[4] speaking to varieties of jasmine when they are madly searching for Krishna,[5] he is also drawn into his full-moon night with the cowherd maidens by both the alluring sight and fragrance of pervasive jasmine flowers in full night bloom.[6] Such night-blooming flowers are essential to the story since it is these flowers that inaugurate the Rāsa Līlā drama and enhance it as it unfolds.

In the first act, Krishna suggests to his beloveds that their coming to the forest is due to the alluring beauty of the flower-filled scene. He also gathers flowers for the special Gopī with whom he disappears, and the other Gopīs observe that "here, flowers were gathered by the lover for his beloved."[7] At the conclusion of the drama, Krishna roams the banks of the Yamunā River "in the direction of the gentle breeze that was carrying the fragrances of flowers over the land and the water."[8]

Jasmine flowers assume a diverse role throughout the drama and appear in the very first verse in which the Beloved Lord is inspired toward love. These autumn nights are curiously filled with "blooming jasmine flowers." This is surprising, since the plant typically does not produce blossoms in the harvest season, but only throughout the spring and summer—an indication of

[4] RL 2.11.
[5] RL 2.8.
[6] RL 1.1.
[7] RL 2.32.
[8] RL 5.25.

the exceptional nature of these nights. It would be equally remarkable if the full moon lasted for the several strikingly beautiful "nights" during which the dance occurs! For that matter, in the eternal Vraja, the moon is always full and the dance never-ending.

Particularly known for its intoxicating fragrance capable of arousing amorous and erotic feelings,[9] the scent of jasmine pervades the air of the Vraja forest. This delicate, star-shaped flower of white, pink, and yellow shades is worn on this special night by the Gopīs, who playfully compare Krishna's teeth to jasmine flowers.

Along with the jasmine, blossoming lotus flowers are also used by the narrator to convey the unequaled beauty and passion of the Gopīs' amorous feelings for Krishna. On thirty separate occasions, lotus flowers appear as frequent symbols of love throughout the poem, starting with the first scene in which the night comes alive with the opening of lotus flowers beneath the rising moon. Krishna is pleased by their appearance[10] and later by their scent: "He delighted in breezes that carried the fragrance of white lotuses, joyfully dancing in the waves of the river."[11]

The lotus flower is a frequently occurring symbol among Indian religious traditions,[12] which describe the state of enlightenment—as well as the heavenly realm of Vraja—with a fully blossomed lotus flower.[13] As ultimate enlightenment in *bhakti* is one of divine love, lotuses are abundant in the Rāsa Līlā. While searching for Krishna, the Gopīs identify their beloved as the one who holds a

[9] The powerful scent of jasmine is conveyed in RL 4.11.

[10] RL 1.3.

[11] RL 1.45cd.

[12] See verse illumination to RL 1.3.

[13] The lotus can represent cosmic evolution, since the creator deity, Brahmā, is born from the lotus. Forms of the powerful Vishnu are found standing on lotus flowers, and the lotus is one of several possible items that a Vishnu form may be holding in one of his four hands.

lotus flower. When Krishna goes missing in the woods, the Gopīs find him by following his lotus-embellished footprints, and the blue-lotus scent wafting from his body. Even the celestials shower lotuses upon Krishna and the cowherd maidens as they perform the Rāsa dance.

Night-blooming lotuses, such as the ones in this poem, differ from their forest varieties, as they are born from the water. This is mentioned earlier in the tenth book of the Bhāgavata, where the special power of such flowers is indicated:

> When the sun rises
>   water-born flowers blossom,
>   except for night-blooming lotus flowers,
> As subjects in the presence of their ruler
>   are without fear, O king,
>   except for the thieves.[14]

This thief-like trait of the night-blooming lotuses is also a characteristic of the hero of the story, since Krishna, in his boyhood, is known for stealing butter from the women of Vraja in order to feed the monkeys. He is called Hari ("one who steals") because he "steals" the hearts of his devotees. And in the Rāsa Līlā, he steals the hearts of the Gopīs.[15] Yet these night-blooming flowers are able to steal even the mind and heart of Krishna.

A great female devotee of Krishna—even a consort of Vishnu—who has taken the bodily form of a plant named *tulasī* also plays a prominent role in the drama, as it does in the lives of *bhakti* practitioners. This plant is worshiped on a daily basis in Vaishnava temples and homes, used to garnish food preparations for sacred offerings, and its leaves are found decorating the feet of sacred images of Krishna. The wood of expired *tulasī* plants is carved into

[14] BhP 10.20.47.
[15] RL 1.8.

beads that are worn around the neck by Vaishnavas and also used as a rosary, or *japa-māla*, or a "garland" of beads for the repeated recitation of a sacred *mantra*.

The special significance of the *tulasī* plant is recognized by the Gopīs when they speak of *tulasī* and Śrī (Lakṣmī): "The Goddess Śrī desires, along with the sacred *tulasī* plant, the dust of your lotus feet."[16] As Krishna's garland is made up of the delicate and fragrant flowerets produced from the sacred plant, in the second act—after Krishna suddenly disappears—the Gopīs inquire from the *tulasī* plant concerning Krishna's whereabouts. Though first the Gopīs speak to the larger plant life in the Vraja forest—specifically the trees—when they get no response, they approach plants of all kinds and sizes in desperation, including varieties of jasmine and, eventually, sacred *tulasī* herself.

Singing like madwomen, as they frantically question the trees in the forest for any indication of Krishna's whereabouts,[17] the maidens perceive these various plants and trees as beings "whose very existence is for the sake of others," thereby indirectly expressing how they feel that their own existence is for the sake of Krishna.[18] Convinced that the vines on the trees must have had contact with their beloved Lord, the Gopīs feel that their textured bodily surfaces are actually "ecstatic eruptions" (*utpulakāni*) caused by his divine touch.[19] They envision the trees and plants, the branches of which are heavy with fruits and flowers during the harvest season, to be bowing before Krishna, whom they have just seen pass by.[20]

The natural surroundings of Vraja sweetly assist in the loving rendezvous between Krishna and the Gopīs when they are apart from each other. Through the intimate dialogue Krishna and the Gopīs have (independently of each other) with the enchanting

[16] RL 1.37.
[17] RL 2.4.
[18] RL 2.9.
[19] RL 2.13.
[20] RL 2.12.

landscape, they are moved to behave in ways that lead to their reunion. These ways of intimately relating to, or communicating personally with, the beauteous Vraja setting—especially during periods of separation—serve to enhance their love play.

As such, the landscape is very much in the foreground when the hero and heroines are apart from one another, and in the background when Krishna and the Gopīs come together in the first and final acts. During these times, they roam the forest and frolic along the shores of the Yamunā, before bathing in the river to cool off. Thus the Vraja forest provides an enchanting arena for the Rāsa dance itself, and becomes a place of recreation following the dance, where both hero and heroines feel their love increase because of it. It is the delightful power known as Yogamāyā that arranges for the divine cowherd and his maidens to relish love at such depths in this paradisal landscape of love known as Vraja, when they unite, as much as when they are apart.

5

Yogamāyā: Potency for Intimacy

The form of the Goddess named Yogamāyā is the most subtle and elusive of the four principals of the Rāsa Līlā to comprehend. Often called simply Māyā, she is a mysterious power that escapes the understanding of souls and even of the divinity himself. Indeed, the Bhāgavata warns the reader: "If the supreme Soul himself does not understand the nature of Māyā, what to speak of others?"[1] For it is upon the enigmatic Yogamāyā that divinity relies to make all the mysterious, colorful, and complex preparations that bring souls closer to him.

Māyā has a transforming function for souls in either divine consciousness or worldly consciousness. Daniel H. H. Ingalls states, "Māyā is one of the most beautiful concepts in the history of religion."[2] It is she who reveals or conceals divinity's identity to souls in this world according to their own heart's desires. Her power constructs the perfect arrangement for the selfless love between divinity and devotee, or for the selfish conditioned love often found in this world.

The term Yogamāyā consists of two words: *yoga* and *māyā*. Though it is often abbreviated as Māyā,[3] it is the complete term

[1] BhP 3.6.39.

[2] Noel Sheth, *The Divinity of Krishna* (New Delhi: Munshiram Manoharlal Publishers, 1982), p. xii. In his Foreword to this book, Ingalls defines the concept of *māyā*, then briefly observes interesting parallels to similar themes in western literature. See pp. xii–xiii.

[3] Most often throughout the Bhāgavata text, the concept of *māyā* carries a metaphysical sense, specifically denoting the realm of "physical nature" (*prakṛti*). Even more specifically, the phrase *māyā-guṇa* is used to refer to the illusory realm of the qualities of nature that originate in Sāṁkhya philosophy and also appear in the Bhagavad Gītā (*tri-guṇa*).

The Yoga of Love. Graham M. Schweig, Oxford University Press. © Oxford University Press 2025.
DOI: 10.1093/oso/9780197768426.003.0006

that is especially significant in the Bhāgavata, where it appears in well over two hundred instances as an important theological idea. Within the Rāsa Līlā itself, the few times it is presented it carries a different sense each time. Several uses of *māyā* in the Bhāgavata indicate that this half of the compound phrase has the sense of "magic spell," "trick," "deceit," or in general "deception." The specific sense of the word *yoga* in Yogamāyā is "joining things together" or "making connections" for God's intimate *līlās*.[4] The compound could be translated literally as "the power of union" or "the power of illusion," whereas connotatively, Yogamāyā refers to the magical power that inspires intimacy.

Yogamāyā has two major functions: creating arrangements for the various events and causing forgetfulness in order to facilitate loving intimacy between God and the soul. In the Rāsa Līlā drama we see these functions unfold, though the word *māyā* appears only three times in the Rāsa Līlā's five acts. Among them, the exact compound phrase Yogamāyā appears only once, in the very first verse, where it is spoken directly by the poet-narrator Śuka as theological explanation: "Even the Beloved Lord . . . turned his mind toward love's delights, fully taking refuge in Yogamāyā's illusive powers."[5]

The other instance of *māyā* appearing in the narrative is the following: "The husband cowherds of Vraja felt no jealousy whatsoever toward Krishna" because they were "deluded by his power of Māyā."[6] Here, the function of "delusion" is demonstrated by the word *mohita*, a state caused by the power of *māyā*. The single instance of *māyā* found in dialogue is in Krishna's words to the Gopīs

[4] As with the word *māyā*, the word *yoga* carries independent senses. The literal meanings of the word from lexical sources are "union," "junction," "connection," "combination," or even "mixture." It is derivative of the verb root *yuj*, which can be translated by the cognate "to yoke." The word can refer to "the eight-fold path of mystic discipline," *aṣṭāṅga-yoga*, in which practitioners attempt to develop various mystical powers or "perfections," *siddhis*.

[5] RL 1.1.

[6] RL 5.38.

from the first act: "For every woman the highest *dharma* is to serve her husband without falsity (*māyā*)."[7]

It is significant that the drama begins with an announcement of Krishna's, or Bhagavān's, dependence upon Yogamāyā to orchestrate the love-inspiring world of paradisal beauty, facilitating the quenching of his divine desires. We see this in the fourth *pāda* (quarter verse) of the opening verse: Yogamāyā *upāśritaḥ* ("fully taking refuge in Yogamāyā's illusive powers"). Paradoxically, Bhagavān, however, as the supreme person in whom the very power of Yogamāyā originates, is never subject to the control of Māyā the way a worldly soul is:

> It is logically wrong to speak of Bhagavān,
> who is the supreme controller and ever liberated,
> As one who could be subject to Māyā,
> not to speak of the weakness of bondage.[8]

Therefore, it is an exceptional and unexpected event that the Lord should submit himself fully to Yogamāyā. The word *upāśritaḥ*, "fully taking refuge," is not engaged anywhere else in the entire Bhāgavata text to describe Bhagavān's dependency on anyone, including Yogamāyā, with the exception of this instance within the first verse of the Rāsa Līlā.[9]

Perhaps though, this is not surprising, as Māyā is full of amazing powers. In the Bhagavad Gītā, the word appears in six verses

[7] RL 1.24.

[8] BhP 3.7.9.

[9] Among the eight instances throughout the Bhāgavata text in which the word *upāśritaḥ* is found, two observations can be drawn. First, the word is never found in conjunction with the concept of *māyā* or *yoga-māyā*, except in the case of the first verse of the Rāsa Līlā. The word stem *āśritaḥ*, without the prefix *upa-*, is found in only one other instance in conjunction with the word *māyā*, and here it is describing souls who are conditioned by the illusory power of *māyā*, *māyāśritānām*. Second, in every instance other than the Rāsa Līlā's first verse, one finds the word *upāśritaḥ* being used to describe the dependency of the soul on the divine. This is also the case in the couple of instances found in the text of the Bhagavad Gītā.

that introduce two essential dimensions of the concept. Krishna explains that his divinity is hidden from unqualified persons by this yogic power, as expressed in the Gītā's single instance in which the full term Yogamāyā is found:

> I am not revealed to everyone,
> being concealed by
> the divine power of yoga,
> Yogamāyā.
> This bewildered world
> does not recognize me
> as the unborn and everpresent.[10]

In addition to concealing reality from deluded souls, the power of Māyā reveals the Lord's divine nature to deserving souls: "By controlling physical nature which belongs to me, I reveal myself through my own power, Māyā."[11] These functions of Māyā in the Bhagavad Gītā anticipate other dimensions of her powers found in the Bhāgavata.

Repeatedly throughout the Bhāgavata text, we are reminded that Māyā is a power that belongs to divinity. One finds the word in compound phrases along with names of the divine masculine, such as "the Māyā of Vishnu," or with epithets of the divine, such as "the Māyā of Bhagavān."[12] Yogamāyā is dependent on divinity, originates in divinity, and cannot exist or act without the sanction of divinity. Yet Māyā is simultaneously an independent power,

[10] BG 7.25.

[11] BG 4.6.

[12] These phrases include: "the great power of Vishnu" (*viṣṇoḥ mahā-māyā*); "the *māyā* of Krishna" (*kṛṣṇa-māyā*); "the *māyā* of Bhagavān" (*māyā-bhagavataḥ*); "the *māyā* of God" (*deva-māyā*); "the Lord of *māyā*" (*māyeśa*); and "the *māyā* of the Lord" (*īśa-māyā*). The possessive suffix *sva-* and the reflexive use of *ātmā* are also found coupled with the word *māyā*, to indicate the divine source and possession of *māyā*. For example, phrases such as "his own *māyā*" (*sva-māyā* or *ātmā-māyā*); and "with the yoga of my own *māyā*" (*ātma-māyā-yogena*); as well as "my *māyā*" (*mat-māyā*) are found throughout the text.

completely separate from divinity's own personal manifestations. If this were not the case, Krishna would not be able to submit himself to it, as he does in the first verse of the Rāsa Līlā.

Yogamāyā is an autonomous divine force intended for Krishna's direct use in his *līlā* of loving intimacy. We see this in Brahmā's prayers to Krishna, in which he addresses the Lord as Yogeśvara, "O master of yogic power," and proclaims that all of Krishna's manifestations are made possible through the power of his Yogamāyā energy that extends into every universe.[13] Even the construction of the universe itself, and "of all the worlds"—which includes Krishna's eternal abode of affectionate play[14]—can be credited to Māyā, having emerged, in a sense, from her womb.

Māyā's divine femininity, and the multiple personifications she assumes, are asserted by Krishna when he explains to Yogamāyā herself that her personae will be identified by various names, such as Durgā and Vaiṣṇavī.[15] The power of this divine feminine force is emphasized by the author of the Bhāgavata through this nomenclature, clearly identifying this power as a *śakti* ("feminine power" or "energy") of divinity. This *śakti* casts spells of enchantment upon us according to our desires: the individual contents of each of our hearts.

Māyā exhibits both concealing and revealing functions: she conceals the true nature of the self as a lover of divinity through delusion: "This whole world is bewildered by such a power in which persons are constantly forgetful of their [true] selves."[16] And she conceals the truth of the divinity from lovers of God through deception, as to a true lover of divinity, God appears to be just like an ordinary human.[17] Therefore, Māyā's spell enchants not only

[13] BhP 10.14.21.
[14] BhP 10.28.6.
[15] "People from all over the earth will give you various names, such as Durgā, Bhadrakālī, Vijayā and Vaiṣṇavī, Kumudā, Caṇḍikā, Kṛṣṇā, Mādhavī and Kanyakā, Māyā, Nārāyaṇī, Īśānī, Śāradā, and Ambikā" (BhP 10.2.11–12).
[16] BhP 10.14.44cd.
[17] BhP 10.17.22.

the bewildered souls of this world, but also from the most liberated souls of the supremely celestial realms.

A classic example is that of the divine mother of the Lord from whom Krishna's divinity is concealed for the purpose of preserving their loving relationship.[18] In this episode, Krishna's foster mother, Yaśodā, inspects her child's opened mouth for dirt particles. While she does so, an overwhelming and tremendous vision of the universe is revealed to her. The potency of Māyā thereafter conceals this awe-inspiring, or *aiśvarya*, manifestation of God, deceiving Yaśodā so that she will not be distracted from her maternal affection for Krishna, who is, after all, playing the role of her loving child.[19]

Concealing the greatness, *aiśvarya*, in order for the sweetness, *mādhurya*, of the divinity to be revealed is a primary function of Māyā. Divinity's most intimate companions are "covered by a curtain of divine illusion," so that any awareness of his majesty is eclipsed, allowing for more affectionate exchanges with the deity.

Throughout the tenth book one finds the phrase *māyā-mohita*, "bewildered by Māyā," in relation to those who are closest to Krishna.[20] The word *mohita*, meaning "stupefied," "bewildered," "infatuated," or "deluded," is used to describe the state of mind in which such special souls find themselves:

> Thus both of them [Krishna's mother and father]
> who were bewildered (*mohita*)
> by the words of the Soul of all, who is Hari,
> Whose appearance in the human form
> was made possible by Māyā,
> joyfully placed him on their laps and embraced him.[21]

[18] BhP 10.8.
[19] BhP 10.8.43–44.
[20] Instances of *māyā-mohita* can be found in BhP 10.13.42, 10.14.44, 10.23.50–51, and 10.63.40.
[21] BhP 10.45.10.

This feminine force of Māyā acts as a veritable catalyst for loving interaction with the divine. She allows the Lord to camouflage manifestations of his power and greatness by providing him with a form or "disguise" that his devotees then relate to affectionately and sweetly.[22] Conversely, for those who are bound to this world, the Lord's disguise acts as smoke covers the light of a fire,[23] causing him to appear as an ordinary human to them: as unremarkable as he is lovable to those bound to him by devotion.[24]

At times, Māyā even allows the more formal aspect of God's *aiśvarya* to appear in the consciousness of intimate devotees, as in the following verse spoken by the Gopīs. Here, the cowherd maidens praise Krishna's feet as objects of worship for those who relate to him in his *aiśvarya* aspect, whereas the Gopīs themselves—who are immersed in the sweetness of *mādhurya-rasa*—look to his feet to satisfy their burning desire:

> Your lotus feet fulfill
> the desires of all
> who humbly submit to them.
> Worshiped by the one
> born from the lotus flower,
> they are the ornament of the earth.
> They are to be meditated upon
> during times of distress, for
> they grant the highest satisfaction.
> O charming lover,
> please place upon our breasts
> your lotus feet, O slayer of misery.
>
> (RL 3.13)

[22] BhP 10.84.16.
[23] BhP 10.70.37.
[24] This type of human-like appearance by God is expressed in phrases such as *māyā-manuṣya*, "the appearance as a human"; *māyā-martya*, "appearance of an ordinary mortal"; and *māyā-manujam*, "appearance like a human being."

Such alternating shifts between feelings for divinity's greatness and feelings for his sweetness are made possible by Yogamāyā, as—for his devotees—experiencing divinity's *aiśvarya* heightens feelings of separation from his *mādhurya*. The Rāsa Līlā is thus sprinkled with verses that swing between the Gopīs' appreciation of Krishna's supreme majesty and greatness and their passion and affection for him as his beloveds. This delightful tug between awe and passion feeds their divine hearts. In such an amorous context, feelings of awe toward divinity assume the extraordinary function of intensifying the sweetness exchanged—*mādhurya-rasa*—between divinity and his most intimately loving companions.

In the final act of the Rāsa Līlā, Māyā makes it possible for each of the Gopīs to become Krishna's dancing companion on that magical night by producing a "double" for each of them. For how else were they to leave their husbands to meet with another male in the middle of the night? Yogamāyā creates situations in which ethical and social reconciliation occurs: Compensating for their absence in their homes, the Gopīs' "doubles" take on their duties as chaste wives, allowing the husbands and family members to experience the full presence of those cowherd maidens, even though they have escaped into the forest to frolic with Krishna. Once there, Yogamāyā works her magic again, so that Krishna's own sense of infinite divine power and the Gopīs' sense of finitude do not interfere with the affectionate reciprocation between them.

Yogamāyā's main function is to nourish the flow of affection between divinity and souls. The Bhāgavata uses the metaphor of a dramatic play to explain the way in which she does this.[25] Although God authors the play, and creates and sustains the very stage on which the play is enacted, he cannot simultaneously participate as one of the actors—completely losing himself in *līlā*—without the

[25] "You [Krishna] are covered by a curtain of illusory power (*māyā*), and you who are imperishable are beyond the range of perception (*ajñādhokṣaja*) for ignorant persons. You are not perceived by the vision of deluded persons, just as an actor is not perceived when he is dressed for a drama" (BhP 1.8.19).

essential, enabling power of Yogamāyā. For it is the divine feminine as Yogamāyā who arranges the stage sets and directs the play. It is her uniting influence alone that allows the spiritual actor and actresses—divinity and the pure souls—to verily lose themselves in this divine play of *līlā*, in which everything unfolds for the purpose of increasing the intensity and intimacy of their love.

6
Krishna: Lord of Love, Beauty, and Play

The rich plot of the Rāsa Līlā drama begins with Krishna's intoxicating flute playing. The powerful effect of Krishna's flute music on all who hear it is extraordinary. In the Bhāgavata tradition, the Lord's flute enchants all the worlds, lovingly calling souls back to him, as it did the young women of Vraja. Portrayed here in the tenth book as the supreme person who resides in his abode known as Goloka—the highest of the heavenly worlds—Krishna, as the supreme Lord of love, captures all devotional hearts with his divine flute music.

The mesmerizing music of Krishna's flute affects living and nonliving beings in various ways. Trees and vines exhibit bodily ecstasy and overflow with fruits and flowers upon hearing the divine flute. Clouds become generous, providing a gentle mist of rain and a percussive accompaniment of thunder. Flowing currents in the rivers are broken and begin to swirl, offering lotus flowers to the cowherd Lord. Birds close their eyes, listening intently to the music, and peacocks dance in madness. Nursing calves become still with wonder, their eyes filled with tears. All moving creatures become stunned, and stationary beings begin to move. Even the wives of the heavenly denizens are entranced as their hair and clothing loosen. Such wondrous effects of hearing Krishna's divine flute playing are described in the Bhāgavata's chapter known as the "Song of the Flute," the Veṇu Gīta.

This particular verse by a traditional Vaishnava poet expresses this phenomenon, in which the devotee appreciates Krishna's flute

The Yoga of Love. Graham M. Schweig, Oxford University Press. © Oxford University Press 2025.
DOI: 10.1093/oso/9780197768426.003.0007

music not only in terms of the *mādhurya* or intimate activities of Krishna, but also as it is connected to the *aiśvarya*, or cosmological and ontological dimensions of his lordship:

> All hail to the child's flute notes coming forth so
> that Om might sound.
> The flute notes cause the worlds to exult, the Vedas to
> sound, trees to rejoice,
> mountains to fly, deer to be tame, cows blissful,
> and cowherds bewildered, ascetics' flesh to
> rise and the seven basic notes to sound.[1]

There is no other deity within the Hindu complex of religion, perhaps even among the religious traditions of the world, who is as amorous, personable, and playful as Krishna, and the tenth book celebrates this divine persona. Whereas in most of the Bhāgavata text, Krishna is presented as the cosmic Vishnu—the supremely powerful deity under whom all other partial divinities work—here, the supreme Lord is utterly adored by his devotees as a young and playful cowherd, carrying a bamboo flute. As compared with the numerous four-armed forms of Vishnu—which hold combinations of the disc, conch, club, and lotus—the special symbol of the intimate deity of Krishna is clearly the flute, held sweetly to his mouth by his two lotus-like hands (see Figure 3).

Along with his playful movements, affectionate smiles, enticing glances, and eloquent speech, Krishna enchants the entire universe with his irresistible flute music. As such, his flute playing and related intimate *līlās* are occurring eternally, and yet his "day" is divided into morning, afternoon, and evening types of play: in the morning, Krishna behaves just like a mischievous child with his parents; he frolics in the fields of Vraja with cows and cowherd

[1] *The Love of Krishna: The Kṛṣṇakarṇāmṛta of Līlāśuka Bilvamaṅgala*, ed. and trans. by Frances Wilson (Philadelphia: University of Pennsylvania Press, 1975), II.110.

Figure 3. Decorative hand-cut stencil of Krishna in his classical bodily formation, with peacock feather in his headdress, playing the flute. 8″ × 10″ plastic sheet cut-out. Courtesy of S. S. Rangoli Art, Mathura, Uttar Pradesh, India.

friends in the afternoon; and in the evening, he engages in sweet amorous play with the cowherd girls.

Just as all entities are affected by Krishna's flute music, all who are touched by him, including plant and animal life, experience blissful, rapturous feelings throughout their bodies. Krishna awakens amorous feelings in the cowherd maidens with his affectionate touch and enticing manner. He even allows his feet to touch the breasts of the Gopīs, which represents their unique way of worshiping the feet of their beloved Lord.[2]

Krishna's feet are distinguishable by the signs appearing on their soles, such as the flag and thunderbolt.[3] Gods, goddesses, mystics, and lovers alike especially long for his feet because, along with other desired effects, they dispel all misfortune and inauspiciousness. In India, the feet of sages, and even more the feet of *avatāra* forms of the divinity (including sacred images of the deity Krishna) are considered holy and worthy of worship, and persons place the dust from such feet on their heads as an act of humility and devotion. At other times, persons worship the feet simply by bowing down to the ground near saintly souls, or where their feet have tread. Thus, dust itself becomes sanctified when in contact, no matter how briefly, with holy feet. As for the dust from Krishna's feet, "Even Brahmā, Śiva, and the Goddess Ramā place this dust upon their heads, in order to dispel their impurities."[4] The devotee, however, bows down to Krishna's alluring beauty as an expression of being fully captivated by his divine form.

The beauty of Krishna's form is elaborately described throughout the Bhāgavata text and is depicted as "glowing brilliantly"—"the only source of beauty pervading all the three worlds." The imagery of this intimate deity is consistently vivid, intricate, and naturalistic. He is known by his effulgent, dark bluish hue. His face, eyes, hands,

[2] RL 3.13.
[3] RL 2.25.
[4] RL 2.29.

and feet are often compared to the loveliness of the lotus flower. Always dressed and decorated in distinctive ways, he wears yellow silken garments, brilliant as gold. On his head of dark curling locks of hair, Krishna wears an ornament adorned with a peacock feather. Ornate earrings decorate either side of his soft glowing face, and he wears a garland made of various colored forest flowers and leaves. He is often found equipped with a herding stick and buffalo horn.

The many names and epithets ascribed to Krishna in the Rāsa Līlā reflect various colorful aspects of his beautiful being. Though Vaishnava worshipers honor "the thousand names of Vishnu" in the well-known traditional work *Viṣṇu Sahasra Nāma*—consisting exclusively of one thousand names of Krishna or Vishnu—the nomenclature for Krishna that appears throughout the Rāsa Līlā drama is the most adored, for no one can resist the lure of Krishna's sacred love-call. An overview of the most prominent names reveals much about his identity.

The specific name Krishna appears a total of twenty-seven times in the Rāsa Līlā text, more than any other name for the deity.[5] The meaning of the name is literally "dark blue" or "blackish," referring to Krishna's dark complexion, which is described poetically as the color of a beautiful new monsoon cloud. When he dances with the Gopīs in the circle of the Rāsa dance, his lovely color is compared to that of "dark clouds" of a thunderstorm.[6]

The name Krishna is derived from the verbal root *kṛṣ* (from which the precise transliterated form "Kṛṣṇa" comes), which means "to draw," or even more applicable here, "to draw into one's power," and hence the meaning "attractive." Theologians from the Chaitanya school claim that the name means "supremely attractive." The divine cowherd certainly possesses this drawing power, dramatically expressed in the first scene of the text in which he

[5] The name Krishna appears in the following verses: 1.4, 1.7, 1.9, 1.12, 1.16, 1.30, 1.47 / 2.3, 2.9, 2.14, 2.15, 2.16, 2.17, 2.18, 2.19, 2.24, 2.31–32, 2.35, 2.38, 2.44 / 4.1 / 5.3, 5.8, 5.9, 5.12, 5.19, 5.38.

[6] RL 5.8.

allures the chaste cowherd maidens from their homes into the forest. Moreover, when Krishna's name first appears in the fourth verse of the text, this power is revealed:

> Upon hearing that sweet music,
> their passion for him swelling,
> The young women of Vraja whose
> minds were captured by Krishna,
> Unaware of one another,
> ran off toward the place
> Where their beloved was waiting,
> with their earrings swinging wildly.[7]

The name Krishna identifies the intimate deity of the godhead. Other names of Krishna found in the text are similarly associated with his more personal and affectionate nature, such as Govinda,[8] or "one who tends the cows," referring to this pastoral deity in the rural region of Vraja; Vāsudeva, "the son of Vasudeva";[9] Keśava, "the one with beautiful hair";[10] Mādhava,[11] "the one who is sweet"; and Hari, or "one who steals our hearts."[12] Other names of Krishna express his grand or powerful nature, such as Mukunda, "the one who grants liberation."[13] These names appear far fewer times than his more intimate ones, clearly indicating the emphasis in the drama on the sweet and loving attributes of the deity.

[7] RL 1.4.

[8] RL 1.8, 1.28/2.7, 2.28, 2.29, 2.30/5.2.

[9] RL 5.39.

[10] RL 1.48/2.10, 2.37/4.9.

[11] RL 2.8 and 2.41.

[12] RL 1.15/2.28.

[13] Other such names also appearing are: Śauri, "the heroic descendent of the Śura dynasty" (RL 4.2, 4.4); Adhokṣaja, "one who is beyond the range of the senses" (RL 1.13); Hṛṣīkeśa, "the Lord of the senses" (1.13); Varāha, "the divine boar" (RL 2.10); and the avatāric manifestations of Urukrama, "the great striding one" (2.10). In the benedictory last verse of the text, the narrator identifies Krishna with Vishnu, as "the all-pervading one" (RL 5.40).

The epithet Bhagavān is especially recognized as a name for Vishnu or Krishna.[14] The hero is immediately introduced in the first verse as Bhagavān, and with the exception of the name Krishna, Bhagavān is the most utilized name in the story, appearing a total of twenty times.[15] My translation of this significant epithet is "the Beloved Lord," intended to express both powerful and intimate aspects of the deity. The word Bhagavān breaks down into two parts: the noun *bhaga* and the suffix *-vān* (*-vat*), meaning "one who possesses (*-vān*) all *bhaga*." The lexical senses of *bhaga* convey either the manifestation of supreme power or excellence (*aiśvarya*), expressed by the word "Lord" in the phrase; or the manifestation of supreme sweetness (*mādhurya*), expressed by the word "Beloved." The word *bhaga* carries both *aiśvarya*-related meanings such as "good fortune," "omnipotence," "virtue," "fame," or "excellence," and *mādhurya*-related meanings such as "love," "loveliness," "affection," "amorous dalliance," or even "sexual inclination."

There are also other names in the narration that express Krishna's power, assuring the reader that this deity, typically known for his playful and intimate nature, is nonetheless the supreme deity.[16] Although Krishna's identity is primarily that of an independent divinity, he places himself in a dependent position in order to enjoy love. This dependency, however, is itself an expression of his power and supremacy. After all, it is Krishna's *divine will* to submit himself fully to Yogamāyā, his potency for making loving arrangements.

[14] The word in other traditional contexts can also refer to the god Śiva, to the Buddha, or even to a Bodhisattva (MW).

[15] "The Beloved Lord," or *bhagavān*, is found in the following acts and verses: 1.1, 1.14, 1.16, 1.17, 1.18, 1.47, 2.1, 2.14, 2.28, 2.40, 4.10, 4.14, 4.17, 5.1, 5.7, 5.16, 5.20, 5.27, 5.39, and 5.40. References here to verses 1.18 and 4.17 refer to the introductory phrase "The Beloved Lord spoke." All other instances of *bhagavān* are embedded within verse lines.

[16] Krishna is referred to as the Supreme in verses 1.11, 1.32, and 2.24. A variety of names express his "supreme" status, such as "Soul" (*ātmā* RL 1.14, 1.32, 1.33, 2.28, and 4.14); "supreme Soul" (*paramātmā* RL 1.11, 2.24); "great Soul" (*mahatma* RL 1.47, 2.31–32); "Person" (*puruṣa* RL 2.4 and 4.10); "Lord" (*īśvara* or *parameśvara* RL1.33); "supreme Lord of Yoga" (RL 1.16, 1.42, 4.14, and 5.3); and the "the supreme God of love" (literally, the "God of love among all love gods," RL 4.2).

Another name of Krishna, Acyuta, appearing nine times in the text, indicates Krishna's supremacy and invulnerability. Unlike any other name of the deity, including the name Krishna itself, Acyuta is the only name that is found at least once in each of the five acts.[17] The author of the text may have utilized the name throughout in order to emphasize that Krishna is not an ordinary soul, but rather the "supreme" soul. The name Acyuta means "the infallible one" or, literally, "the unshaken one" or "the one who is not fallen." The connotation is that he, as the supreme soul, does "not fall" to this world in which finite souls experience the endless cycles of birth and rebirth (*saṁsāra*).

When Krishna, who is full and complete in himself, engages in love's delights with the cowherd maidens, he is not conforming to the ways of this world. Rather, he is allowing his devotee and himself to love intimately and freely in a realm that transcends the everyday world—and transcends *even* himself. This is tied into the essential message behind the name Acyuta—that despite Krishna's erotic sports with the Gopīs, he does not fall into sexual relations with them—and is a powerful and consistent theme running through the text.

The narrator of the story carefully explains that Krishna's erotic play is due to the delight of *rasa* within the divine. In other words, a dramatic clue for appreciating this paradoxical theological theme can be found in the use of the word "even" in the first verse. As mentioned above, the epithetical nomenclature Bhagavān, "the Beloved Lord," expresses to the reader that Krishna is powerful as well as intimate, and full in all excellences. The adversative particle "even" (*api*), subjoined to the subject noun of the verse, "the Beloved Lord," further heightens the extraordinary event that is occurring.

[17] The name Acyuta appears in the following acts: RL 1.10, 1.43/2.7, 2.11, 2.30/3.16/4.10/5.14, and 5.15. It is telling that no other name of Krishna appears in the third act of the RL.

All beauty and all loveliness are contained in Krishna, yet "those nights in autumn filled with blooming jasmine flowers" inspire *even* the supreme Lord. *Even* he is moved "toward love's delights"; though pleasure exists fully within himself, he succumbs to beauty and love. Moreover, *even* he takes full "refuge in Yogamāyā," desiring assistance from the Goddess for his intimate *līlā*, though he is unlimitedly powerful. Thus Krishna's supremacy is challenged and his intimate attributes augmented in this theological paradox.

Krishna delights more in reciprocating the love of his devotees in *rasa* than he does in deriving pleasure from within his supreme self. In a verse depicting Krishna's dalliance with a special Gopī, it is stated: "He delighted in loving her, yet he delights in the self and takes pleasure in the self, for he is complete."[18] Another verse describes Krishna's interactions with the collective Gopīs: "He, who himself possesses all pleasure, took pleasure in loving them, playing like the king of elephants."[19] Through these verses and others, it is clear that the supreme Lord is complete, without limitation or need, inexhaustible, and fully content, yet he is moved by the beauteous scene and submits himself to love.

Although loving play occurs for the pleasure of his intimate devotees and his own delight, it also teaches those who read or hear about it, as expressed by the narrator who interprets these teachings in theological apologia throughout the story. Thus Krishna is a teacher to souls in this world through constituent phases of love play that take place in his own divine world. Such playfulness teaches souls that Krishna preserves the worldly ethical conventions and, at the same time, transcends them, as will be discussed further below.

Divinity disappears from the soul who exhibits pride. While engaged in play with his most intimate female associates, Krishna teaches his reader that pride is the enemy of love and devotion.

18 RL 2.34.
19 RL 5.24. See other similar expressions in RL 1.42 and 5.20.

Even though such pride, as displayed in the Gopīs, is a component of their passionate devotion, the narrator uses the example of their "otherworldly" pride to teach an indispensable lesson about worldly pride. This lesson is indeed so important that he teaches it twice—first with the group of Gopīs at the end of the first act, then with the special Gopī in the second scene of the second act. After Krishna agrees to let the cowherd maidens stay with him and then disappears due to their pride, he later reappears to join them in the Rāsa dance.

This dialectical movement between divine absence and presence, between the hiddenness and revelation of the intimate divinity (perhaps the tradition's version of the Christian notions of *deus absconditus* and *deus revelatus*), creating a kind of "hide and seek" of love, is not only didactic but also part of Krishna's sportiveness. In the fourth act, the supreme Lord again exhibits his lesson-giving when he delivers to the maidens a discourse on the nature of love, which also imparts wisdom to the reader.[20] Thus, both the Gopīs and the reader benefit from Krishna's didactic words, often taught through his love play with his dearest devotees.

David Kinsley observes about the divinity of Krishna: "Play as divine activity in India is nowhere more fully illustrated."[21] As we have shown, this playfulness of Krishna often takes on a paradoxical character, appearing to be subversive, all the while demonstrating itself to be elevating and transcending. The author-narrator makes it tacitly clear that the pleasure Krishna experiences with his dearest cowherd maidens is not transgressive, nor is it limited or compromised by worldly interactions; rather, his pleasure takes place in a realm of pure poetry and divine aesthetics:

[20] RL 4.17–20.

[21] David R. Kinsley, *The Divine Player: A Study of Kṛṣṇa Līlā* (Delhi: Motilal Banarsidass, 1979), p. 56. This book presents a comprehensive study of the idea of "play" in traditions surrounding the worship of Krishna and, additionally, throughout Indian religion in general.

Thus he allowed himself to be
subdued by these nights
made so brilliant
by the rays of the moon—
He was perfectly
fulfilled in all desires
and pure within himself;
While with that group of maidens
so passionately attached to him,
sexual enjoyment was of no issue—
Inspired by the narrations
and poetry of autumn,
all those moonlit nights
found their refuge in *rasa*.[22]

The Beloved Lord's ultimate play manifests as dancing and singing with the Gopīs in the Rāsa dance. Afterward, they delight in sporting together in the forest and cooling rivers.

[22] RL 5.26.

7

The Gopīs: Beloveds of Krishna

The Gopīs are portrayed as extraordinary souls who are the dearest beloveds of Krishna. This special and exalted position given to the divine feminine reflects the prominent goddess worship that saturated ancient cultures, including the one from which the Bhāgavata emerged.

In the Rāsa Līlā story, the Gopīs' love for Krishna is in fact so exceptional that Krishna himself questions if he can reciprocate it as purely as it was offered to him.[1] Later, in the eleventh book, Krishna even asserts that the only way that he can be attained is through the love of the Gopīs: their path being superior to all other paths leading to the divinity. Krishna then reminisces about the Gopīs' love during those autumn nights of the Rāsa and compares these divine females in their devotion to sages who merge their spirits into the supreme reality, like rivers into the ocean.[2]

In the latter part of the tenth book, Uddhava—the special friend sent by Krishna to console the cowherd maidens—does the same. Astonished by their unexcelled love, Uddhava declares that even great sages have difficulty attaining their level of devotion.[3] The Gopīs are thus recognized as the paradigms of devotion, which—in their case—is so powerful that it bestows grace upon anyone who observes it.[4] We hear Uddhava completely overtaken by this grace in the verses that follow, where he effusively praises the maidens for their exemplary love of Krishna.[5]

[1] RL 4.20–22.
[2] BhP 11.12.8–13.
[3] BhP 10.47.25.
[4] BhP 10.47.27.
[5] BhP 10.47.58–63.

The Yoga of Love. Graham M. Schweig, Oxford University Press. © Oxford University Press 2025.
DOI: 10.1093/oso/9780197768426.003.0008

The name "Gopī," meaning "a cowherdess" or "cowherd maiden," appears in the plural form in the majority of instances within the Rāsa Līlā, since the maidens relate to Krishna as a group more often than not. It is by far the most utilized epithet for the consorts, appearing twenty-four times within the five acts.[6] No personal names are found for the cowherd maidens, who even refer to themselves as *gopīs*.[7]

Many other colorful epithets appear in the drama, through which we learn about the identity of the maidens. They are called "those ladies with beautiful eyes,"[8] "ones with beautiful waists,"[9] and "jewel-like women."[10] Names of servitude are presented throughout by the Gopīs themselves, such as "undemanding maidservants."[11] There are several epithets identifying the village of Vraja in relation to the maidens, who are called "the beautiful women of Vraja."[12] Epithets of affection are also found repeatedly. The cowherd maidens are referred to as "dear ones," "beloved ones," or "lovers," even "those who are dear to the Lord." In addition, the narrator calls the Gopīs "the delighted lovers." They are further described as "those who desire him," and the one special Gopī as "the girl desirous of love."

The nomenclature used in the Rāsa Līlā leads to a complex portrait of the maidens when it comes to their marital status, for they are presented as both the wives of cowherd men, as well as wives of Krishna—or simply, as unmarried girls who have become the young wives of Krishna. The Gopīs are called "women," "brides,"

[6] There are twenty-two instances of the plural of Gopī, and two of the singular. Three of the plural instances are found in introductory lines external to the actual verses, as in "The beautiful Gopīs spoke."

[7] RL 2.30–31.

[8] RL 1.3.

[9] RL 1.19, 4.18.

[10] RL 5.2.

[11] For example, the words "of your maidservants" (*kiṅkarīṇām*, RL 1.41), "undemanding maidservants" (*aśulka-dāsikā*, RL 3.2), and "maidservants" (*vidhi-karīr*, RL 3.8) are found. The phrase "your miserable maidservant" (*dāsyās te kṛpaṇāyā*, RL 2.39) is cried out by the special Gopī when she is deserted by Krishna.

[12] *Vraja-sundarī*, RL 1.46 and 5.17; other examples are: *vraja-striyaḥ*, RL 1.4, 5.16; *vraja-yoṣitaḥ*, RL 1.17; *vrajāṅganāḥ*, RL 2.1; and *vraja-vadhūbhir*, RL 5.40.

and "young wives" in different instances.[13] In the climactic verse of the drama they are referred to as *kṛṣṇa-vadhvaḥ*, which could easily be understood as "the wives of Krishna."[14] Yet the inquiring king calls them "others' wives,"[15] while the narrator refers to them both as ones who are "faithful" to Krishna[16] and as "ladies of the cowherd men."[17] Ironically, Krishna calls the Gopīs "chaste ladies,"[18] and even "friends."[19] The mystery of the married or unmarried status of the Gopīs—which is addressed in "Ethical Boundaries and Boundless Love" below—has been a debated issue in the Chaitanya school.

As the social status of the Gopīs shifts between married and unmarried, the voice of the Gopīs shifts between plural (as the complete group or partial groups) and singular. At times it is difficult to discern whether one of the Gopīs is speaking on behalf of the group, or whether the maidens as a group are speaking in unison, like a Greek chorus. This shifting between singular and collective voices, as well as ambiguity in the number of voices, is intentional on the part of the Bhāgavata's author. It conveys a deep sense of intimacy within the community of cowherd maidens and, at the same time, supports the various personalities of the individual Gopīs. Moreover, their collective and individual voices and actions are mutually interdependent; that is, the individual voice is expressive of the collective voice, which in turn is expressive of each of the individual voices.

This dialectical relationship between the collective and individual maidens is especially highlighted during the Rāsa dance

[13] Words meaning "women" are the following: *striyāḥ*, 1.19, 2.35, 2.42, and 5.2; *vadhū*, RL 1.26, 2.31–32, 2.38, 5.8, and 5.40; *abalāḥ*, RL 4.21, and *yuvatīḥ*, RL 5.24. The word *vadhū* can mean simply "woman," but the word's more essential meaning is "bride," "newly married woman," or "young wife" (MW).

[14] RL 5.8.

[15] *Para-dāra*, RL 5.28.

[16] RL 5.2.

[17] RL 5.20.

[18] RL 1.22.

[19] RL 4.20.

and becomes a major symbolic motif: all the Gopīs together form the Rāsa dance circle, yet, simultaneously, each one experiences Krishna's exclusive attention. Even as early as the first two verses, the introduction of the one and the many voices is conveyed by way of metaphor. The author establishes the cowherd maidens as a group in the first verse, then as a singular presence in the second verse. These two presentations anticipate the continuous movement in the story line between the Gopīs as a group and as individuals.

Perhaps this movement is most dramatically expressed through the metaphorical use of the word "nights" (*rātrī*), found in the opening verse of the work. The term *rātrī*—a feminine noun stem in the plural[20]—is one among many words in Sanskrit that have the meaning of "night." Yet, appropriately, it is the only word for "night" that is used to refer to the Goddess of the Night in the ancient Ṛg Veda text. The image here is of many "nights" adorned with beautiful jasmine—the scented flower commonly found ornamenting the hair of Indian women and girls of any social status—in order to attract the attention of a male.

These "nights decorated with jasmine" is seen as a metaphor for the many cowherd maidens, who also decorate themselves with jasmine in order to attract Krishna, the supreme male (RL 5.11). Just as this special jasmine blooms at night, the Gopīs' love for Krishna is to blossom that very night. And just as jasmine is "not supposed" to appear in the autumn season, the Gopīs are "not supposed" to appear in the forest after nightfall. This love story's forbidden and otherworldly quality is conveyed through this complex metaphor.

[20] Words for night in Sanskrit are many, including *rātra*, *niśā*, *rajanī*, *kṣaṇadā*, *kṣapā*, and so on. The idea of *rātrī* functioning metaphorically as the Goddess Nights, as the tenor of the metaphor, is supported by modern dramatic performance. It is interesting to note that in such modern pilgrimage plays of the Rāsa Līlā story, the Goddess is not only personified as "Nights," but her role includes a dialogue with Krishna! See John Stratton Hawley in association with Shrivatsa Goswami, "The Great Circle Dance," in *At Play with Krishna: Pilgrimage Dramas of Brindavan* (Princeton: Princeton University Press, 1981), p. 184.

The collective heroines of the story emerge through the metaphorical vehicle of the Night goddess when presented in the plural. For both the cowherd maidens and the Night goddess are ephemeral, enticingly beautiful and come alive at night. Thus, in this introductory verse, "those nights in autumn" represent the Night goddess, who reveals Krishna's own night goddesses, the heroines of the story, the Gopīs. Like the spellbinding autumn nights, the Gopīs are ripe for love in this festive and celebratory season, setting the ideal scene for the Rāsa dance.

The cowherd maidens' love for Krishna awakens in the third verse. Here, the Gopīs—presented explicitly as a group—open their eyes widely with affection and anticipation. Drawn to the flute music, their minds so enraptured by Krishna, they have no choice but to join him. What follows in verses five through eight is a peek into the various activities occupying the Gopīs before they burst forth into the forest, such as the milking of cows, the feeding of their children and husbands, and so on.

Despite being under the care of their husbands, fathers, or brothers, in verses six and eight, the cowherd maidens swiftly abandon their caretakers to be with Krishna.[21] We then discover, in verses nine through eleven, that some of the Gopīs were not able to sneak away as easily. Instead, they enter into deep meditation, embracing their Beloved inside their hearts, like sages do with Divinity. In the last verse of this scene, it becomes clear that the Gopīs are not ordinary souls, since they have "relinquished their bodies composed of physical elements."[22]

The extraordinary nature of the cowherd maidens becomes the topic for discourse between the narrator and listener in the second didactic scene. The king observes that the maidens know Krishna as "the greatest lover," and not as "the source of Brahman." He inquires of the sage how it is that they are able to escape the influence of the

[21] In Indian society, women are traditionally under the care of a male, if not father or husband, then a brother or other male in the family. However, the Gopīs abandoned any male caretaker for the purpose of being with Krishna.

[22] RL 1.11.

underlying forces of nature, while remaining passionately in love with Krishna. The narrating sage offers two responses to his question: the Gopīs' deepest emotions are focused on Krishna, for they are "fully absorbed in God"; and the Lord liberates all, including persons who are hateful toward him, not to mention those who are in love with him.

After the Gopīs and Krishna meet, share sweet words, and frolic in the forest, Krishna suddenly vanishes, ostensibly because of the pride of the maidens. Pride, though usually regarded as a negative quality for developing love of God—either as a self-indulgent or an arrogant state of mind—in this instance is understood by the Chaitanya school to be an expression of the purity and intensity of the Gopīs' love. Jīva Gosvāmī explains that their pride is that of "loving intimacy" and would only cause Krishna to favor them. Although it appears that he rejects the cowherd maidens in order to subdue their pride,[23] it is revealed by Krishna himself that he disappears in order to increase their love for him.[24]

There is ample evidence that the Gopīs "know" the various majestic and cosmic forms of Krishna, but it is his more intimate nature on which they focus, especially when their beloved is personally present before them. Theologians have observed, as mentioned above, that *aiśvarya* becomes prominent for the Gopīs when they are feeling some level of separation from Krishna, either anticipatory or actual. During periods of separation, they recall the formal, powerful aspect of Krishna, as in Scene 1 of Act Two, and Act Three. This is a matter taken up by Nārada in his *Bhakti Sūtra*, in which he recognizes the Gopīs as the foremost examples of *bhakti.*[25] Nārada points out that they "know" Krishna's supreme greatness. However, it appears as if they do not recognize it at times, due to forgetfulness caused by their passionate devotion to him.[26]

In the second act, the maidens desperately search for Krishna. Their madness, caused by intense love, is observable in their

[23] RL 1.48.
[24] RL 4.20–21.
[25] NBS 20.
[26] NBS 21–24.

"deranged" behavior of speaking to the plants and vines of the forest:

> Singing out loud about him
> like deranged persons,
> Together they searched
> from forest to forest.
> They inquired from trees,
> the lords of the forest,
> about the supreme Person
> Who is present internally and
> externally for all living beings,
> as heavenly air pervades all beings,
> within and without.[27]

According to Jīva, this madness is an appreciation of God's presence based on pure love, allowing one to see God manifest in everything.

The Gopīs then begin to imitate the behavior of Krishna, due to identifying so deeply and dramatically with him:

> Through their movements,
> smiles, glances, speech,
> and other gestures,
> The bodily forms of his lovers
> became similar
> to those of their beloved.
> The young women,
> their selves fully absorbed in him,
> thus declared, "I am he!"
> Their amorous,
> playful gestures
> were those of Krishna.[28]

[27] RL 2.4.
[28] RL 2.3.

This condition of the Gopīs is one in which the various movements of Krishna take over their minds and senses, and their very selves assume a likeness to their beloved. Viśvanātha Cakravartin—a prominent eighteenth-century commentator in the Chaitanya school—explains that this state of divine madness, or *unmāda*, is characterized by taking on the bodily movements and behavioral qualities of the supreme Beloved. This madness of the cowherd maidens, as described in the Bhāgavata, in turn becomes the model for Chaitanya, whose life is famous for his ecstatic madness in devotion to Krishna.

While imitating Krishna, the Gopīs are a unified group of heroines who are collectively presented, but who exhibit individual activities. This interesting relation between the group and individual Gopīs is especially accentuated when the group finds a solitary Gopī abandoned in the forest. By the end of the first act, Krishna has left the collective maidens, and in the second act, the reader is informed that he has run off with one particular Gopī from whom he also disappears, ostensibly due to her pride. After this special maiden relates to the inquiring group of maidens what has happened to her, she rejoins them in their search for Krishna.

The third act consists of nineteen verses of song in which the Gopīs use their collective voice to pray, remember, and yearn for Krishna. By the time the drama reaches the fourth act, then, the primary portrait the reader has of the Gopīs is one of separation from their beloved, and longing for union with him. When Krishna suddenly reappears at the beginning of the act, the reactions and emotions of specific maidens are described in verses RL 4.4–7. The group of maidens "stood up at once, as if their very lives had just been returned to their bodies."[29] By the middle of the act, the Gopīs collectively

[29] RL 4.3.

inquire from Krishna about the nature of love, and he responds in several verses.[30]

The Gopīs' narrative on the nature of love is given to us by the author's description of their utterly lovestruck condition. In the forth and first acts a certain phenomenon of psychosomatic bliss occurs in the Gopīs, as a result of directly experiencing Krishna's presence—either through physical contact or through contemplation. It mirrors a similar reaction that occurs in others when they come in contact with Krishna: "Seeing your beauty, the most magnificent in all the three worlds, the animals, trees, birds, and cows are elated with bodily ripplings of bliss."[31]

My translation of Sanskrit words that convey this experience of bliss attempts to uncover the essential meaning of these words, signifying a certain condition of ecstatic rapture caused by divine love: a condition for which we find no comparable English term. Yet the ancient culture that birthed these verses had plentiful words that described states of bliss and their accompanying phenomena in magnificent detail.

The words *pulaka-aṅgī*, referring to the Gopīs, literally mean "the [hairs] of the limbs standing," which I have translated as "elated with bodily ripplings of joy."[32] Similarly, in the fifth act, the words *hṛṣṭa-romā*, meaning literally "having hairs that are thrilled," have been translated as "elated with bodily ripplings of bliss."[33] Both these verses utilize one of two verbs that are characteristically used to describe this phenomenon; in fact, most of the words used throughout the complete Bhāgavata text to express this experience

[30] RL 4.17–22.

[31] RL 1.40.

[32] RL 4.8. Verse RL 2.10, however, is one instance in which I retain much of the literal translation of *pulaka*. My choice to do so was influenced by the imagery projected by the verse, which poetically engages imagery from the literal translation of the words. In addition, the surrounding supporting words lend themselves to this treatment.

[33] RL 5.12.

are derivative words from the verbs *hṛṣ-* "to excite" and *pul-* "to be high or stand."[34] In each of these instances, the meaning of the derivatives has the positive sense of delight and rarely carries the negative sense of fear[35] typically found in English expressions that many translators employ to describe this phenomenon.[36]

[34] Derivative words from *hṛṣ-* are as follows: *prahṛṣṭa-romā*, "with bristling or thrilling of hair"; *roma-harṣa*, "hairs thrilled or bristled"; *harṣa*, "bristling or erection (esp. of hair in a thrill of rapture or delight [MW])"; *prema-hṛṣṭa-tanu*, "a body with hairs standing out of love"; and *hṛṣyat tanū-ruhaḥ bhāva*, "due to loving emotion, the hair on the body was thrilled." Derivative words from *pul-* are the following: *utpulaka*, "hairs standing up"; *pulakācitāṅga*, "the body covered with raised hairs"; and *pulaka*, "raised hairs." Examples of less frequently used alternative expressions are *roma-utsava*, "standing up of hair" and *premṇā ūrdhva roma*, "with hairs standing due to love." Both of these phrases utilize the word for hair, "*roma*," and another word indicating its upward direction, "*utsava*" or "*ūrdhva*."

[35] Only in the Bhagavad Gītā (from the greater text of the Mahābhārata) do we have a usage that conveys both the negative sense of fear before the universal form and, simultaneously, the positive sense of jubilation.

[36] The negative sense of fear, associated with a variety of English words or phrases, is often conveyed through translations of Sanskrit words or phrases originally intended by ancient authors to indicate a positive experience of joy or bliss. In other words, the negative English connotation conflicts with the positive intent behind the Sanskrit words. Therefore, I have avoided engaging such English expressions in a literal translation of the Sanskrit. Words or phrases such as "chills," "shivers," "goose flesh," or "goose pimples" generally convey reactions to the unpleasant emotions of fear or horror. Although these can indicate the more positive emotion of "excitement," they still fail to communicate the full experience intended by the Sanskrit. "Horripilation," which would be a convenient one-word translation of the Sanskrit, is another unsuitable word choice. The word means, "a bristling of the hair of the head or body (as from disease, terror, or chilliness)" [WEB], and furthermore, etymologically, is related to the word "horror," thereby carrying negative senses. The word "eruptions" also indicates negative qualities since one of its definitions is "the breaking out of an exanthem [eruptive disease] on the skin."

English words with more positive associations, on the other hand, are too often inadequate. The lexical meaning of the word "thrill" as "an instantaneous excitement: a tingling of or as if of the nerves produced by a sudden emotional reaction" [WEB], carries only a partial sense, failing to depict the full depth of the complexion of this phenomenon, as described in the flood of bliss the *yogī* experiences (RL 4.8). Moreover, "thrill" can be associated with fear; thus a horror story is called a "thriller." And one cannot ignore the word's affiliation with negative colloquial connotations like "cheap thrill," which is clearly more fleeting and superficial than the experience conveyed through the Sanskrit terms. The phrase "sending chills up the spine" could be considered, but again, inadequately conveys the sustained intensity and superlative spiritual nature of the experience. Furthermore, the phrase can carry the sense of reaction to fear, which is certainly not the intended meaning, as already discussed above.

This state of ecstasy—experienced by the cowherd maidens—is caused by contact with Krishna: either in his presence or absence through meditating on him. To convey it fully, Sanskrit words like *pulaka* distinguish between the positive and negative senses. The literal meaning of *pulaka* in its plural form, *pulakāni*, is "erection or bristling of the hairs of the body (considered to be occasioned by delight or rapture rather than by fear)."[37] The word *pulakāni*—along with other similar terms—is intended to convey more than just the physical reactions. Instead, it clearly points to the deeper stirrings of the soul that give rise to such pronounced physical signs: the inner experience of overwhelming joy and blissfulness, which in turn makes their bodies ripple in delight.

The Rāsa Līlā's narrator draws a bridge between the rapturous sensation occurring in the Gopīs and the meditating *yogī* who becomes "flooded with bliss."[38] Both great *yogīs* and the Gopīs are touched by Divinity. This divine touch then sends them into a state of ecstasy including "ripplings" of divine bliss. The complete phrase, "elated with bodily ripplings of bliss," possesses several senses that facilitate an understanding of this complex experience, including the joyful thrill and rapturous sensation, the resulting bumpy eruptions of the skin, and the sustaining waves or undulating movement of bliss that takes over the body.

The word "ripplings" within the phrase "elated with bodily ripplings of bliss" expresses the two ways in which this phenomenon is manifest in the Gopīs: either rising from within the body and moving to the body's surface, or coming from an outside stimulus that affects the surface of the body. In either case, their skin displays eruptions. When the Gopīs meditate upon their beloved Lord, it is the former, and when they are physically touched by him, it is the latter. Like water running through a shallow stream undulates while flowing over a rocky bottom, the surface of the

[37] MW.
[38] RL 4.8.

Gopīs' skins undulates when stimulated by an inner bliss. Likewise, when Krishna touches[39] the Gopīs directly, it is like the ripples that winds create upon the formerly flat surfaces of a lakes.

While winds may wane, the continuing joyfulness that constitutes this phenomenon of being touched by Krishna—or Divinity—is sustained. For this reason—although English lexical sources do not recognize the plural form of the word rippling, as "ripplings"—I have created it in order to emphasize this unique, on-going sensation, rather than a short-lived, fleeting one. It is a state of rapturous bliss that is sustained according to how sustained our love flow toward Divinity is. There is one Gopī who is sustains this with utmost expertise: her presence is essential to the story.

The Gopīs' presence blossoms poetically in the four opening verses, like a lotus flower spreading her petals at the touch of light. In the first two verses, the petals begin to open, or the Gopīs' presence begins to unfold. In the third, their presence blossoms, and by the fourth they have almost fully bloomed, as the plot of the drama develops. The plot's flower then fully blooms when Krishna joins the Gopīs in the dance known as the Rāsa,[40] described in the fifth and final act: the apex of the sacred love story.

The word "Rāsa" indicates an ancient, circular dance form assuming the appearance of a multi-petaled flower, composed of many male and female dancers. The arms, or hands, of the female dancers are interlocked with one another in a chainlike manner, while that of their male dancing partners are interlocked around their necks. In this particular Rāsa dance, however, it is Krishna who—by duplicating himself from the center of the divine circle

[39] The definitions of the word as a verb, "to ripple," further express the specific bodily condition related to this phenomenon. The experience described is not merely the "hairs standing on end," but it is the body as it "becomes fretted or lightly ruffled on the surface (as water)" (WEB). Also, the body may "become covered with or form in small waves or undulations" (WEB), or "move with an undulating motion or so as to cause ripples" (WEB).

[40] RL 5.2.

through his mystic power—becomes the sole male partner for each maiden.[41]

As the Gopīs begin to dance, each one experiences the exclusive attention of Krishna, and "each thought she alone was at his side." Together, they sing songs of love in chorus with their beloved Lord. This portrait of Krishna and the cowherd maidens is colorfully described a few verses later, just before the climactic verse of the story:

> There, glowing brilliantly among them,
> was the Beloved Lord, son of Devakī—
> In a setting of golden ornaments,
> he appeared like a magnificent emerald![42]

It is significant that Krishna, whose complexion is usually compared to a deep blue sapphire, appears like a brilliant green emerald as he mingles with all of the golden-complexioned Gopīs in the wondrous ring of the Rāsa dance.

Among those beautiful maidens of golden complexions is the very special Gopī favored by Krishna. As the very first verse of the drama introduces us to the heroines of the story as a group of Gopīs—through the poetic metaphor of the Night goddess—the second verse speaks of a single lover and beloved, secretly anticipating the special maiden whom Krishna whisks off into the woods to have all to himself: "Then the moon, king among stars, arose, spreading soothing reddish rays over the face of the eastern horizon as a lover caresses his beloved's blushed face, consoling her after long separation."[43] Who is this special Gopī that the other Gopīs later discover abandoned in the forest?

[41] RL 5.3.
[42] RL 5.7.
[43] RL 1.2.

8

The Special Gopī: Rādhā

The special Gopī selected by Krishna—among all others—to venture alone with him to a secret place, is identified by the Chaitanya school as Rādhā. The Bhāgavata author presents Rādhā in the second scene of the second act. There, it is described how during a feverish search for Krishna, the maidens find alongside his own footprints, those of a young woman.[1]

The group of Gopīs then gives the reason why this particular maiden must have been considered so attractive in Krishna's eyes: she must have worshiped him perfectly, and therefore he was pleased with her:

> The Beloved Lord,
> the supreme Lord Hari,
> was worshiped by her perfectly.
> Having abandoned us,
> being so pleased with her,
> Govinda led her to a secret place.[2]

Verses 30–38 in the second act proceed to present this favored cowherd maiden not merely as an individual Gopī who is mingling with the others, but as one who has been uniquely chosen by Krishna for his exclusive attention. This sequence of verses is the only place where the special Gopī is explicitly described.

[1] RL 2.25–27.
[2] RL 2.28.

The Yoga of Love. Graham M. Schweig, Oxford University Press. © Oxford University Press 2025.
DOI: 10.1093/oso/9780197768426.003.0009

The Chaitanya school believes that the name and identity of Rādhā are both revealed and concealed in the verse quoted above, in the phrase, "the one who worships Krishna perfectly" (*anayārādhitaḥ*—note the letters *rādh* in the middle of this phrase, indicating Rādhā's name). The tradition gives Rādhā a very prominent position in the performance of the Rāsa dance itself, without any implicit or explicit indication of this in the narrative. In fact, the Chaitanya school cannot envision the Rāsa Līlā without Rādhā in the center of the Rāsa *maṇḍala*, "the circle of the Rāsa dance," with Krishna.[3] Rāmānanda Rāya, speaking to Chaitanya, reflects on the importance of Rādhā's place within the Rāsa Līlā:

> The Rāsa Līlā is the full essence
> of Krishna's desire.
> Rādhā is the binding link
> in his desire for the Rāsa Līlā.
>
> Without her, the Rāsa Līlā
> does not radiate in his heart.
> Leaving the circle of the Rāsa,
> he went to search for Rādhā.[4]

Here, Rāmānanda describes Krishna as leaving "the circle of the Rāsa" to search for Rādhā. In the Bhāgavata version of the story, Krishna deserts the group of Gopīs as they are frolicking in the forest at the end of the first act, yet there is no mention of him leaving them during the Rāsa dance, in the fifth act. This vision of Krishna departing from the circle of the Rāsa is an embellishment or variation on the theme of the story that is likely to have been taken from the vision of Jayadeva in his *Gīta Govinda*. The

[3] CC 2.8.109 and 3.14.19.
[4] CC 2.8.113–114.

capacity of the tradition's esoteric eye to reveal its secrets is essential to understanding Rādhā, and her followers.

Upon lifting the esoteric veil, teachings uncover that each of the Gopīs is a partial manifestation of the unique Gopī, Rādhā. Although personal names of the Gopīs are absent from the Rāsa Līla and the rest of the Bhāgavata text, many of their names—along with Rādhā's—appear in several other *purāṇas.* With the aid of these *purāṇas* and other sources, teachers of the Chaitanya school have identified the names of various voices of cowherd maidens in the story, as well as elaborated upon intricate details concerning the maidens.

As a major theologian of the school, Krishnadāsa further explains that not only are all the Gopīs found in Rādhā but all other goddesses are found in Rādhā as well! Indeed, Rādhā is the supreme Goddess: the embodiment of all divine women. Krishnadāsa identifies her as the particular Gopī who appears in the second act of the Rāsa Līlā,[5] and she is also understood to be the supreme *śakti* ("energy") of Krishna, who is the *śaktimat* ("the possessor of that energy"). Furthermore, we learn that Rādhā and Krishna are one and yet different from each other:

> Rādhā and Krishna are of one Soul,
>   although they bear two bodies
> So they can enjoy the experience
>   of *rasa* with one another.[6]

Thus, the ultimate focal point of worship for the Chaitanya school is this divine couple: Rādhā and Krishna. Their *līlā* is at the core of the tradition's devotion, *bhakti.* In order to appreciate the full esoteric significance of the Rāsa Līlā, we need to understand more about the supreme position of Rādhā in Chaitanya theology.

[5] CC 1.4.87–88.
[6] CC 1.4.56.

Just as Krishna manifests in various *avatāra* forms, or divine forms of descent, so, also, the tradition holds, does Rādhā appear in various forms.[7] Three types of manifestation coming from Rādhā are described: the forms of Lakṣmī, the consort Goddess of the cosmic Vishnu; the queens of Dvāraka and Mathurā, who are married to the regal form of Krishna; and the Gopī consorts of Vraja. Of these, the Gopīs are presented as superior to the other two types of feminine counterparts, not only because Rādhā herself is a cowherd maiden and the origin of all Gopīs, but also because they are the consorts who participate in the Rāsa Līlā, the most significant of all *līlās*. The theologians of the school delight in the supremacy of Rādhā, who exceeds all other goddesses, since it is explicated that all such goddesses are but manifestations of her divinity:

> The Goddess filled with Krishna
> is known as Rādhikā,
> the supreme divinity.
> She is the one in whom all Lakṣmīs
> and all loveliness are found.
> She is utterly confounding
> and she is beyond all others.[8]

Remarkably, then, Rādhā manifests in various multiple forms,[9] paralleling the way Krishna multiplies himself in the Rāsa dance (see Figure 4).

Thus, the Gopīs—according to the esoteric vision of the school—are truly parts of Rādhā, who accommodates Krishna with various manifestations of her own bodily form. These maidens are independent, partial but pure, alter-ego personifications of Rādhā. Each of the Gopīs is presented as a personified embodiment of

[7] CC 1.4.76.
[8] CC 1.4.83.
[9] CC 2.8.165.

Figure 4. Miniature painting of Rādhā and Krishna. Color paints on ivory, 6″ × 3.75″. Artist unknown. Located in the private collection of the author.

each of the particular emotions in Radha's wide range of feelings. Although each of the Gopīs expresses a singular part of Rādhā's rich and complex personality, Rādhā expresses them all, signifying her superlative, divine status and elevating her beyond the sum total of all the Gopīs, combined. Rādhā is therefore envisioned as the special Gopī at the center of the Rāsa *maṇḍala*: the one whom Krishna manifests multiple duplicates of himself for, just so that he can sensitively respond and reciprocate with each and every one of her feelings—feelings that delightfully encircle Krishna as cowherd maidens. As such, the Rāsa Līlā is essentially an expression of Rādhā-Krishna *līlā*.

In the Rāsa Līlā drama, we thus see a portrait of the divine couple—Rādhā and Krishna—as well as a portrait of each of the Gopīs with her beloved Krishna. Although an explicit description of Rādhā's place in the Rāsa dance is absent from the text—and the uncultivated eye does not see her at the center of the Rāsa *maṇḍala* with Krishna—she is surely there, as so many artistic renderings reveal. Not only is Krishna in the middle of the circle of the Rāsa dance, but, according to the teachers of the Chaitanya school, he is there with "the queen of Vrindāvana, Rādhā," because she is the superlative Gopī and the "cause" of the Rāsa dance itself.

Rādhā's role, which was once obscure, has now become widely accepted and recognized by all Hindus as central in this most worshiped portion of the Bhāgavata. In modern-day pilgrimage dramas and artistic renderings, Rādhā appears most often at the center of the Rāsa dance, along with her beloved Krishna: a beautiful reflection of the central position she holds in the hearts of her followers.

PART III

DANCE OF DIVINE LOVE

The Rāsa Līlā

Dramatis Personae

(in order of appearance)

SON OF VYĀSA / ŚUKA, *the narrator*

BELOVED LORD / KRISHNA, *the protagonist of the story*

Other personal names used for Krishna (in order of appearance): Govinda, Acyuta, Hṛṣīkeśa, Adhokṣaja, Hari, Keśava, Mādhava, Urukrama, Varāha, Śauri, Mukunda, Vāsudeva, and Vishnu

GOPĪS, *married and unmarried cowherd maidens, the heroines of the story*

as all of the Gopīs

as a partial group of Gopīs

as individual Gopīs (often speaking on behalf of other Gopīs)

PARIKṢIT, *the king for whom the story is narrated and from whom questions arise*

SPECIAL GOPĪ *(most often identified as Rādhā), the maiden with whom Krishna runs off*

Non-Speaking

YOGAMĀYĀ (or MĀYĀ), *the Goddess who directs the illusive power of divine loving union*

COWHERD MEN, *husbands of the Gopīs*

FAMILIES OR RELATIVES, *of the Gopīs*

COWS, *milked by the Gopīs*

TREES, PLANTS, FLOWERS, AND VINES, *spoken to by the Gopīs in the Vraja forest*

The Yoga of Love. Graham M. Schweig, Oxford University Press. © Oxford University Press 2025.
DOI: 10.1093/oso/9780197768426.003.0010

TULASĪ, *most sacred plant of Krishna flourishing in the Vraja forest*
THE EARTH, *consulted by the Gopīs in their search for Krishna*
WIFE OF THE DEER, *consulted by the Gopīs in their search for Krishna*
BEES *around Krishna's garland and as a chorus for Rāsa dance*
DENIZENS OF THE HEAVENS AND THEIR WIVES, *from their celestial chariots in the sky*
GANDHARVA SINGERS AND THEIR WIVES, *from their celestial chariots in the sky*

SCENES

The region of Vraja: a rural area located in central northern India about eighty miles south of Delhi, near Agra (home of the Taj Mahal);
a paradisal natural countryside with many forests
and the Yamunā River running through it

The village of Vraja: also known as Vrindāvana,
located within the region of Vraja,
bordering the Yamunā River;
home of Krishna, the Gopīs, and their families

DANCE OF DIVINE LOVE
THE RĀSA LĪLĀ

ACT ONE

KRISHNA ATTRACTS THE GOPĪS AND DISAPPEARS
Bhāgavata Purāṇa, Book 10, Chapter 29

Scene 1

The illustrious son of Vyāsa spoke:

Even the Beloved Lord,
seeing those nights
in autumn filled with
blooming jasmine flowers,
Turned his mind toward
love's delights,
fully taking refuge in
Yogamāyā's illusive powers.[1] 1

[1] Son of Vyāsa: Śuka, the sage who narrates this story.

The Beloved Lord: God, as Krishna, the intimate persona and ultimate deity of the godhead, the divine hero of this story. The various names and epithetical nomenclature for Krishna throughout this text will be briefly explained in these footnotes.

Those nights in autumn filled with blooming jasmine flowers: jasmine amazingly blossoms here during "those nights in autumn," even though the flower only blossoms in the spring and summer in India. "Those nights" metaphorically introduce the cowherd maidens of Vraja, or the Gopīs, who are explicitly introduced for the first time two verses later.

Yogamāyā: Divine feminine power or the Great Goddess for arranging loving exchanges between God and his devotee.

Then the moon,
  king among stars, arose,
Spreading soothing reddish rays
  over the face of the eastern horizon;
Dispelling the sorrow
  from those who looked on,
As a lover caresses his beloved's blushed face,
  consoling her after long separation. 2

Seeing lotus flowers bloom
  and the perfect circle of the moon
Beaming like the face of Ramā,
  reddish as fresh *kuṅkuma*;
Seeing the forest colored
  by the moon's gentle rays,
He began to make sweet music,
  melting the hearts of fair maidens
  with beautiful eyes.[2] 3

Upon hearing that sweet music,
  their passion for him swelling,
The young women of Vraja whose
  minds were captured by Krishna,
Unaware of one another,
  ran off toward the place
Where their beloved was waiting,
  with their earrings swinging wildly.[3] 4

[2] Ramā: the Goddess Lakṣmī, consort of Vishnu (Krishna's cosmic persona and form of four arms), not to be confused with Rāma (note the macron over the first "a" rather than the second), the brother of Krishna or the consort of Sītā as the *avatāra* or divine descent of Vishnu.

kuṅkuma: vermilion; a brilliant but deep reddish colored powder.

Fair maidens with beautiful eyes: the cowherd heroines of the story, known as the Gopīs.

[3] Vraja: the beautiful village of and surrounding rural area in central northern India, considered a divine manifestation of the highest heaven in this world.

Krishna: "the dark-complexioned one" or "the divinely attractive one"; primary name of the Beloved Lord, who is both supremely powerful and supremely intimate.

Figure 5. Love call of the divine: Krishna's intense yearning. Pen and ink, with opaque watercolor, acrylic gouache, and pastel on archival cold press illustration board, 30" x 24". Painting by Kim Waters. Located in the private collection of the author.

Some left abruptly
while milking the cows—
due to excitement
the milking had ceased.
Some left the milk
as it boiled over;
others departed
leaving cakes on the hearth. 5

Some suddenly stopped
dressing themselves;
others no longer
fed children their milk.
Some left their husbands
who had not yet been served;
others while eating
abandoned their meals. 6

Some were massaging
their bodies with oils
or cleansing themselves;
others applying
ointment to their eyes.
Their garments
and ornaments
in utter disarray,
they hastened
to be with Krishna. 7

Figure 6. When divinity calls our souls to dance: A Vraja Gopikā running to Krishna in the night. Pen and ink, with opaque watercolor, acrylic gouache, and pastel on archival cold press illustration board, 30" x 24". Painting by Kim Waters.

Their husbands,
fathers, brothers—
all relatives endeavored
to detain them.
Since their hearts
had been stolen by Govinda,
they who were entranced
did not turn back.[4] 8

Some Gopīs,
unable to leave,
had gone inside their homes.
With eyes closed,
fully absorbed in love,
they meditated upon Krishna.[5] 9

The intense burning
of unbearable separation
from their dearest beloved
disrupted all inauspiciousness;
Due to the joy
of embracing Acyuta
attained through meditation,
even their worldly happiness was lost.[6] 10

Certainly, he is the supreme Soul,
though they knew him
intimately as their lover.
They relinquished their bodies
composed of physical elements,
and any worldly bondage
was instantly destroyed. 11

[4] Govinda: Krishna, "one who lovingly tends the cows."
[5] Gopīs: "cowherd maidens"; the fair young women of Vraja; the collective heroines of the story.
[6] Acyuta: Krishna, "the infallible one."

Figure 7. Embracing divinity from within the heart by means of Yoga Meditation. Pen and ink, with opaque watercolor, acrylic gouache, and pastel on archival cold press illustration board, 30" x 24". Painting by Kim Waters.

Scene 2

The celebrated king Parīkṣit spoke:

They knew Krishna, however,
as the greatest lover and
not as the source of Brahman.
O sage, how did the underlying
current of natural forces
stop affecting their minds
controlled by such forces?[7] 12

The sage Śuka spoke:

This was explained to you previously:
if the king of Cedi could
achieve perfection
Even while despising Hṛṣīkeśa,
why would not they,
so dear to Adhokṣaja,
be much more likely to do so?[8] 13

[7] Parīkṣit: the king to whom the sage Śuka narrates this story.

Brahman: the word used to indicate the "ultimate reality" or "supreme being" in the Upanishads and Vedānta philosophical texts.

underlying current of natural forces: the three constituent *guṇas* or qualities underlying the natural world as well as human conditioning and qualities of human interactions. These forces refer to the three *guṇas*, *sattva* (light, clarity or goodness), *rajas* (haziness, mixture of goodness and ignorance), and *tamas* (darkness or ignorance). In verse 14, the same word is translated as "underlying forces of nature."

[8] King of Cedi: Śīṣupāla, who insulted Krishna; Krishna granted liberation to Śīṣupāla by killing him.

Hṛṣīkeśa: Krishna, "the Lord of the senses."

Adhokṣaja: Krishna, "the Lord who is beyond the perception of the senses."

For the purpose of
benefiting all, O king,
the Beloved Lord
manifests himself.
He is imperishable, immeasurable,
unbound by the forces of nature—
the Soul from whom
such powerful forces arise.[9] 14

Desire, anger, fear, and
certainly loving attachment,
intimacy and affection
Should always be directed toward Hari;
by so doing, persons become
fully absorbed in God.[10] 15

Surely this should not surprise you;
the Beloved Lord exists without birth.
He is Krishna, the supreme Lord of yoga;
by him this entire world is liberated.[11] 16

Scene 3

Seeing they had arrived nearby,
the Beloved Lord then approached
the young women of Vraja.
He, most eloquent of all speakers,
began to converse with them,
bewildering them with playful words. 17

[9] Forces of Nature: The "*guṇas*." Krishna as Lord is the original source of these basic forces of nature and therefore is not bound by them. These same forces are spoken of earlier in Verse 12 as "underlying current of natural forces."

[10] Hari: Krishna, "one who steals the heart," or "one who takes away suffering."

[11] Supreme Lord of yoga: Krishna; yoga refers here to the divine supernatural powers that unite the soul with supreme reality.

The Beloved Lord spoke:

Welcome, most fortunate ladies!
  What can I do to please you?
Is all going well in Vraja?
  Please explain the purpose of your arrival. 18

Night has a frightening appearance;
  inhabiting this place are
  fearsome creatures!
Please return to Vraja—
  women should not remain here,
  O ones with beautiful waists.[12] 19

Your mothers, fathers, sons,
  Brothers, and husbands cannot find you.
They are searching for you—
  do not create anxiety for your families.[13] 20

[12] This verse and several following verses possess double entendre meanings, cleverly expressing Krishna's ethical and trans-ethical intentions. Traditional commentators recognize the opposite meanings that are simultaneously expressed in these verses. An opposite meaning for this verse can read as follows:

Night is without a frightening appearance;
  inhabiting this place are
  creatures that are not fearsome.
Please do not return to Vraja—
  women should remain here,
  O ones with beautiful waists.

[13] A clever alternative reading of this verse is the following:

Your mothers, fathers, sons,
  brothers, and husbands cannot find you.
Even though they are searching for you,
  you must not be anxious for your families.

You have seen the forest
  filled with flowers,
  glowing with the rays
  of the full moon;
Made beautiful by leaves of trees,
  playfully shimmering
  from the gentle breeze
  off the river Yamunā.[14] 21

Please go to the village without delay!
  O chaste ladies, attend your husbands.
Your calves and children are crying for you—
  you must go feed and nurse them.[15] 22

Or perhaps your hearts are bound
  out of deep affection for me;
Since all living beings are dear to me,
  you also must have come to be near me. 23

For every woman the highest *dharma*
  is to serve her husband without falsity,
Be agreeable toward his family members,
  and nourish the children.[16] 24

[14] Yamunā: the river that runs through Vraja that is dearest to Krishna, and therefore most sacred.

[15] An alternative reading of this verse is the following:

> Please do not go back right away
>   to attend your husbands, O chaste ladies.
> Your calves and children are crying for others [not for you!];
>   you need not feed and nurse them.

[16] An alternative reading of this verse is the following:

> For the *dharma* of all other women
>   is to serve false husbands,
> Be agreeable toward their family members
>   and nourish the children.

Dharma: one's essential purpose in life; one's "duty" in this world that also links one to the divine; a sense of one's place in the cosmic scheme of things that is intimately related to one's place in the total social order; the ultimate matrix of divine and social law combined that places the individual perfectly within the universe.

Even if unpleasant, unfortunate,
old, decrepit, sickly or poor,
if not morally fallen,
The husband should not be deserted
by women desiring a better
position in the next world. 25

For this does not lead to heaven
nor to good reputation;
instead it brings undesirable,
painful, fearful results.
Certainly adultery
is condemned everywhere
by women from good families.[17] 26

By hearing about me,
seeing me,
meditating on me,
and praising me,
you feel love for me—
Not by being in my presence.
Therefore you
should return
to your homes. 27

The sage Śuka spoke:

Having heard these unpleasant
words of Govinda,
the Gopīs felt great sadness.
Their expectations broken,
they felt unbearable anxiety
too difficult to overcome. 28

[17] The second half of this verse can also be read as the following:

Women from good families know
adultery is found everywhere [with their own husbands],
and it should be condemned.

Bowing their heads in sorrow,
with reddened lips dried
by heavy breathing,
Scratching the ground with their feet,
they were burdened
with intense distress;
With streaming tears
washing away
the *kuṅkuma* on their breasts,
And *kajjala* running
down from their eyes,
they stood there in silence.[18] 29

Having discarded all desires for the sake
of their most beloved Krishna,
Who had addressed them
as if uninterested in love,
Wiping their eyes while
trying to stop crying,
Those impassioned ones, choked up,
spoke with faltering voices. 30

The beautiful Gopīs said:

O all-pervading one,
you should not speak
so cruelly to us!
We have fully abandoned
all objects of desire
for the soles of your feet.
O unattainable one,
do not reject us—
accept us as your devotees
Just as you, the Lord,
the original Person,
accept those who desire liberation. 31

[18] *Kajjala*: a black ointment eyeliner used by Indian women and men.

O dear one, as you
who knows *dharma*
have stated,
The proper duty for women
is to be loyal to husbands,
children, and close friends.
Let this *dharma* of ours be for you,
O Lord, since you are
the true object of such teachings.
Truly you are the dearest
beloved of all living beings,
the most intimate relation,
for you are the supreme Soul. 32

O Soul, the spiritually advanced
certainly feel attraction to you
as their eternal beloved.
With these husbands, children, and
others causing much trouble,
what is to be done?
O supreme Lord,
please be merciful unto us.
O one with eyes like lotus flowers,
do not destroy our hopes
that we have held for so long. 33

While in our homes, our minds
were easily stolen by you;
So also were our hands
engaged in housework.
Our feet will not move even one step
from the soles of your feet.
How shall we return to Vraja—
what would we do there? 34

O dear one,
with the flood of nectar
coming from your lips,
Extinguish the fire
burning within our hearts
born of your sweet music,
your glances and laughter.
For if you don't,
we shall place
our bodies in the fire
born of separation from you.
Then, O friend,
by means of meditation
we shall go to the abode of your feet. 35

O lotus-eyed one,
so dear to sages
residing in the forest,
From the moment we touched
the soles of your feet,
a moment rarely granted
even to the Goddess Ramā,
From that time on,
we have been unable to stand
directly in the presence
of any other man;
Indeed, we have become
filled with joy
because of you. 36

The Goddess Śrī,
  though having obtained
  a place on your chest,
And for whose very glance
  the gods ultimately aspire,
Desires, along with
  the sacred *tulasī* plant,
  the dust of your lotus feet.
It is the same way for us—
  our shelter is the dust of your feet.[19] 37

O destroyer of affliction,
  please have mercy on us.
Having found the soles of your feet,
  we have abandoned our homes
  with the hope of worshiping you.
O jewel among men,
  please grant unto us
Whose hearts are burning
  with intense desire,
  inspired by your beautiful
  glances and smiles,
  the chance to serve you. 38

Upon seeing your face encircled
  by curling locks of hair,
  your lips of sweet nectar,
The earrings on your beautiful cheeks,
  and your glances and smiles;
Seeing your strong arms
  which award fearlessness,
And your chest, the only
  pleasure for the Goddess Śrī—
  we must become your maidservants! 39

[19] Goddess Śrī: Lakṣmī, the consort of Vishnu.
Tulasī: name of the aromatic flowering plant dearest to Krishna; the most sacred plant of all plants.

O dear one, what woman
in the three worlds
would not abandon
her noble character,
After being overcome
by the sweet melodious
music of your flute?
Seeing your beauty,
the most magnificent
in all the three worlds,
The animals, trees,
birds, and cows are elated
with bodily ripplings of bliss.[20] 40

Clearly, you are the one
who removes the suffering
of the people of Vraja,
As you, the Lord,
the original Person,
protect the celestial
world of the divinities.
O friend of the distressed,
place your hand,
beautiful like the lotus,
On the heads
and impassioned breasts
of your maidservants. 41

[20] Elated with bodily ripplings of bliss: the positive experience of bodily hairs standing on end.

Scene 4

The sage Śuka said:

Thus the supreme Lord
among masters of yoga
heard their despondent words.
Laughing, yet with compassion,
he, possessing all
pleasure within himself,
still arranged for
the pleasure of the Gopīs. 42

Acyuta, whose actions are exalted,
whose jasmine-like teeth
Shone forth from his eloquent smile,
joined together with all of them,
Whose faces were blossoming
with loving glances;
He was glowing like the full moon
surrounded by stars. 43

Being praised through song,
then singing in response,
he was the leader of
hundreds of young women.
Wearing the garland Vaijayantī
while moving among them,
he was decorating the forest.[21] 44

[21] Vaijayantī: "victory," name of Krishna's garland consisting of five different colored flowers strung together.

Upon reaching the riverbank
with its cool sands,
accompanied by the Gopīs,
He delighted in breezes
that carried the fragrance of
white lotuses, joyfully dancing
in the waves of that river. 45

Embracing them with wandering arms;
playfully touching their hands
with the tips of his fingernails
Which then fell upon their breasts,
belts, thighs, and hair;
Conversing coyly
with glances and laughter,
He joyfully awakened the god of love
in those beautiful young women from Vraja. 46

Thus, those who received honor
from the Beloved Lord,
Krishna, the great Soul,
Thought themselves the best
among all women in the world—
they then became filled with pride. 47

Keśava could see how they
had become intoxicated
with their good fortune;
Bestowing upon them his grace,
in order to quell their pride,
suddenly, right before them,
he disappeared.[22] 48

[22] Keśava: Krishna, "one with beautiful long hair."

Act Two

The Gopīs Search for Krishna

Bhāgavata Purāṇa, Book 10, Chapter 30

Scene 1

The sage Śuka spoke:

When the Beloved Lord
disappeared so suddenly,
the young women of Vraja
could no longer see him.
They felt greatly tormented,
like female elephants
who have lost
their male leader. 1

By his movements,
affectionate smiles,
passionate glances,
His attractive speaking
and the passion of
his playfulness,
Their hearts were captivated;
those crazed women
began to imitate various
Actions of the Lord of Ramā,
losing themselves,
fully absorbed in him.[23] 2

[23] Lord of Ramā: Krishna; "Lord of the Goddess Lakṣmī," or Vishnu, whom the Gopīs identify here as Krishna.

Through their movements,
smiles, glances, speech,
and other gestures,
The bodily forms of his lovers
became similar
to those of their beloved.
The young women,
their selves fully absorbed in him,
thus declared, "I am he!"
Their amorous,
playful gestures
were those of Krishna. 3

Singing out loud about him
like deranged persons,
Together they searched
from forest to forest.
They inquired from trees,
the lords of the forest,
about the supreme Person
Who is present internally and
externally for all living beings,
as heavenly air pervades all beings,
within and without. 4

[The Gopīs spoke:]

O Aśvattha fig tree,
Plakṣa and Nyagrodha trees,
have you seen the son of Nanda?
He has stolen our minds
with smiles and
glances of pure love.[24] 5

[24] Son of Nanda: Krishna; the foster father of Krishna is Nanda.

O Kurabaka tree,
Aśoka and Nāga trees,
O Punnāga and Campaka plants,
Has the younger brother of Rāma
passed this way?
His smile steals the conceit
of all proud women.[25] 6

O most fortunate Tulasī
to whom the feet
of Govinda are so dear,
Have you seen Acyuta, our beloved,
wandering about in this forest
followed by a swarm of bees? 7

O Mālatī, Mallikā, Jātī, and
Yūthikā jasmine flowers,
have you seen him?
When Mādhava was passing by,
did he cause you great delight
with the gentle touch of his hand?[26] 8

O Cūta mango and Priyāla trees,
Panasa jackfruit tree,
Āsana and Kovidāra trees;
O Jambu rose-apple tree, small Arka plant,
Bilva wood-apple tree, Bakula mimosa,
Āmra mango and Nīpa trees;
O all other plants and trees
growing by the banks
of the Yamunā
Whose lives are devoted
to the service of others—
please show us the path to Krishna,
for we are losing our minds! 9

[25] Younger brother of Rāma: Krishna; the older brother of Krishna is Rāma, or Balarāma. Do not confuse with Ramā, a name for the Goddess.

[26] Mādhava: Krishna; a name derived from the word *madhu*, meaning "honey," or "sweet."

O Earth,
what severe austerity
have you performed?
Ah, you appear resplendent
with the grass hairs of your body
blissfully standing erect, elated
from the touch of Keśava's feet.
Is this perhaps
the result of footsteps coming
from his earlier descent
as Urukrama?
Or, even before that, is it
coming from the embrace
of his divine form of Varāha?[27] 10

O wife of the deer,
have you encountered Acyuta
in this place with his beloved?
O friend, have your widened eyes
received great pleasure from
the sight of his beautiful limbs?
The garland of jasmine
worn by the Lord of this group
is tinged with *kuṅkuma* powder
Coming from the breasts of his lover
whom he has embraced;
its scent is blowing in our direction.[28] 11

[27] Urukrama: Krishna, "the wide-striding one," the divine form whose two steps spanned the whole earth.
Varāha: Krishna who takes the form of a "divine boar," lifting the earth with his tusks to protect it.
[28] Wife of the deer: a doe, a female deer with whom the Gopīs identify.

Perhaps the younger brother of Rāma,
holding a lotus flower in one hand
and resting his other arm
on the shoulder of his beloved,
Was followed here by a swarm of bees
hovering around his garland of *tulasī*,
all of them blinded by madness.
O trees,
when walking by,
Did he graciously accept
your respectful bowing
with his affectionate glances?[29] 12

Let us inquire from these vines,
even though they are embracing
the branch-like arms
of their tree-husband.
Certainly they must have been
touched by his fingernails—
just see how they are elated
with bodily ripplings of bliss! 13

[Śuka spoke:]

Thus the Gopis, discouraged
by their search for Krishna,
uttered these irrational words.
They began to act out
the *līlā* of their Beloved Lord,
for they were wholly absorbed in him.[30] 14

[29] Younger brother of Rāma: Krishna.
[30] *Līlā*: the divine play or drama of God.

One of them mimicked Pūtanā,
while another imitated Krishna
who drank from her breast.
Yet another acted like a crying infant;
with her foot she kicked one
who pretended to be a cart.[31] 15

One imitated a demon
carrying away another who
pretended to be Krishna as an infant.
Another crawled around,
dragging her two feet
with the tinkling of ankle bells.[32] 16

Some performed like Krishna and Rāma,
others acted like their cowherd friends.
One mimicked the slaying of the calf demon,
another the slaying of the crane.[33] 17

One of them called for the cows
who had wandered off,
just as Krishna would;
then, imitating him,
She pretended to sport about
while making music with a flute.
Others praised her,
saying "Well done!" 18

[31] Pūtanā: the demonness who tried to kill Krishna as a baby by nursing from her poisoned breast.

One who pretended to be a cart: imitation of the "cart demon," Śakaṭa.

[32] A demon carrying away another: refers to the "whirlwind demon" Tṛṇāvarta who carried away Krishna.

Tinkling of ankle bells: Krishna is adored as an infant whose feet are adorned with this sounding jewelry.

[33] Rāma: short for Balarāma; the older brother of Krishna (distinguished from Ramā, the Goddess Lakṣmī).

Calf demon: Vatsāsura.

Crane: the demon Baka.

One of them,
placing her arm on another girl,
sauntered about and declared,
"I am Krishna!
Look at my graceful gait."
Their minds were absorbed in him. 19

"Don't be afraid
of the wind and rain—
I have arranged for your protection."
Another said,
lifting her upper garment
with her hand as if to shield them.[34] 20

One of them rose,
climbed up and placed
her foot on the other's head,
saying, "O wicked snake, go away!
Indeed, I have been
born as the one
who gives punishment
to those who are evil."[35] 21

Then another one declared,
"O cowherd boys,
look at the raging forest fire—
Quickly close your eyes!
I shall easily arrange
for your protection."[36] 22

[34] Lifting her upper garment with her hand: imitating Krishna who lifted Govardhana hill with his finger to protect the residents of Vraja from Indra's wrath in the form of great rainstorms and thunderbolts.

[35] "O wicked snake": refers to the multi-hooded poisonous serpent Kāliya; Krishna as a young boy, upon subduing and conquering the serpent, performs a dance on his hoods.

[36] Raging forest fire: a great fire that Krishna extinguishes by swallowing it up in order to protect his cowherd friends.

One of them, with a garland,
was tied to a grinding mortar
by a slender maiden
Who said, "I am binding
the one who has
broken the butter pots
and stolen the butter!"
Another covered her
face and beautiful eyes,
pretending to be afraid.[37] 23

Scene 2

Just then,
as they inquired about Krishna
from the trees and vines of Vrindāvana,
They saw,
in an area of the forest,
the footprints of the supreme Soul.[38] 24

[The Gopīs spoke:]

Clearly these are footprints
of the great Soul,
the son of Nanda.
Here they can be identified by
the flag, lotus, thunderbolt,
elephant goad, and barley seed,
along with other signs.[39] 25

[37] The Gopīs imitate Krishna as a mischievous butter thief and his mother, Yaśodā, who attempts to control him.

[38] Vrindāvana: is the village within the greater region of Vraja, sometimes interchangeable with Vraja; "the forest of *tulasī*."
Supreme Soul: Krishna.

[39] Flag, lotus, thunderbolt, elephant goad, and barley seed: symbols found on the soles of the feet of various *avatāra* ("divine descent") manifestations of Vishnu or Krishna.

[Śuka spoke:]

Those maidens went forward by
tracing various footprints
along his path.
Discovering in the pattern of footprints
those of a young woman,
they became distressed
and spoke these words:[40] 26

[The Gopīs spoke:]

Whose footprints are these?
Someone was walking
with the son of Nanda!
He must have placed
his arm on her shoulder,
just as an elephant
rests his trunk on a mate. 27

The Beloved Lord,
the supreme Lord Hari,
was worshiped by her perfectly.
Having abandoned us,
being so pleased with her,
Govinda led her to a secret place.[41] 28

[40] Young woman: commonly identified as Rādhā, the Gopī who is Krishna's supreme beloved. This verse and the following verses through verse 41 describe this special Gopī, or Rādhā.

[41] Hari: Krishna.

Ah, this dust
from the lotus feet
of Govinda
is sanctified, O friends!
Even Brahmā, Śiva, and
the Goddess Ramā
place this dust
upon their heads,
in order to remove
their impurities.[42] 29

These footprints of hers
cause great pain for us
since she alone,
Among all the Gopīs,
was taken to a secret place
and now enjoys the lips of Acyuta. 30

Her footprints
are not visible over here;
the soles of her soft feet certainly
Were hurting from
the sprouting blades of grass;
the lover must have lifted up his beloved. 31a

[42] Brahmā: deity of cosmic creation, most often associated with cosmic deities of Vishnu and Śiva.
Śiva: the deity of cosmic dissolution.
The Goddess Ramā: the Goddess Lakṣmī, consort of Vishnu.

These footprints
are sunken from
carrying this maiden.
O Gopīs, look! Krishna,
the amorous one, became
heavy from bearing her weight.
There, the great Soul
must have set her down
to gather flowers. 31b

Here, flowers were gathered
by the lover for his beloved.
Just see these incomplete footprints,
leaving impressions only of his toes. 32

Then, this impassioned lover
decorated the hair
of his beloved over here.
He undoubtedly was seated
while making for his dearest
a crown of flowers. 33

[Śuka spoke:]

He delighted in loving her,
yet he delights in the self
and takes pleasure in the self,
for he is complete.
By contrast, then, he revealed
the abased condition
of lustful men with
bad-hearted women. 34

Thus, showing each other
patterns of footprints
while wandering about,
the Gopīs became bewildered.
They concluded that
Krishna had departed
with one special Gopī,
leaving behind the other
young women in the forest. 35

She believed herself to be
best among all women
and she considered,
"Abandoning the other Gopīs,
struck by passionate love,
he adores me as his only beloved." 36

Then, reaching a certain place in the forest,
she became proud and said to Keśava:
"I am unable to walk any further—
please take me wherever you desire." 37

Thus addressed by his beloved,
he replied, "Please climb on my shoulder."
Then Krishna suddenly disappeared;
the young woman was devastated. 38

[The Gopī spoke:]

O my Lord! My pleasure!
My dearest! Where are you?
Where are you,
mighty-armed Lord?
O Friend!
I am your miserable
maidservant—
please show me
that you are near! 39

Figure 8. Intense longing and searching for the divine: Footprints of Krishna with another Gopikā. Pen and ink, with opaque watercolor, acrylic gouache, and pastel on archival cold press illustration board, 30" × 24". Painting by Kim Waters.

The sage Śuka spoke:

As the Gopīs were
following the path
of their Beloved Lord,
not far away,
They caught a glimpse
of their grieving friend,
overwhelmed by separation
from her beloved. 40

They intently listened to her story;
how she first received
honor from Mādhava,
Then, due to self-indulgence,
how she was dishonored;
they were completely amazed. 41

Upon entering the forest,
they continued their search
until they no longer could see
by the light of the moon.
Then, finding themselves
surrounded by darkness,
the young women
turned back. 42

Their minds were
filled with thoughts of him;
they spoke about him constantly;
their movements
were no longer their own
for they were fully absorbed in him.
While praising
his qualities in song
they forgot their homes;
indeed, they even forgot themselves. 43

They again returned
to the banks of the Kālindī,
immersed in their feelings for Krishna.
Sitting together,
singing about Krishna,
they ardently longed for his return.[43] 44

[43] Kālindī: the Yamunā River.

Act Three

Song of the Gopīs: The Gopī Gīta

Bhāgavata Purāṇa, Book 10 Chapter 31

Scene: Monologue

The Gopīs spoke:

Glorious is Vraja, surpassing all,
for it is the land of your birth.
Indeed, the Goddess Indirā
resides in this place forever.
O beloved, please allow
your maidservants to see you!
Their very life-breath is sustained in you,
and they search for you everywhere.[44] 1

With your eyes,
you steal the beauty
of the center
Of an exquisite fully bloomed
lotus flower, rising out
of a serene autumn pond,
O Lord of love,
and it is killing us,
your voluntary maidservants—
O bestower of benedictions,
in this world,
is this not murder? 2

[44] Indirā: Name for the Goddess Lakṣmī, goddess of prosperity, consort of Nārāyaṇa.

Whether it be
from poisonous waters
or a fearsome demon;
From torrential rains,
windstorms, and
fiery thunderbolts;
From the bull demon,
the son of Maya, or from
any other fearful predicament;
O almighty one,
you have been our protector
time and time again.[45] 3

Clearly you are not
the son of a Gopī;
you are the Witness
Residing in the hearts
of all embodied beings.
When Vikhanas
prayed to you for
the protection of the universe,
O friend, you appeared
in the dynasty of the Sātvatas.[46] 4

[45] Poisonous waters: caused by the demon serpent Kāliya, on whose multiple heads Krishna dances.

Fearsome demon: commonly understood as the gigantic, wicked snake Agha, whom Krishna slays.

Torrential rains: alluding to Indra in the Govardhana *līlā*, or the demonic activities of Tṛṇāvarta.

Fiery thunderbolts: could again be referring to the god Indra in Govardhana *līlā*.

The bull demon: referring to the demon Ariṣṭa or Vatsāsura, whom Krishna slays.

Son of Maya: the demon Vyomāsura, whom Krishna slays.

[46] Witness: Krishna as the indwelling Lord within the heart of all beings.

Vikhanas: the cosmic creator deity, Brahmā.

Dynasty of the Sātvatas: name for the Yādava dynasty, the Yadus who worship Krishna.

O leader of the Vṛṣṇis,
those who fear the cycle
of endless suffering
Approach your feet,
which grant fearlessness.
O beloved,
please place on our heads
Your hand, beautiful as a lotus,
that fulfills all wishes
and holds the hand of Śrī.[47] 5

O destroyer of suffering
for the residents of Vraja;
O hero of all women
whose smile crushes
the pride of your devotees;
O friend,
please accept us
as your maidservants—
Show us the beauty
of your lotus-like face! 6

Your lotus feet remove
all misfortunes of those who
have offered themselves unto you.
Your feet, the resting place
of the Goddess Śrī,
follow cows out to graze.
May your lotus feet,
once placed on
the hoods of a serpent,
Be placed upon our breasts—
please crush this passion
lying within our hearts![48] 7

[47] Vṛṣnis: the dynasty in which Krishna appears.
[48] The hoods of a serpent: refers to the serpent demon Kāliya.

By your sweet voicc
and charming words
So attractive to the wise,
O one with lotus eyes,
These maidservants
are becoming delirious—
O hero, please revive us
with your intoxicating lips! 8

Your words of nectar
described by sages and poets
Are life for the suffering,
destroy all misfortunes,
and are auspicious to hear.
Those who extol your praises
throughout the world
Are the most generous persons,
bestowing the greatest riches. 9

Your smiles,
your glances of pure love
for your beloved ones,
And your intimate
playful ways
are auspicious meditations;
Also the promises
you made to us in secret—
all have touched our hearts.
O cunning one,
indeed, these things
agitate our minds. 10

When you leave Vraja
while herding the cows,
Your feet, O Lord,
beautiful as a lotus,
May be hurt by stones,
grasses, and grains;
O beloved, our hearts
become disturbed.[49] 11

At the close of each day,
your face, encircled by
Dark blue locks of hair,
like the lotus enveloped
by forest foliage,
Displays thickly smeared
dust from cows.
O hero, you constantly place
this loving memory
within our hearts. 12

Your lotus feet fulfill
the desires of all
who humbly submit to them.
Worshiped by the one
born from the lotus flower,
they are the ornament of the earth.
They are to be meditated upon
during times of distress, for
they grant the highest satisfaction.
O charming lover,
please place upon our breasts
your lotus feet, O slayer of misery.[50] 13

[49] Vraja: the village within the Vraja region.
[50] The one born from the lotus flower: Brahmā, the god of creation who is born from the navel of Vishnu.

The nectar that
strengthens our love
and vanquishes our grief;
The nectar that
is abundantly kissed
by the flute you play,
Making everyone forget
all other attachments;
O hero, please bestow
upon us this nectar
of your lips! 14

During the day when
you go off to the forest,
we cannot see you.
The smallest fraction
of a moment seems
like thousands of years.
When we eagerly behold
again your beautiful face
with curling locks of hair,
It seems the creator was mindless,
making eyelids to cover our eyes. 15

Our husbands, sons, brothers,
ancestors, and all others
Have been completely forsaken, O Acyuta,
so we could be in your presence.
You know why we have come here—
we were captured by your alluring song.
O deceiver, who would abandon
such women in the middle of the night? [51] 16

[51] Alluring song: The sound of Krishna's flute.

The promises you made
  to us in secret and
  the passionate feelings
  rising in our hearts;
Your smiling face and
  glances of pure love;
Your broad chest,
  the abode of Śrī;
Recalling all this,
  we feel constant,
  unbearable longing for you
  and our minds become bewildered. 17

O dearest one,
  by manifesting yourself,
You remove the distress
  of the inhabitants
  of the forest of Vraja.
Please give to us, whose
  hearts are longing for you,
That medicine which brings relief
  to our tormented hearts,
  fully devoted to you. 18

Your fine feet,
  delicate like the lotus,
  we gently place upon our breasts
Which we fear, O dear one,
  may be too rough for you.
When you roam the forest,
  we wonder, are your feet not hurt
By small stones and other harsh objects?
  Our minds are turning and reeling—
  our very lives are only for you. 19

ACT FOUR

KRISHNA REAPPEARS AND SPEAKS OF LOVE

Bhāgavata Purāṇa, Book 10, Chapter 32

Scene 1

The sage Śuka said:

Thus after the Gopīs sang out for him,
lamenting in these wondrous ways,
They burst into tears, O king,
longing for the vision of Krishna. 1

Then, right before them,
the heroic Śauri appeared,
his face blossoming like a lotus
and beaming with a smile.
Wearing yellow garments and
adorned with a flower garland,
the supreme God of Love
stood directly before them,
alluring even the love-god
who himself charms all others.[52] 2

With eyes opening wide,
the maidens became
filled with love
upon seeing their
dearest beloved return.
All of them stood up at once,
as if the breath of life
had just returned
to their bodies. 3

[52] Śauri: Krishna, appearing very powerful as a descendent of the Śura dynasty.
The love-god: known as Kāmadeva, the "Cupid" of India who functions similarly to the Greek god.

One of them reverently held
in her joined palms
the hand of Śauri,
beautiful as the lotus;
Another placed his arm,
covered with the balm
of sandalwood,
on her shoulder. 4

One slender maiden held
his chewed betel nut
in her joined palms;
Another, burning with desire,
placed his lotus feet
on her breasts. 5

One of them,
straining her eyebrows,
was beside herself
with a fury due to pure love.
With accusing glances
as if to injure him,
she glared at him,
biting her lip. 6

Still another,
though greatly delighted
as she gazed with unblinking eyes
at the beauty of his lotus-like face,
Could not be satisfied,
just as saintly persons who
meditate upon his feet
remain insatiable. 7

One of them took him
into her heart through
the aperture of her eyes;
then closing her eyes,
she embraced him within.
She became elated with
bodily ripplings of joy,
as the body of a *yogī*
is overcome with bliss.[53] 8

All of them,
as their tranquility
fully blossomed by fixing
their gaze upon Keśava,
Put aside their sorrow
born of separation,
as persons who are blessed
with the presence of a wise sage. 9

The Beloved Lord, Acyuta,
was surrounded by those
whose sorrow had dispersed.
O dear king,
he appeared radiant,
like the supreme Person
with his splendorous powers. 10

Having taken them
to the river Kālindī,
the almighty one
approached the sandy shore,
Where a light breeze
carried fragrances of blooming
jasmine and coral trees,
attracting many bees. 11

[53] *Yogī*: one who practices the arduous physical, mental, and spiritual disciplines of yoga.

The darkness of the night
was graciously dispelled
by an abundance of rays
from the autumn moon,
While the water
of the Kṛṣṇā river
gathered soft sands
with her rippling hands.[54] 12

The pain in their hearts
was driven away
by the delight of seeing him;
Their hearts' bliss
reached its limits as if
the goal of the revealed scriptures
had been attained.
Using their delicate shawls,
colored by reddish *kuṅkuma*
from their breasts,
They arranged a seat
for the true companion
of all souls.[55] 13

The Beloved Lord was seated
there among them
as the supreme Lord,
Who arranges for himself
a seat within the hearts of all,
as the supreme Lord of yoga.
Appearing resplendent,
he was worshiped in
that assembly of Gopīs;
He exhibited his form as
the only source of beauty
pervading all the three worlds. 14

[54] Kṛṣṇā: the Yamunā River.

[55] Shawls: the light-weight " upper coverings" of the Gopīs used not so much for warmth, but for modesty.

Scene 2

Honoring the one who ignited
the passion of their love,
With their sporting eyebrows,
playful glances and smiles;
Placing his limbs on their laps
while gently touching both
his feet and hands;
Offering effusive praises,
though mildly angered,
they spoke. 15

The Gopīs spoke:

Some love only
those who love in return;
some, however, love those
who may not return their love;
Some do not love
in either of these ways;
please explain this
clearly to us, O dear one. 16

The Beloved Lord spoke:

Friends who love each other,
yet ultimately strive
for their own self-interest,
Do not find endearment
nor fulfill *dharma*;
indeed, such friends
have no purpose
other than self-interest. 17

Those who love others who
 may not offer love in return,
 in which manner parents or
 compassionate persons truly do,
They are persons of *dharma*
 who are without fault
 and are truly endearing,
 O ladies with beautiful waists. 18

Some do not love even
 those who offer them love,
 let alone those who are
 not loving toward them.
Such persons may be
 satisfied by the self
 and fulfilled in all desires,
 or they may be ungrateful,
 even hateful, toward the venerable. 19

Now, O friends, in order
 to strengthen their love,
I may not return even the love
 of those who love me;
Like a poor man who obtains
 a treasure and then loses it,
Such a person knows nothing else,
 filled with no other thought
 than regaining that treasure. 20

Dear ladies,
indeed, for my sake alone
You have abandoned the world,
the Vedas, and
even your relatives,
out of love for me.
It was out of love for you
that I became invisible,
though you were never
removed from my sight.
Therefore, you should not be
discontented with me—
O dearest ones,
I am your beloved![56] 21

I am unable to reciprocate
your faultless love for me,
your own purity,
And all that you have
sacrificed for me,
even over the lifetime
of a great divinity.
Severing strong ties
to your homes, so difficult
to overcome, you have
lovingly worshiped me.
May your reward be
your own purity. 22

[56] The Vedas: the foundational Sanskrit sacred texts of India, the texts symbolizing complete knowledge.

ACT FIVE

KRISHNA JOINS THE GOPĪS IN THE RĀSA DANCE

Bhāgavata Purāṇa, Book 10, Chapter 33

Scene 1

The sage Śuka spoke:

Thus having heard
 the enchanting words
 of their Beloved Lord,
The Gopīs forgot the agony
 caused by separation from him;
 their desires were fulfilled
 simply by touching his limbs. 1

Then Govinda
 commenced the play
 of the Rāsa dance
 with his devoted ones;
Those jewel-like maidens,
 joined together
 by pure love,
 linked their arms
 with one another.[57] 2

[57] Rāsa dance: "rāsa" is the name of a special kind of ancient circular dance, which also includes singing on the part of the dancers.

The Rāsa dance and its festival
fully blossomed with
the perfect turning forth
of Vraja Gopikās in a circular
movement so beautifully adorned.
The supreme Lord of yoga,
Krishna, then entered
among them
between each pair—
Each thought she alone
was at his side
as he placed his arms
around the necks
of those young women. 3

Then hundreds
of celestial chariots
crowded the sky,
Carrying the captivated denizens
of the heavens, along with their wives,
their souls anxious to behold that scene.[58] 4

Kettledrums resounded
while showers of blossoms
fell to the ground.
The leading Gandharvas
and their wives sang
about his perfect glory.[59] 5

The bracelets, ankle bells, and
bells decorating the waists
of those young women,
Each with her own beloved,
created a tumultuous sound
in the circle of the Rāsa dance. 6

[58] Celestial chariots: heavenly beings ride in "*vimānas*," or chariots that float through the heavens.

[59] Gandharvas: name of celestial singers who produce exquisite music with instruments.

There, glowing brilliantly among them,
was the Beloved Lord, son of Devakī—
In a setting of golden ornaments,
he appeared like a magnificent emerald! [60] 7

With their feet
stepping to the dance;
with gestures of their hands,
loving smiles and sporting eyebrows;
With waists bending
and the rhythmic movements
of garments covering their breasts;
with earrings swinging
on their cheeks;
The spiritual wives of Krishna,
with moistened faces
and braids and belts
tied tightly,
sang his praises—
They appeared
like lustrous flashes
of radiant lightning
engulfed by a ring of dark clouds. 8

While dancing,
they sang out loud,
and the throats of those
so delighted by love
became reddened.
Overjoyed by
the touch of Krishna,
the whole universe
became filled
with their song. 9

[60] Devakī: Krishna's original birth mother and the wife of Vāsudeva.

One of them, together with Mukunda,
sang out in pure embellished tones,
freely improvising on a melody.
Pleased by her performance
he honored her, saying
"Well done!" "Well done!"
Another one sang out that melody
in a stylized rhythmic pattern,
and he offered her much praise.[61] 10

Another, weary from
the Rāsa dance,
stood beside the one
who carried a baton;
Placing her arm
around his shoulder,
her jasmine flowers
and bracelets slackened. 11

Then one of them placed
on her shoulder
the arm of Krishna,
with the fragrance
of a blue lotus.
Upon smelling this scent,
blended with the balm
of sandalwood,
she became elated
with bodily ripplings of bliss
and kissed his arm tenderly. 12

[61] Mukunda: Krishna, "one who grants liberation, or *mukti*."
In a specific musical style: known as *dhruvam*, a particular measure of music.

One, decorated with
shimmering earrings
that swayed to the dance,
placed her cheek next to his.
With his cheek
touching hers,
he gave her
the betel nut he was chewing. 13

Another, whose ankle bells
and bells of her belt
were accompanying
the singing and dancing,
stood by his side.
Becoming weary,
she tenderly brought
the lotus-like hand of Acyuta
to her breasts. 14

The Gopīs had obtained Acyuta,
the exclusive beloved of Śrī,
as their lover.
With their necks
embraced by his arms,
they delighted in singing about him. 15

The beauty of their faces was enhanced
by droplets of perspiration
decorating their cheeks, and
By lotus flowers in their hair
and behind their ears.
With music resounding from
their bracelets and ankle bells,
and garlands falling from their hair,
The Gopīs danced
together with their Beloved Lord;
bees became a chorus of singers
in that assembly of the Rāsa dance. 16

Thus with his hands
touching them in embraces,
With broad playful smiles
and affectionate glances,
The Lord of Ramā delighted in
loving the fair maidens of Vraja
Just as a small child plays
with his own reflection. 17

From their contact with his limbs,
their senses were filled with joy.
The young women of Vraja
could hardly keep their hair,
Skirts and upper garments
that covered their breasts
From becoming disheveled, and
their garlands and ornaments
from scattering, O leader of the Kurus.[62] 18

[62] Leader of the Kurus: the king Parīkṣit to whom the Rāsa Līlā is being narrated.

Observing the play of Krishna,
celestial ladies
moving in the sky
became enchanted and
Passion arose in them—
even the moon
with its constellations
became amazed. 19

Having multiplied himself
in as many forms as there
were cowherd women,
He, the Beloved Lord, knowing
all pleasure within himself,
delighted in loving them
in this divine play. 20

Figure 9. The Wondrous Circle Dance of Divine Love: The Eternally Joyful Rāsa Maṇḍala. Painting by Kim Waters.

Scene 2

When he saw how they
had become weary
from their amorous play,
The compassionate one,
with pure love,
wiped their faces,
O king, with his soothing hand. 21

The Gopīs were beautiful
with shining cheeks,
Locks of hair, brilliant gold earrings,
and glances enhanced by sweet smiles.
They honored their hero
and sang of his auspicious acts,
Delighted by the touch
of his fingernails. 22

His garland,
crushed by their limbs
joined together with his,
Was colored with
the reddish *kuṅkuma*
that covered their breasts.
Followed by a chorus of bees
who sang as though they
were the best of Gandharvas,
He swiftly entered the water to dispel
the maidens' fatigue and relax with them,
like a roused elephant along
with his female elephant companions,
breaking down any boundaries in his way. 23

In the water,
  being splashed by the girls,
He gazed upon them with pure love
  as they laughed all around him,
  dear king.
He was worshiped by those
  traveling in celestial vehicles who
  showered lotus flowers upon that scene.
He, who himself possesses all pleasure,
  took pleasure in amorous love,
  playing like the king of elephants. 24

Then he moved along the banks
  of the Kṛṣṇā river
  into a small forest grove,
In the direction of a gentle breeze
  carrying fragrances of flowers
  over land and water.
Surrounded by
  that group of maidens
  who gathered around him like bees,
He was just like a large elephant
  reeling with excitement
  in the company of female elephants. 25

Thus he allowed himself to be
subdued by those nights
made so brilliant
by the rays of the moon—
He was perfectly
fulfilled in all desires
and pure within himself;
While with that group of maidens
so passionately attached to him,
sexual enjoyment was of no issue—
Inspiring the narrations
and poetry of autumn,
all those moonlit nights
found their refuge in *rasa*.[63] 26

Scene 3

The king Parīkṣit spoke:

For the purpose of
establishing *dharma* and
subduing all that opposes it,
The Beloved Lord, accordingly,
descends with his counterpart
as Lord of the universe.[64] 27

How could he—the teacher,
executor and protector
of the limits of *dharma*—
O knower of Brahman,
act in contrary ways
by touching others' wives? 28

[63] *rasa*: "taste," aesthetic experience or poetic delight. The word also connotes a "divine relationship of affection and tenderness." Note that this word is different than Rāsa, Krishna's "wondrous circle dance" with the Gopīs.

[64] Counterpart: Krishna's complementary divine associate(s) and/or divine abode.

With what intention
would the Lord of the Yadus,
whose desires are supremely fulfilled,
Perform such acts that
would usually be condemned?
Please destroy our doubt, O strict sage.[65] 29

The sage Śuka spoke:

Apparent transgressions of *dharma*
in the acts of the most exalted souls
can appear bold or reckless.
Among such powerful beings
there is no adverse effect,
just as fire can devour anything
without being affected. 30

If one, unlike the exalted soul,
is not powerful,
one should never perform
any transgressions,
even within one's mind.
Such a person
who acts foolishly would perish,
as anyone other than Rudra
would be destroyed by poison
generated from the sea.[66] 31

Words from exalted souls,
meant for us, are always true,
though their actions
only sometimes can be followed.
Therefore one who
possesses intelligence
should act in agreement
with their teachings. 32

[65] Lord of the Yadus: Krishna.

[66] Rudra: name for the deity of cosmic dissolution, Śiva.
Poison generated by the sea: Śiva saves the universe by drinking the *kālakūṭa* poison that was produced from the churning of the ocean.

Selfishness in this world
is not found in the behavior
of virtuous persons.
Actions appearing at times
to be contrary, which are
without any false sense of self,
are not without true purpose,
O dear king. 33

Thus, for the Lord, how could
there be good or bad effects
arising from the piety
or impiety of creatures,
Whether they be animals,
human beings,
or inhabitants of heaven,
who are themselves controlled by him? 34

Those whose bondage to karma
has been shaken off
by the power of yoga
Are fully satisfied
by humble service to the dust
of the lotus feet of the Lord.
Such sages act freely
without becoming
bound to this world.
The supreme Lord, who accepts
various revealed forms according
to his own supreme desire,
also acts freely—
how then, for him,
could there possibly be bondage? [67] 35

[67] Karma: the soul's ties to actions and reactions of this world. Karma keeps a soul bound to this world, to the cycle of birth and death, without allowing its final release into the eternal world of Spirit in which the highest abode is Krishna's blissful world of Vraja.

Scene 4

He who dwells within the Gopīs
and within their husbands,
indeed, within all embodied beings
As the internal Witness,
also acts in this world
through his divine dramas,
by assuming various forms.[68] 36

In order to show
special favor to his devotees,
he reveals his personal
human-like form.
Upon hearing
how he affectionately
enacts his divine plays
in this manner,
one becomes fully devoted to him. 37

The husband cowherds of Vraja
felt no jealousy whatsoever
toward Krishna.
Deluded by his special power of Māyā,
each husband thought his wife
had remained all the while by his side.[69] 38

[68] The internal Witness: manifestation of Krishna within the heart of living beings. Assuming various forms: refers to the *avatāra* forms, or "divine descents" of the supreme deity or Vishnu.

[69] Special power of Māyā: the divine illusory power of God causing forgetfulness (see Yogamāyā in verse 1.1).

During the sacred hour before dawn,
at the end of the night of Brahmā,
and with the consent of Vāsudeva,
The Gopīs returned to their homes,
though reluctantly,
for they so loved the Beloved Lord
and they were so loved by him.[70] 39

This is the divine play of Vishnu
with the fair maidens of Vraja.
One who is filled with faith,
who hears or describes this play,
Having regained the highest
devotion for the Beloved Lord,
Has lust, the disease of the heart,
quickly removed without delay—
such a person is peaceful and wise.[71] 40

[70] Vāsudeva: Krishna; son of Vasudeva, Krishna's father and husband of Devakī.

Night of Brahmā: a night of the creator god, Brahmā, is a night in cosmic or heavenly terms, an extraordinary length of time, the equivalent of 4.32 billion human years.

[71] Vishnu: Krishna in his persona as cosmic deity, sustainer of all the universes.

Peaceful and wise: two words that translate the two essential meanings of the word "*dhīra*."

Song of the Flute

—The Veṇu Gīta—

Bhāgavata Purāṇa, Book 10, Chapter 21, Verses 1 through 20

The sage Śuka spoke:

Thus, the forest was filled
with clear autumn waters
and gentle breezes carrying
the sweet scent of lotus flowers.
Entering that scene
together with cows
and cowherd friends,
Acyuta appeared. 1•

Among groves of flowering trees,
and lakes, rivers, and hills
Resounding with flocks of birds
and swarming maddened bees,
Madhupati arrived, accompanied by
Balarāma and the cowherd boys.
While tending the cows
he began to play his flute. 2•

Song of the Flute: in Sanskrit, "Veṇu Gīta." The word "song" in this chapter title has two possible meanings. It can mean the "song about Krishna's flute" and also the "song-like music coming from Krishna's flute."

•1 Śuka: the sage-narrator of this passage.
Acyuta: Krishna, "the infallible one."

•2 Madhupati: Krishna, epithet meaning "chief of the Madhu dynasty."
Balarāma: the older brother of Krishna.

The Yoga of Love. Graham M. Schweig, Oxford University Press. © Oxford University Press 2025.
DOI: 10.1093/oso/9780197768426.003.0011

Those young women of Vraja
were aroused by Passion
after hearing
the song of his flute.
Some of them, in his absence,
were moved to describe
the qualities of Krishna
to their intimate friends. 3•

As they began to describe him,
they remembered
the playful activities of Krishna.
Their minds again became
disturbed by the force of Passion
and they could no longer speak, O king. 4•

Adorned with a crown
of peacock feathers
and blue *karṇikāra* flowers
ornamenting his ears,
He, most excellent of dancers,
wearing the Vaijayantī garland
and yellow garments brilliant as gold,
Filled the holes of his flute
with the nectar of his lips
while his praises were
being sung by cowherd friends.
He then entered
the Vrindāvana forest,
made beautiful by his footprints. 5•

•3 Vraja: the rural region in which Krishna and the Gopīs reside.
Passion: Amorous love personified, Krishna as the God of Love.
•4 King: Parīkṣit, the listener to whom this passage is being narrated.
•5 *Karṇikāra* flowers: the pericarp portion of lotus flowers.
Vaijayantī: the name of Krishna's garland consisting of flowers of five colors.
Vṛndāvana: the village in which Krishna and the Gopīs reside.

Thus hearing, O king,
the sound of the flute
that captivates
the hearts of all beings,
The young women of Vraja
began describing
that alluring sound yet again,
embracing him within their minds. 6

The beautiful Gopīs spoke:

O friends,
for those who have eyes,
we know of no greater
reward than this—
Entering the forest
with their companions and
herding the cows before them,
The two sons of the ruler of Vraja,
whose faces are adorned
by the flutes they play,
Cast loving glances
all around them—
it is this vision that
is constantly imbibed 7

Dressed in a splendid array
of garments; decorated
with tender mango leaves,
Peacock feathers and bunches
of flowers; and wearing
garlands of lotuses and lilies;
The two of them
are exceedingly beautiful,
sometimes singing
Among their cowherd friends,
and appearing like the most
excellent of dancers on a stage. 8

O Gopīs, what auspicious acts
  must have been performed
  by this flute,
For it enjoys the nectar flowing
  from the lips of Dāmodara,
  leaving only a taste for us cowherd girls
  to whom this nectar truly belongs.
The rivers, themselves
  mothers of the bamboo
  from which the flute is made,
  feel jubilant with blooming lotuses;
And the forefathers of the flute,
  the bamboo trees, shed tears
  of joy with their flowing sap. 9•

O friend,
  Vrindāvana enhances
  the beauty of the earth
With treasure obtained
  from the lotus feet
  of the son of Devakī.
Upon hearing
  the flute of Govinda,
  peacocks dance in rapture—
Observing their dancing from hilltops,
  all other creatures
  become stunned. 10•

•9 Dāmodara: Krishna, the "one whose waist (*-udara*) is bound (*dama-*)," referring to the *līlā* in BhP 10.9.
•10 Devakī: Krishna's birth mother.
Govinda: Krishna, the protector of the cows.
O friend: A form of address of one Gopī to another.

Blessed, surely,
  in spite of their ignorance,
Are these female deer
  who have taken birth as animals.
Upon hearing the exquisitely dressed
  son of Nanda sound his divine flute,
They offer him worship
  through affectionate glances,
  along with their black deer mates. 11•

Gazing at Krishna whose
  pleasing form and behavior
  are utterly elating for all women,
And hearing
  the enchanting music
  emanating from his flute,
The hearts of the gods' wives
  are agitated by Passion while
  they move in heavenly chariots;
They become bewildered
  and their belts loosen,
  as flowers fall from their hair. 12•

Cows, too, drink the nectar
  of the song of the flute
Coming forth from Krishna's mouth
  into the vessels of their up-raised ears.
Indeed, calves stand still,
  their mouths filled with milk
  flowing from their mothers' teats.
Watching with tearful eyes,
  they embrace Govinda
  within their hearts. 13

•11 Nanda: Krishna's foster father, husband of Yaśodā.
•12 The gods' wives: Translates *devyāḥ*.
Heavenly chariots: Translates *vimāna*.

In this forest, O mother, the birds
are most certainly great sages.
Beholding Krishna playing
the melodious song of his flute,
They rise to branches of trees
covered with beautiful foliage.
With unblinking eyes they listen,
while all other sounds cease. 14•

When rivers hear
the music of Mukunda,
their flowing currents are broken
And their waters swirl
out of intense love for him.
The two feet of Murāri
are made stationary,
seized by the embrace of
Arm-like waves that present
offerings of lotus flowers. 15•

Seeing how he tends
the animals of Vraja
in the heat of the sun,
Along with Balarāma
and the cowherd boys;
and how he follows the cows
while playing his flute;
The rain-cloud,
rising high in the sky
with love overflowing,
Creates from its own form
an umbrella for its friend,
showering flower-like raindrops. 16

•14 Mother: A form of address of certain Gopīs for other Gopīs.
•15 Mukunda: Krishna, the bestower of liberation.
Murāri: Krishna, the slayer of the Mura demon.

The native women of Pulinda
  are fully satisfied by contact with
The *kuṅkuma* powder that decorates
  the breasts of his beloveds,
  released from the beautiful
  reddish lotus feet
  of the greatly praised Lord.
Even though they feel
  tormented by the sight
  of reddened blades of grass,
They also experience relief from
  the pangs of that vision of Passion
  when they spread the powder upon
  their own faces and breasts. 17•

Ah! This hill is best among all
  the servants of Hari, O friends.
It delights in the touch of the feet
  of Krishna and Balarāma,
Offering respects to them both,
  along with their cows
  and cowherd friends,
By supplying fresh water,
  pastures of soft grass,
  sheltering caves and edible roots. 18•

•17 Pulinda: A local indigenous people.
kuṅkuma: A deep reddish powder.
•18 Hari: Krishna, the one who steals the hearts of all.
This hill: Referring to Govardhana, the hill on which Krishna and Balarāma play with the cows, that was effortlessly lifted by Krishna to protect the residents of Vraja from the wrath of the god Indra.

The cows are led through
the forest by the two boys
and their cowherd friends.
They are accompanied by
sweet sounds of melodious notes flowing
from the enchanting flute, O friends,
That cause moving beings not to move,
and non-moving beings like trees
to be elated with ripplings of bliss.
The two boys can be recognized
by the ropes they carry to bind
milking and rambunctious cows—
all of this is wonderful! 19•

[The sage Śuka spoke:]

Thus, the various divine acts
of their Beloved Lord as he
wandered about Vrindāvana
Were being described
by each one of them,
for the Gopīs had attained
complete absorption in him. 20•

•19 Elated with ripplings of bliss: Translates *pulakaḥ*. See footnote for RL 1.40.
•20 Divine acts: Translates *krīḍās*.
Beloved Lord: Krishna; translates *bhagavat*.
Completely absorbed in him: Translates *tan-mayatām*.

Song of the Black Bee

— The Bhramara Gīta —

Bhāgavata Purāṇa, Book 10, Chapter 47 Verses 1 through 21

The sage Śuka spoke:

The women of Vraja were gazing
  upon one companion of Krishna,
Whose arms were long
  and eyes like young lotus flowers.
Wearing a yellow garment
  and a garland of lotuses,
His face, beautiful as a lotus,
  was glowing with shining earrings. 1•

They were astonished
  by his charming appearance:
  "Who is this? From where does he come?
And just whom does he serve?
  His ornaments and clothing
  are like those of Acyuta!"
Speaking these words
  and very excited indeed,
  all of them surrounded him,
Whose shelter was the lotus feet
  of the most excellent and famous one. 2•

•1 One companion of Krishna: Uddhava, Krishna's messenger, whose name is revealed in verse 9.
•2 Acyuta: Krishna, "the infallible one."

The Yoga of Love. Graham M. Schweig, Oxford University Press. © Oxford University Press 2025.
DOI: 10.1093/oso/9780197768426.003.0012

They bowed down to him
  and honored him properly
With modesty, shyness, smiling,
  glances, and pleasing words.
In confidence, they inquired from him
  as he was seated comfortably before them,
For they knew he was carrying a message
  from the Lord of the Goddess Ramā. 3•

The Gopīs spoke:

We know that you have arrived
  as a companion
  of the Lord of the Yadus,
And that you, good sir,
  have been sent here by him
  who desires to give pleasure to his parents. 4•

Otherwise, in these cow pastures of Vraja,
  but for him we see nothing else
  worth remembering—
Certainly the bonds of affection
  in family relations are difficult
  to give up, even for a sage. 5

The most excellent and famous one: name for Krishna or Vishnu; translates the compound Uttamaśloka, more literally meaning, "The one whose hymns of praise (*śloka*) are the greatest or highest (*uttama*)." This epithetical name is also found in verses 13 and 15 below.

•3 The Lord of the Goddess Ramā: Krishna.
•4 The Lord of the Yadus: Krishna.

Friendliness toward others
is displayed for a purpose,
until one's purpose is achieved.
This is the case with men
in relation to women,
and black bees
in relation to flowers. 6

Prostitutes abandon men
who have no money;
citizens abandon
incompetent kings;
Students, their teachers
after completing their education;
and sacrificial priests, their patrons
after receiving their compensation. 7

Birds abandon trees
when their fruits are gone;
guests abandon houses
after they have eaten;
Similarly, animals abandon
burnt-down forests;
and lovers abandon women
after having enjoyed love with them. 8

The sage Śuka spoke:

These were the words of the Gopīs
whose minds, bodies, and speech
were completely devoted to Govinda.
They turned to Uddhava who had just arrived,
for he was a messenger from Krishna,
and they dropped all worldly concerns. 9•

•9 Govinda: Krishna
Uddhava: The name of Krishna's companion-messenger to whom the Gopīs have been speaking.

They sang about the various times
they spent with him, their beloved —
giving up their shyness
they began to cry.
Over and over,
they remembered all the events
of his childhood and youth. 10

One of them, contemplating
her closeness with Krishna,
observed a black bee.
Imagining it to be a messenger
sent to her by her beloved,
she thus began to speak. 11

The Gopī spoke:

O black bee,
friend of a cheater—
please do not touch my feet
with your whiskers,
Which are clearly tinged
by reddish *kuṅkuma* powder
that has fallen onto his garland
from the breasts of rival lovers.
Let the Lord of the Madhu dynasty,
for whom you are the messenger,
bear the marks of favor
from these proud women—
Such behavior would be
the object of ridicule
in the assembly of the Yadus! 12•

•12 The specific group of verses known as the Bhramara Gīta, "Song of the Black Bee," begins with this verse and ends with verse 21 as presented below.

Reddish *kuṅkuma* powder: Saffron or vermilion.

The Lord of the Madhu dynasty: The dynasty in which Krishna appears.

The Yadus: The great and powerful tribe to which Krishna belonged.

After having us drink just once
  the enchanting nectar
  of his own lips,
He suddenly abandoned us,
  just as you may abandon
  blossoming flowers.
Then how is it that the Goddess Padmā
  continues to serve his feet,
  beautiful as the lotus?
Oh! Her mind has certainly been stolen
  by the deceitful speech of the most
  excellent and famous one. 13•

O six-legged creature,
  why are you singing
About the ancient one,
  Lord of the Yadus,
  here before us homeless girls?
Let the singing about him,
  friend of the victorious one,
  be instead for all his lady friends
Whose breasts he now relieves
  of their intense agony—
  those beloved ones of his
  will provide what it is that you desire. 14•

•13 The Goddess Padmā: Another name for Lakṣmī, the divine consort of the cosmic Vishnu.
•14 The friend: Referring to Krishna.
The victorious one: Referring to Arjuna.

Are there any women
in the celestial, earthly,
or lower worlds
Who would not be available to him,
with his playful, arching eyebrows
and deceptive, charming smiles?
After all, what are we to him,
the dust of whose feet is worshiped
by the Goddess Lakṣmī herself?
Nevertheless, those who are destitute
are favored by the words of
the most excellent and famous one. 15•

Please keep your head
away from my foot!
I understand you very well—
You know how to offer flattering words
while acting as his messenger
because you have been trained by Mukunda.
Now he has abandoned us,
who have given up our children, husbands
and all others in the world for his sake.
Therefore, why, since he is ungrateful,
should we make up with him? 16•

•15 Goddess Lakṣmī: The consort of Krishna's cosmic form of Vishnu.
•16 Mukunda: Krishna, the one who grants liberation.

Behaving like
  a cruel-hearted hunter,
  he shot arrows
  at the king of monkeys;
While dominated by one woman,
  he disfigured another
  who approached him
  with passionate desires;
Even after accepting the worship of Bali,
  he tied him up with ropes like a crow
  who, after devouring its prey,
  hovers over it;
So enough of this friendship
  with that dark-complexioned one—
  even if the treasure of such stories
  about him is impossible to give up! 17•

For one who constantly seeks
  to hear of his divine acts,
  the ears are filled with nectar—
A drop of which, if relished even once,
  destroys all attachment to worldly duties
  filled with conflict and duality.
Such irresponsible persons promptly
  give up their families and homes,
  leaving them in a wretched condition.
Here, many of them wander about
  acting as mendicants,
  begging for their livelihood
  like so many birds. 18

•17 A cruel-hearted hunter: Referring to Rāma, the divine manifestation of Krishna, presented fully in the great Sanskrit epic Rāmāyana, and presented briefly in Book 9 of the Bhāgavata Purāṇa.

The king of monkeys: Referring to Vāli.

By one woman: Referring to Sītā, the wife of Rāma.

Disfigured another: Referring to Śūrpaṇakhā.

Accepting the worship of Bali: Referring to Vāmana.

We had faith
  that his deceptive speech was true,
Just as the foolish female companion
  of the black deer is deceived
  by mimicking sounds of a hunter.
We, the maidservants of Krishna,
  have experienced repeatedly
  the pain of his amorous love
Created by the ardent touch of his nails—
  O messenger, please speak of other things! 19

O friend of my dear one,
  have you been sent here
  once again by my beloved?
You ought to be honored
  by me, my friend—
  so what do you wish from me?
How will you lead us who
  remain here to his side,
  he with whom togetherness
  is too difficult to give up?
After all, O gentle one,
  the Goddess Śrī, his consort,
  is forever present with him
  resting upon his chest. 20•

•20 The Goddess Śrī: Another name for the consort of Krishna's cosmic form of Vishnu.

Oh! Indeed, is it not regrettable
that the son of a highly esteemed man
now resides in the city of Mathurā?
O gentle one, does he remember
his father's house, his family relations,
and his cowherd friends?
Does he ever relate to you
any words about us,
his maidservants?
When might he place his hand,
with the fragrant scent of
soothing aloe-wood balm,
on our heads? 21•

•21 The city of Mathurā: The large city about 20 miles south of Vraja.
Aloe-wood balm: Aguru, a fragrant paste coming from Aloe wood tree.

PART IV
BACKGROUND OF THE TEXT

9

Devotional Love as *Rasa*

Literature describing the soul's passionate love for the deity is extensive in India, spanning the course of at least one millennium prior to and following the common era. Consequently, the Bhāgavata Purāṇa's portraits of intimacy with the divinity come out of a colorful and extensive literary past, a heritage reflected in the devotional and aesthetic achievements of the Rāsa Līlā. Sources of such amorous devotion are scriptural, dramatic, and poetic.

Rūpa Gosvāmī (sixteenth century C.E.), along with other disciples of Chaitanya, derived his principles of divine aesthetics from Indian dramaturgy and adapted these to his systematic psychology of divine love. In Sanskrit poetics (*kāvya*) and Indian dramaturgy (*nāṭya*), the word *rasa* (not to be confused with "Rāsa," as in the dance) refers to the pervasive mood or emotion experienced by an audience as aesthetic delight. Based on the concept that God manifests in his *līlā*, or "divine drama," the Gosvāmī applied Indian dramatic theory to the devotional process of reentering God's eternal drama. In his important work *Bhakti Rasāmṛta Sindhu*, "The Ocean of Eternal Rasa in Devotional Love," Rūpa further developed the understanding of *rasa* as the pervasive emotion of relationships found solely within devotional love, *bhakti-rasa*. David L. Haberman observes that the Chaitanya school believes that "love itself is identified as an aspect of the essential nature of God" and notes that it became the task of Chaitanya's disciples, therefore, to elaborate on the love of the divinity.[1] Rūpa's text draws largely from the foundational theory of *rasa*

[1] Haberman has done much to show how Rūpa Gosvāmī's conception of *rasa* has drawn from previous theorists yet makes its own unique contribution to *rasa* theory. See David Haberman's chapters "Religion and Drama in South Asia" and "The Aesthetics

The Yoga of Love. Graham M. Schweig, Oxford University Press.
DOI: 10.1093/oso/9780197768426.003.0013

Figure 10. Marble sacred image of Krishna elaborately worshiped. International Society for Krishna Consciousness, Bury Place, London, UK. Photograph taken by the author in 1974.

formed by Bharata Muni, the originator of Sanskrit dramaturgy, or *Nāṭya Śāstra* (perhaps as early as the second century B.C.E.), and further, from theorists such as Bhoja (eleventh century), Abhinavagupta (twelfth century), and Viśvanātha (fourteenth century).[2]

The teachers of the Chaitanya school, specifically Rūpa Gosvāmī, and following him, Jīva Gosvāmī and Krishnadāsa Kavirāja Gosvāmī, broadly define and describe the relationship with God as *rasa*. The word *rasa* has several meanings worth mentioning here because, collectively, they give us a feel for the word's power and depth in its religious context. It has the sense of "essence" or "taste." It can also mean "the sap of a plant," "the juice of fruit," or more broadly, "the best or finest or prime part of anything," or the "vital essence" of a thing.[3] The word can mean connotatively and more generally "spiritual experience," or more specifically a particular relationship with God.

The Chaitanya Vaishnavas apply the sense of "the prevailing feeling," "religious sentiment," or even "disposition of the heart or mind" to the term *rasa*. Their general connotative meaning is the directly experienced intimate relationship with the divinity. According to the *bhakti* school, God is *rasa*, God supremely enjoys *rasa* and God is the ultimate object of *rasa*. The theological use of the word can be found very early, about two thousand years before the Chaitanya school, in a phrase that the tradition frequently quotes: "Truly, the Lord is *rasa*" (*raso vai saḥ*).[4] This statement expresses the view that God is the one who is the sole object of *rasa*. God is "the greatest connoisseur of *rasa*, or divine loving relation" (*rasika śekhara*).

of Bhakti" in *Acting as a Way of Salvation: A Study of Rāgānugā Bhakti Sādhana* (New York: Oxford University Press, 1988) for a detailed overview of the history and development of *rasa* theory as it establishes itself in the thought of Rūpa Gosvāmī. Another valuable discussion on the background of *rasa* theory and details on Rūpa's conception can be found in the Introduction to Haberman's *The Bhaktirasāmṛtasindhu of Rūpa Gosvāmin*, translated with introduction and notes (New Delhi: Indira Gandhi National Centre for the Arts and Delhi: Motilal Banarsidass Publishers Pvt. Ltd., 2003).

[2] This Viśvanātha of poetics should not be confused with the *bhakti* commentator Viśvanātha Chakravartin of the eighteenth century, whose commentary on the Bhāgavata has been invaluable for this study.

[3] The word can also mean "flavor," or even "love," "affection," or "desire."

[4] Taittirīya Upaniṣad 2.7.1.

Devotion to God as conceived by the Chaitanya school consists of five primary types of loving relations with the deity. The soul's particular relationship with the divinity in devotional love, *rasa*, can closely resemble the variety of loving feelings that humans experience for one another.[5] These types of *rasa* between the soul and divinity can be described as follows:

1. *Reverential Love* (*śānta-rasa*). The soul loves the Beloved from a distance, as a great and powerful emperor is loved by subjects who are not personally serving him. Here the soul is removed from the direct presence of the Beloved, due to the soul's awareness of his or her finite existence in relation to the overwhelming majesty and omnipresence of the Lord. This love is characterized as quiet veneration and admiration; reverential love is passive and contemplative, unlike the dynamic and more intimate forms of love that follow.
2. *Subservient Love* (*dāsya-rasa*). The soul loves the Beloved actively and more closely, as personal servants love and directly serve their king. Here the soul is in a submissive position to the Beloved, who is in a superior position. This love is characterized as obedient service. The distance between the soul and God in reverential love is replaced by dynamic service in subservient love, although the relationship here remains formal.
3. *Mutual Love* (*sakhya-rasa*). The soul loves the Beloved more intimately in mutuality and equality, as a friend loves a companion. The endearing love of close friendships is now experienced with the supreme Beloved, who places himself on an equal level with the soul. This love is characterized by confidential, even playful, and affectionate exchanges. Mutual love

[5] It has even been suggested that the types of experiences within the various *rasas* with Krishna parallel those experiences that Christains can have in particular relationships with Christ. See Sudhindra Chandra Cakravarti's discussion on "Christianity and Bengal Vaiṣṇavism" (Ch. XIV) in his work *Philosophical Foundation of Bengal Vaiṣṇavism* (n/a: Academic Publishers, 1969), especially p. 382.

constitutes a greater level of intimacy with the divine, since the superior position of the Beloved is no longer acknowledged.

4. *Nurturing Love* (*vātsalya-rasa*). The soul loves the Beloved even more deeply and tenderly, as a parent loves a child. The soul's love for the Beloved is from a higher or superior "parental" position as the soul cares for and protects the Beloved, who in turn exhibits dependency upon the soul. This love is characterized by adoration and nurturing affection; here, the carefree and casual familiarity of mutual love is replaced by a constant mindfulness and sense of responsibility for the well-being of the Beloved.
5. *Passionate Love* (*śṛṅgāra-rasa*). The soul loves the Beloved in the most intimate way, as a lover loves a beloved in a conjugal, premarital, or extramarital relationship. It is the most confidential form of love, and the intensity of amorous feelings exchanged represents the greatest attainable intimacy in *rasa*. This love is characterized by total self-surrender of the lover in an exclusive passionate union with the divine, often heightened by periods of intense separation. Essential elements of all four previous *rasas* are present within this highest *rasa*.

The school views these five types of intimacy with the deity collectively, as hierarchically arranged stages of love. Each *rasa*, beginning with the first and proceeding to the fifth, represents a higher intensity of love and progressively greater level of intimacy. Yet each *rasa*, in and of itself, is also recognized as a perfection of love for the divine. Even so, the *rasa* of passionate love is regarded as the ultimate perfection among all perfect *rasas*. It should be noted that these *rasas* are not categories in the strictest sense, because each higher *rasa* incorporates selective aspects from the lower *rasas*.[6]

[6] It is explained that certain elements within each *rasa* are unique, and others are transferred or carried over into the higher *rasas* in more intensified forms. See CC 2.19.

10

Ancient Sources of Devotional Love

Many characteristics of all five *rasas* are found in the Vedic devotional hymns, which display strikingly intimate expressions of love for the divine. Although the formal categorization of these *rasas* in *bhakti* was not developed until the sixteenth century, it could be asserted that the religious experience presented as early as the ancient Ṛg Veda anticipates dimensions of the formal practice of *bhakti*, or devotional love, in the Chaitanya school.

The divinity of the Vedas enters into a variety of love relations with the Vedic worshiper, who relates to the deity as a father, mother, or father and mother together; as a brother, son, or friend; or as a beloved, even as a bride.[1] The "passionate love" of this last worshiper is expressed in these prayerful words: "As yearning wives cleave to their yearning husband, so cleave our hymns to thee, O Lord most potent" (Ṛg Veda 1.62.11), and "As wives embrace their lord, the comely bridegroom" (Ṛg Veda 10.43.1–2).[2] In other examples the soul "strives to win the heart" of the divinity (Ṛg Veda 8.31.18), a sentiment found throughout the Ṛg Veda. Note that the worshiper in the first two instances above is feminine in gender. At other times the worshiper is masculine, as in the following: "I, like a bridegroom thinking of his consort" (Ṛg Veda 4.20.5). Moreover, the divine spouse of the deity himself is also acknowledged in the Vedas: "Vishnu, together with his Spouse" (Ṛg Veda 1.156.2). The soul's passionate love for the deity

[1] Mrinal Das Gupta, "Śraddhā and Bhakti in Vedic Literature," *The Indian Historical Quarterly* 6, no. 2 (June 1930): 325.

[2] *The Hymns of the Ṛgveda*, trans. by Ralph T. H. Griffith (Delhi: Motilal Banarsidass, 1973). The excerpted quotations that follow are taken from this work.

The Yoga of Love. Graham M. Schweig, Oxford University Press. © Oxford University Press 2025.
DOI: 10.1093/oso/9780197768426.003.0014

can therefore be seen to mirror the love found directly within divine conjugal relations.

The other higher *rasas* of nurturing and mutual love are also expressed in Vedic hymns. Nurturing love can be observed in the words, "Thou art a Son to him who duly worships thee" (Ṛg Veda 2.1.9), and in the passage, "Be to us easy of approach, even as a father to his son" (Ṛg Veda 1.1.9).[3] Mutual love between the soul and the divinity is evidenced in the words, "Friend among men" (Ṛg Veda 1.67.1), and "Him, him we seek for friendship" (Ṛg Veda 1.10.6). Much of the Vedic literature is permeated with such heartfelt emotion expressed by the soul to the deity, or about the deity.

The Upanishads, recorded after the Vedas yet hundreds of years before the common era, at times will engage the theme of devotional love. These texts record intimate dialogues between a teacher and student, addressing philosophical and metaphysical questions on the relationship of the soul to "the supreme Self" (the supreme Lord as the soul within the soul) or to "ultimate reality," Brahman. The Upanishadic teacher stresses that the supreme Self is the source of love in human relationships, as demonstrated in this passage:

> Truly, it is not due to the love of a husband
>   that a husband becomes dear,
>   but due to the love of the Divine
>   that a husband becomes dear;
> Truly, it is not due to the love of a wife
>   that a wife becomes dear,
>   but due to the love of the Divine
>   that a wife becomes dear; . . .

[3] In this example of nurturing love, the father is the deity and the son is the dependent soul. Generally, the nurturing *rasa* designates the worshiper as the parental figure, and God as the dependent child. Even when the reverse is found, the *rasa* is considered to be that of nurturing love. Other examples of nurturing love can be found in Ṛg Veda 1.66.1 and Ṛg Veda 6.2.7.

Truly, it is not due to the love of all things
that all things become dear,
but due to the love of the Divine
that all things become dear.
(*Bṛhadāraṇyaka Upaniṣad* 2.4.5)

In the following quotation, a simile drawn from the human experience of conjugal love is engaged, in order to convey the soul's experience of union with the supreme:

As one fully embraced
by one who is dearly beloved
no longer knows
what is without or within,
so a person fully embraced
by the Intelligent Self
no longer knows what
is without or within.
For one who truly has
a desire to reach this state,
whose desire is of the self,
whose nature is without desire,
there is no longer any sorrow within.
(*Bṛhadāraṇyaka Upaniṣad* 4.3.21)

Here, when the soul "embraces" the supreme Soul, an erotic union occurs, characterized by a nondistinction between what is external and what is internal. These examples of passionate devotion of the soul for the divine clearly demonstrate the fervent emotion that filled the heart of the worshiper in post-Vedic times.

The use of the term *bhakti* as the practice of "devotional love for the deity" first appears in the Upanishads (*Śvetāśvatara Upaniṣad* 6.23).[4] It is in the epic literature following the Upanishads, however,

[4] Other Upanishads present a doctrine of grace (*Katha Up.* 1.2.23 and *Mundaka Up.* 3.2.3).

that we find the developed philosophical and doctrinal presentation of *bhakti.* In the Bhagavad Gītā, the small but famous passage within the great Mahābhārata epic, "mutual love" is predominantly exhibited between Krishna and Arjuna. In fact, Krishna declares that he is the "dear friend of all beings" (BG 5.29). The other intimate forms of love are indicated, as well, and "intimacy" with the divinity (*mādhurya*) is emphasized over reverence for the "majesty" of the divinity (*aiśvarya*).

The Bhagavad Gītā thus firmly and comprehensively establishes the concept of intimacy with the deity. When Krishna gives Arjuna a private vision of his unlimited greatness manifest in his "universal form" (*virāṭa-rūpa*), Arjuna yearns to experience once again his more loving relationship with Krishna. He does not desire to serve the Lord in awe and with reverential devotion; rather, he prays to be with Krishna in a personal, affectionate way:

> As a father is to a son,
>   as a friend to a friend,
> As a dearly loved one
>   to a dearly beloved—
>   be pleased to show your
>   loving kindness, O Divinity.
>
> (BG 11.44).

Clearly, the three higher *rasas* are acknowledged and preferred by Arjuna. Although the narrative line of the Bhagavad Gītā places Arjuna and Krishna together as close companions, and their *rasa* is undoubtedly that of mutual love, still some of Krishna's devotional prescriptions resonate with motifs of a more intense love:

> Be mindful of me
>   with love offered to me;
>   sacrificing for me,
>   act out of reverence for me.

Surely you shall
 come to me,
 thus having absorbed
 your self in yoga with
 me as the supreme goal.

(BG 9.34)

These words do not sound like those coming from a friend; rather, the total self-surrender that characterizes passionate love is depicted here, and there are many more such expressions throughout the Bhagavad Gītā's text. The Gopīs, in the Rāsa Līlā, as we shall see, exemplify such passionate devotion for the deity. Indeed, the drama represents a culmination of the history of intimacy with the divine in India. Let us now consider the path of devotional love as it relates to other paths leading to God.

11
Devotional Love as a Path to the Divine

The religious complex that arises from and finds its foundational scriptural authority in the Vedas is commonly known as Hinduism. The word Hindu, oddly enough, is not derived from either of an ancient language or from the many vernacular languages of India.[1] Instead, the word was created by Persian-speaking persons who invaded the northwest corner of India, specifically the area of the Sindhu (Indus) River, around the ninth century of the common era. This nomenclature was adopted at least two millennia after the birth of much Indic religious activity to which we refer when using the name; yet, the word "Hindu" has been firmly integrated into the religious identity of persons within Indic traditions. It is perhaps more accurate to speak of a "Hindu complex" of religion rather than Hindu-*ism*, given the great number and variety of Indic religious traditions that consider the Vedas as their foundation.

The primary Hindu traditions, those that focus upon a particular divinity such as the masculine deity Śiva, the goddess Devī, or the cosmic form of Krishna as Vishnu, regard the Vedas as the original revelation of all knowledge, even if they have no active relationship with the Vedic literature or practices. In some ways, the situation parallels that which is found among the Semitic traditions: Christianity and Islam are traditions in their own right,

[1] It is telling that almost every scholar of "Hinduism" is obliged to elaborately discuss the awkward and un-self-explanatory nomenclature of this religious complex when writing introductory texts on the subject.

The Yoga of Love. Graham M. Schweig, Oxford University Press. © Oxford University Press 2025.
DOI: 10.1093/oso/9780197768426.003.0015

and not merely sects of Judaism; yet both Christian and Islamic traditions rely upon the Jewish Bible at least as a foundation for their faiths, despite their newer, independent revelations and differing forms of worship.

As we can say that Judaism, Christianity, and Islam are the major traditions within the Semitic complex, we can also point to three major South Asian traditions that include the majority of Hindus in India and its northern neighboring country, Nepal. These three traditions—Śaivism, Śaktism, and Vaishnavism—are each named after the ultimate deity upon whom practitioners center their worship. Thus Śaivism focuses on worship of the deity Śiva, known for his universal role in cosmic dissolution; Śaktism involves worship of *śakti*, the supreme feminine power of Devī, or the Goddess; and Vaishnavism is centered on worship of Vishnu, known for his universal role in cosmic sustenance, or Krishna, the intimate and playful deity.

Even though these traditions within the Hindu family of religion do not focus upon the same ultimate deity, they do share the same understanding of the soul's various paths for attaining salvation. Vedic hymns reveal practices that later became formalized as "paths of the soul" (*margas*), which have persisted throughout Indian religious history. Traditions of India may emphasize one of these methods of salvation over the others, or prescribe a combination of the three, which are as follows: the path of "action" (*karma*), in which one "works" for one's salvation; the path of "knowledge" (*jñāna*), in which one undergoes a process of study, meditation, and introspection; and the path of "devotional love" (*bhakti*), in which one is actively dedicated to the deity in loving service and experiences the reciprocal "grace" of the deity.

Although a pan-Indian phenomenon, *bhakti* is particularly associated with Vaishnava traditions and the Bhāgavata text, emphasizing deep devotional love and affectionate self-surrender offered to a singular personal supreme deity, along with God's transforming grace for the worshiper. It is primarily the Vaishnava sects across India that developed *bhakti* into sophisticated theologies and practices, especially during the *bhakti* renaissance of the medieval period (eleventh through seventeenth centuries).

Philosophers of *bhakti* are quick to point out that the paths of action and knowledge, along with all other paths apart from *bhakti*, can become egocentric and self-interested, and therefore lack the purity of heart found in *bhakti*. Although they acknowledge that other paths lead to transcendence and are effective spiritual achievements for the soul, they insist that such religious endeavors are intrinsically self-centered and are not ultimately carried out for the pleasure of God; whereas in *bhakti*, self-sacrifice and lack of self-concern are both conducive to complete theocentrism, or god-centeredness. Thus, the Bhāgavata and Vaishnava traditions extol devotional love in *bhakti* as the superior path to salvation, while also recognizing the presence of the other two paths, *jñāna* and *karma*. Such paths are considered valid, however, only if they lead to or are naturally incorporated in *bhakti*; they are not regarded as valuable paths independent of *bhakti*.

For all practitioners within the Hindu complex, the ultimate truth and reality is known as Brahman. The goal of Hindu religion has consistently been the union of the individual soul (*ātman*) with the supreme reality, Brahman. While some traditions understand Brahman to be the supreme *personal* being, others regard Brahman as the supreme state of *impersonal* being.[2] Many accept that the supreme reality contains both personal and impersonal dimensions, but the question remains as to the priority and superiority of one over the other. If a tradition asserts that Brahman at its highest is a supreme personal being from whom all living beings and realities originate, and the very source from which the impersonal Brahman emanates, then it presents a theism. On the other hand,

[2] In Christian theology, these types of distinctions are made with the terms *via positiva* (or *via affirmativa*) and *via negativa*, or cataphatic and apophatic distinctions, respectively.

if a tradition asserts that Brahman at its highest is a supreme state of impersonal being in which there are no longer any distinctions among souls, divinity, and Brahman, then such a tradition presents a monism. In theistic Brahman, the soul and divinity remain distinct and eternally related entities between whom a supreme love is forever sustained. By contrast, in monistic Brahman, there is no scope for love since the relationship between soul and divinity is ultimately dissolved.

Vaishnava traditions from the Hindu complex of religion are theistic in that they consider the process of devotion to the supreme deity to be salvation itself, and not merely a means to salvation. In other words, they accept the means and the end of devotion to be the same. Rudolf Otto, the famous twentieth-century German comparative theologian, recognized Vaishnavism as possessing a profound sense of theism. After searching the religions of the world for Christianity's greatest "competitor," he found that the Vaishnava tradition was worthy of being compared to Christianity precisely because of its theological sophistication.[3] Other traditions, such as the Śaiva and Śakta sects, typically retain a curtain of monism behind their devotional and theistic practices. Such non-Vaishnava traditions can exhibit the appearance of a theism, since *bhakti* is engaged. However, their ultimate goal is to go beyond a relationship with the deity to attain an eternal state of impersonal oneness. Vaishnavism could thus be considered the most strictly theistic among traditions within the Hindu complex, for it sustains theism in the fullest sense.

[3] In this matter, Rudolf Otto states, ". . . the special problems of the doctrine of grace have been developed more acutely and in greater detail among the Vishnu-*bhaktas* than among those of Śiva" (*India's Religion of Grace and Christianity Compared and Contrasted*, trans. by Frank Hugh Foster [New York: Macmillan, 1930], 27). In spite of the evolved forms of *bhakti* in the Śaiva tradition, especially in the Śaiva Siddhānta of South India, an ultimate veil of monism, in my estimation, seems to eclipse a fully developed *bhakti* theism of the sort found in Vaishnava sects.

12
Forms of the Deity Vishnu

Vaishnava practitioners understand Vishnu to be identical to the supreme personal Brahman to whom all worshipers return. Vishnu is also regarded as the supreme personal being who is the very source of Brahman, and who fills the cosmos with a stratified government of minor divinities working under his divine direction. Moreover, Vishnu plays a role in the triune cosmic godly functions, with Brahmā serving as the god of creation, Vishnu as the god of sustenance, and Śiva as the god of destruction. From the Vaishnava theological perspective, Brahmā and Śiva, though extraordinarily powerful minor divinities within the complex cosmic government, do not have the supreme divine status of Vishnu.

Vishnu exhibits various cosmic or divine forms in his transcendent spiritual realms, and simultaneously appears in this world in varying manifestations, each known as an *avatāra* or "divine descent." Although the word *avatāra* is often translated by both Western and Indian scholars as "incarnation," Vishnu is not technically in-carnate; rather, he manifests a divine descent of his own form.[1] Thus when he condescends to this world, it is understood that Vishnu comes in his very own form, spiritual and omnipotent.

Commonly held Hindu belief recognizes that when Krishna comes to this world as the manifest divinity, he does so as an *avatāra* of Vishnu. In fact, Krishna is listed in the *Bhāgavata* as

[1] The English word "incarnation" unavoidably possesses certain Christian senses that are not present in the word it attempts to translate. Etymologically, "incarnation" and "*avatāra*" have very different senses. The word "incarnation" means "the act of coming into a carnal body," and *avatāra* means a "con-descent" of a divine body (literally, *ava-* = "down" and *-tāra* = "a crossing over").

The Yoga of Love. Graham M. Schweig, Oxford University Press. © Oxford University Press 2025.
DOI: 10.1093/oso/9780197768426.003.0016

the twentieth *avatāra* manifestation (BhP 1.3.23). Within those Vaishnava traditions for whom the form of Krishna is the ultimate form of the divinity, however, he is both a "divine descent" and "the original person of the godhead" (*ādipuruṣa-devatā*). He is the very source of even Vishnu, who is in turn the source of Brahman. Krishna is understood, then, as the supremely intimate deity from whom all-powerful and cosmic forms of the divinity emanate.

Krishna is also known as *pūrṇāvatāra,* the "full descent of the deity." Thus, the Vaishnavas regard Krishna as descending to earth through the power of his Vishnu form. These three levels of divinity are schematized in Table 2.

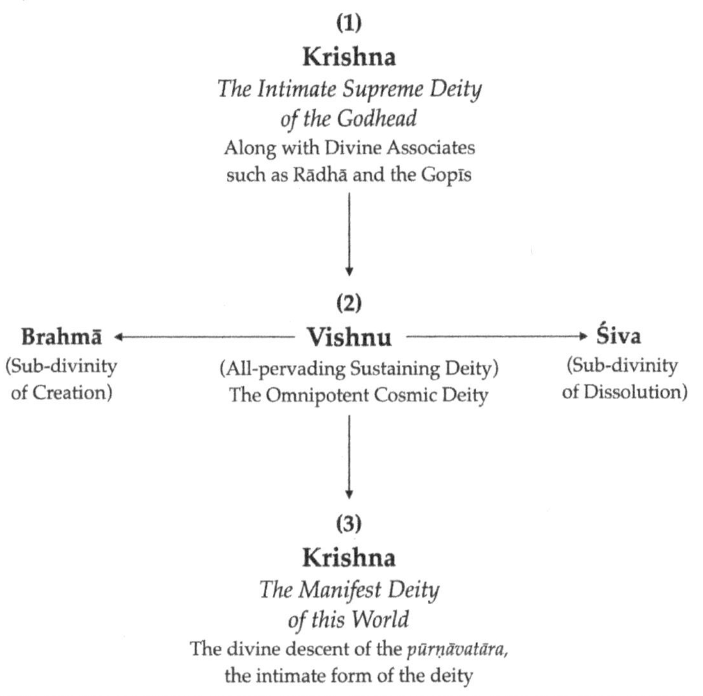

Table 2. Intimate, cosmic, and compassionate manifestations of Krishna.

The most intimate form of God is also the ultimate form of the deity, which I have termed "The Intimate Supreme Deity of the Godhead." From this foundational level comes "The Omnipotent Cosmic Deity," who is Vishnu, "the manifestation of God's sustaining power and almightiness," along with Brahmā (as the Creator) and Śiva (as the Annihilator). Vishnu, then, is the immediate source of the divinity of this world, the manifest deity Krishna, as well as other *avatāra* manifestations.

Furthermore, inasmuch as the identities of Krishna and Vishnu are distinctive, they are also identical and interchangeable. One observes an interesting twist in the last verse of the Rāsa Līlā, the only instance of the drama in which the name Vishnu occurs: "This is the divine play of Vishnu with the young women of Vraja" (RL 5.40). Here, Krishna, who has been the hero all along, is unexpectedly named Vishnu as the narrator concludes the story, identifying Vishnu rather than Krishna as the hero of the drama.

Although there are many *avatāra* forms of Vishnu honored and celebrated by Hindus, the most famous are those of Rāma and Krishna. The scholar A. L. Basham characterizes the *avatāra* Rāma as a deity of loyalty and righteousness: "Rāma and his faithful wife Sītā combine the ideals of heroism, long suffering, righteousness, loyalty, and justice in a story so full of exciting incident that it has become part of the tradition not only of India, but also of most of South-East Asia."[2] The Rāmāyaṇa of Vālmīki, which describes the deeds of Rāma, is without question one of the most loved sacred texts for Hindus.

By comparison, the deity Krishna shares more personal and loving relationships with his worshipers. Basham confirms this in the following portrait of Krishna's personality:

> Krishna, probably even more popular than Rāma, is a divinity of a rare completeness and catholicity, meeting almost every

[2] A. L. Basham, ed., *A Cultural History of India* (Oxford: Oxford University Press, 1975), pp. 80–81.

> human need. As the divine child he satisfies the warm maternal drives of Indian womanhood. As the divine lover, he provides romantic wish fulfillment in a society still tightly controlled by ancient norms of behaviour which give little scope for freedom of expression in sexual relations. As charioteer of the hero Arjuna on the battlefield of Kurukshetra, he is the helper of all those who turn to him, even saving the sinner from evil rebirths, if he has sufficient faith in the Lord.[3]

While Basham observes correctly Krishna's popularity and completeness as a divinity, his explanation of Krishna's role as "the divine lover" seems shortsighted. After all, the famed *Kāma Sūtra*, a veritable manual of passionate love and sexuality, has arisen out of Indian culture, which certainly could lead one to believe that India possesses a great deal of "freedom of expression in sexual relations."

Basham describes what I have termed the "intimate deity" of Krishna. This more personal form of the divinity is elaborately presented in the great classical texts of India, the Mahābhārata and the Bhāgavata Purāṇa. Intimate *līlās* of the deity are not associated exclusively with the *avatāra* form; rather, they are a manifestation, according to certain Vaishnava sects, of the ultimate deity and his activities from within the very center of the godhead. In other words, the deity's activities are taking place eternally in the spiritual realm and are simultaneously manifest by the deity in this world at special times in the revolution of the cosmos.

[3] A. L. Basham, ed., *A Cultural History of India* (Oxford: Oxford University Press, 1975), p. 81.

PART V

MESSAGES OF THE TEXT

13

Devotional Yoga Transcends Death

Love and death powerfully intersect in the Rāsa Līlā. While the biblical Song of Solomon tells us that, "love is as strong as death,"[1] in devotional yoga—or *bhakti*—love becomes even *stronger* than death. Thus, those who fully absorb themselves in love gain a taste of immortality, savoring what Nārada describes in the *Bhakti Sūtra* as "the essential nature of devotional love" (NBS 3–4). Through passionately orienting their hearts and minds around their beloved Krishna, the heroines of the story—the Gopīs—become masters of this yoga. Appropriately, Krishna is referred to throughout the drama as *yogeśvareśvara*, or "the Lord of all masters of yoga."

Through these master *yoginīs* of love we are given a peek into the mysterious relationship between devoted souls and death. Passages into immortality—moving from one world to another—is a subtle but prominent theme in the Rāsa Līlā story line. Greater though than the passage of death is the passage of love, through which the Gopīs travel to leave their worlds and enter Krishna's world in the forest. This journey beyond death—even while the soul is in the embodied state prior to death—is a unique phenomenon experienced only by those who have mastered *bhakti* yoga. The Gopīs exhibit this shift into immortality when entranced with Krishna's flute music: a divine state the Rāsa Līlā's narrator illustrates by describing the Gopīs as possessing three types of bodies: physical, nonphysical, and illusory.

The Gopīs' first kind of body is "composed of physical elements": a body influenced by the "underlying forces of nature"

[1] Song of Solomon 8:4.

The Yoga of Love. Graham M. Schweig, Oxford University Press. © Oxford University Press 2025.
DOI: 10.1093/oso/9780197768426.003.0017

that is abandoned upon hearing Krishna's flute (RL 1.11). This body fulfills the responsibilities of an ideal village woman as dictated by *dharma*, by maintaining faithfulness to the family, performing household work, milking cows, and feeding the children and husband (RL 1.5–7). The abrupt abandonment, or death, of the physical body occurs in the first scene of the drama, when the Gopīs suddenly drop all types of vital household activities upon hearing the flute music of their beloved Lord.

The second type of body appears to be a body not composed of physical elements and not influenced by the forces of nature; it is a perfected spiritual body suitable for relating to God, facilitating the passionate love of the cowherd maidens. The Gopīs give up their physical, dharmic bodies as they abandon their duties, either by escaping outwardly to the forest or inwardly into meditation. The author of the *Bhāgavata*, however, addresses this new body only in relation to the maidens who are unable to be with Krishna, in the following verse:

> Certainly, he is the supreme Soul,
>   though they knew him
>   intimately as their lover.
> They relinquished their bodies
>   composed of physical elements,
>   and any worldly bondage
>   was instantly destroyed.
>
> (RL 1.11)

Thus, the Gopīs who cannot depart from their families instead depart by means of yogic meditation, embracing Krishna from within. In either case, the physical body is abandoned, and they find themselves in a new body that is perfect for engaging in loving affairs with their beloved.

The maidens lose themselves in their Lord in utter self-forgetfulness, whether they move inwardly, embracing Krishna deeply within the heart, or outwardly, embracing him in the forest of Vraja. The Gopīs interact with Krishna throughout the drama in this devotional body, which can be understood either as a transformation of the original body or a different body into which the soul has been transported (although, in the latter scenario, there is no explicit mention of a body that remains behind, as in an ordinary death, as typically understood).

We do not hear of the third type—the illusory body—until the final scene of the drama. Arranged by Yogamāyā, this body is designed to create an appearance of the maidens in their homes as if they had never left. The illusory or substitute body is maintained while, simultaneously, the Gopīs are engaged in *līlā* with Krishna, in their nonphysical, devotional bodies. We are told that the cowherd husbands continue to feel the presence of their wives in their homes and are peaceful, apparently unaware of the dual role that their wives are playing:

> The husband cowherds of Vraja
> felt no jealousy whatsoever
> toward Krishna.
> Deluded by his power of Māyā,
> each husband thought his wife
> had remained all the while by his side.
>
> (RL 5.38)

Mysteriously, the cowherd maidens, at the end of the night of the Rāsa dance, return to their homes: "During the sacred hour before dawn, the Gopīs returned to their homes, although reluctantly, for they so loved the Beloved Lord" (RL 5.39). It is certainly enigmatic that the devotional body returns home, where the illusory body has remained all along. This apparent discrepancy actually serves to reveal treasured yoga secrets.

Those cowherd maidens who are not able to abandon their everyday lives by externally leaving are, nevertheless, successful in giving up their lives, through the internal yogic means of deep devotional contemplation:

> Some Gopīs,
>   unable to leave,
>   had gone inside their homes.
> With eyes closed,
>   fully absorbed in love,
>   they meditated upon Krishna.
>
> The intense burning
>   of unbearable separation
>   from their dearest beloved
>   disrupted all inauspiciousness;
> Due to the joy
>   of embracing Acyuta
>   attained through meditation,
>   even their worldly happiness was lost.
>
> (RL 1.9–10)

The Gopīs referred to here are forced to turn inward due to their family circumstances, and it may appear as if this is their misfortune. However, Krishna himself coyly prescribes meditation, or *dhyāna*—as it is called in the yoga tradition—even to the maidens who have successfully united with him in the forest, in lieu of leaving their homes at such a questionable hour (RL 1.27).

It is not surprising that yoga is entwined with *bhakti* throughout the Bhāgavata text. The relationship of yoga to *bhakti* had been already established in the Bhagavad Gītā, as well as in the Yoga Sūtra of Patañjali—the famous classical and comprehensive exposition on the practice and philosophy of yoga—which also recognizes devotion to the deity within its prescribed practice. Though the Vaishnava commentators from the Chaitanya school make virtually no comment on the application of yoga in the devotion of the

Gopīs, yoga is clearly at the heart of it. In fact, the narrator of the Rāsa Līlā confirms that service to the feet of the supreme deity is achieved by the power of yoga: "They whose bondage to karma has been shaken off by the power of yoga are fully satisfied by humble service to the dust of the lotus feet of the Lord" (RL 5.35ab).

The meditation of the Gopīs who could not escape to the forest constitutes the penultimate step, called *dhyāna*, of the "eight-limbed" (*aṣṭāṅga*) system of yoga.[2] Meditation (*dhyāna*) is defined as "the single continuous movement [of the mind] toward an object," and in this case the object of the Gopīs' meditation is their beloved Krishna, in whose beauty they revel unceasingly. It is through their meditation that the Gopīs are able to overcome the pain of being separated from Krishna (RL 1.10).

The detained maidens then go on to further achieve the perfection of yoga as *samādhi*, the final step of the eightfold process of yoga, that is, meditation in its purest and deepest form.[3] Such meditation allows them to be "fully absorbed in love" as they are able to experience the "joy of embracing Acyuta" (RL 1.9–10). Although the Yoga Sūtra and Bhāgavata both promote loving meditation on a personal and worshipful deity,[4] the Bhāgavata's focus is especially on the beautiful and adorable attributes of divinity as the intimate deity, which effectively transforms *dhyāna* and *samādhi* into more spontaneous and erotically intense experiences within *bhakti*.[5]

[2] The eight limbs of yoga are as follows: (1) *yama*: principles of self-restraint, (2) *niyama*: established observances, (3) *āsana*: physical postures, (4) *prāṇāyāma*: deepending and control over the breathing, (5) *pratyāhāra*: withdrawal of the senses from sense objects, (6) *dhāraṇā*: concentration, (7) *dhyāna*: meditation, and (8) *samādhi*: total ecstatic absorption (YS 2.29).

[3] "Total ecstatic absorption, and the perfection of this state, is achieved because one's relationship with the divine source of all reality has been reached by moving deeply into the space within the heart" (*samādhi-siddhi īśvara-praṇidhānāt*, YS 2.45). See also other texts that emphasize *īśvara-praṇidhāna*: YS 1.23, 2.1, and 2.32.

[4] See YS 1.24, which equates *īśvara* ("the supreme Lord") with *puruṣa* ("the supreme person").

[5] It is interesting to note that Krishna, in the Bhagavad Gītā, declares that a *yogī* ultimately becomes a *bhakta* or devotee (BG 6.47). The cowherd maidens, however, have already perfected the process of yoga in their meditation on Krishna, and they resort to yoga as an expression of their intense love for him. Such practice does not merely legitimize the devotion of the Gopīs; the cowherd maidens utilize yoga as a technique for intimacy.

Yoga is also used by the Gopīs as a threat directed toward Krishna in their songs of longing. The cowherd maidens boldly ask Krishna to "extinguish the fire burning within our hearts." They then threaten him with these words: "For if you don't, we shall place our bodies in the fire of separation from you. Then, O friend, by means of meditation, we shall go to the abode of your feet" (RL 1.35). It is significant that some Gopīs choose to connect with Krishna by meditating on his beautiful form, even while in his presence:

> One of them took him
> into her heart through
> the aperture of her eyes;
> then closing her eyes,
> she embraced him within.
> She became elated with
> bodily ripplings of joy,
> just as the body of a *yogī*
> is overcome with bliss.
>
> (RL 4.8)

This verse makes it clear that yoga, in the devotion of the Gopīs, is used as a means of enhancing experiences of love.

Whether the Gopīs attain Krishna's audience through appearing before him or through internal yogic meditation, the tradition understands this "new" body of each of the maidens to be a spiritual, perfected body (*siddha-deha*): a body that the devoted soul ultimately develops during the course of pursuing the process of *bhakti*.[6]

[6] The process of *bhakti* has two general phases: the first is *vaidhī-bhakti*, "devotional love in the various forms of discipline"; and the second is *rāgānuga-bhakti*, "devotional love following the *rāga-bhaktas*, or pure spontaneous associates of the Lord," in which a spiritual body is said to develop. For a thorough treatment of *rāgānuga-bhakti*, see David L. Haberman, *Acting as a Way of Salvation: A Study of Rāgānugā Bhakti Sādhana* (New York: Oxford University Press, 1988).

It is in such a spiritual body that complete absorption in the service of the Lord becomes possible:

> Within the mind of one whose
> own body is spiritually perfect,
> One contemplates day and night
> the service of Krishna in Vraja.
>
> (CC 2.22.157)

The development of a spiritual body does not, however, preclude the possibility of maintaining a physical body. In other words, it is plausible to remain in this world while living in a spiritual body. This is illustrated by the cowherd maidens who, at the end of the drama, return to their homes. The tradition suggests that the life of a practitioner becomes this coalescence of the devotional body with the physical body—performing in the world according to *dharma* while simultaneously living in the devotional world of the heart.

Indeed, for the Chaitanya school, meditation on the Rāsa Līlā, enables the absorbed devotee to develop a spiritual form so that one is able to be even more fully immersed in devotion:

> For one who hears or recites [the Rāsa Līlā]
> the benefit for such a person is
> Full absorption in love,
> serving [the Lord] day and night.
>
> What can be said of the benefit for such a person?
> It is simply impossible to convey.
> One is eternally perfect,
> and one acquires a perfect body.
>
> (CC 3.5.49–50)

Having acquired such a perfected spiritual body, the devotee is only concerned about devotional service, no matter where it may take place, in this world or the next. The desire to please the deity lifts the devotee from the world, even while living in it. This transcendent, uplifted state shines with the nature of love, death, and immortality: all constituents of a singular, divine realm into which devotional love delivers us.

Death, then, becomes a shift in our hearts and consciousness, and does not consist merely of being released from the world, as the devotee is already liberated from this world through his or her loving service to God (*sevā*). This unique vision of death given to us by the Chaitanya tradition presents an understanding distinctly opposing that of the greater Hindu complex. Whereas the former sees death as the result of attracting God's grace (the Chaitanya school's concept of *anugraha* or *kṛpā*), the latter relates to death as the cumulative result of one's own actions and what one has earned (the traditional concept of karma).

The *bhakti* tradition puts forward a process that ultimately transcends any of the pan-Hindu requirements. This is possible because in the practice of *bhakti* the journey and the destination eventually become one: loving divinity leads us to purer experiences of love. Like the Gopīs in their illusory bodies, the devoted soul remains active in this world, and similar to the Gopīs in their devotional bodies, the devotee's heart and mind is all the while diving deeply into divinity. This rich inner life is what ultimately allows one to be engaged in worldly affairs while being simultaneously detached from them. For such a soul—deeply absorbed in loving service to the deity—the death of one's physical body becomes inconsequential, and the liberation sought by *yogīs* has already been attained.

According to the Bhagavad Gītā, after obtaining such an elevated state of devotion, the soul is guaranteed to join the supreme upon departure from this world (BG 8.5). After all, one's hearts and minds have already reached that destination. As such, it is the way of life that determines the outcome of death for the devotee. For such devotional souls, externals such as the cause, time, and place of the physical death become inconsequential compared to how absorbed they were during their lives in loving their beloved Lord.

When both the cause and result of being so absorbed are the same (the singular attention of the devoted soul being fully directed to their divine beloved), the reward for such complete absorption is the absorption itself. The following *sūtra* text—describing such devotion—is reminiscent of that of the Gopīs: master *yoginīs* of love from whom we've gained a peek into the mysterious and powerful relationship between love and death.

> Having attained
> this purest love, *premā*,
> it is only the Beloved
> one sees before one's eyes;
> it is only the Beloved
> whom one hears;
> it is only the Beloved
> about whom one speaks;
> it is only the Beloved
> one contemplates.
>
> (NBS 55)

14
Ethical Boundaries and Boundless Love

We have already seen how the boundless love of the Gopīs causes them to cross bodily boundaries and manifest other types of bodies. Such boundless love also crosses social and ethical boundaries for both Krishna and the Gopīs. It is Krishna's identity as the divine lover of the cowherd maidens that raises the question of ethics. The Chaitanya school considers the play of the amorous and erotic Krishna with Rādhā and her cowherd girlfriends as the ultimate display of pure love between the deity and devotee. At the same time, the divine cowherd is understood as the originator of all religious and ethical principles (*dharma*). Some scholars, even among specialists in the Chaitanya tradition, have been confounded as to how God, the source of *dharma*, can also be the amorous deity whose affairs with the Gopīs can appear to be unethical.[1] Indeed, even the king to whom the story is narrated inquires from the narrator, Śuka, regarding this ethical question:

How could he—the teacher,
executor, and protector
of the limits of *dharma*—

[1] Perhaps the most thoroughgoing scholarship on the Chaitanya school has been presented by S. K. De in his *Early History of the Vaiṣṇava Faith and Movement in Bengal* (Calcutta: Firma K. L. Mukhopadhyay, 1961). In this rich presentation of the historical, literary, and theological tradition, the one confounding factor for De was the question of ethics in relation to the tradition's erotic mysticism of Krishna. See the chapter, "Ritualism and Devotional Practices," especially section three of this chapter, entitled "Ethics of Bengal Vaisnavism" (542–555). Also, see his criticism of Krishnadas Kaviraja's *Govinda Līlāmṛta* as an erotic text that ignores the ethical and presents what he describes as an "excessive load of sexual passion" (610–611).

The Yoga of Love. Graham M. Schweig, Oxford University Press. © Oxford University Press 2025.
DOI: 10.1093/oso/9780197768426.003.0018

O knower of Brahman,
act in contrary ways
by touching others' wives?

(RL 5.28)

The answer to the king's question lies not so much in the narrator's direct response as in the divine identities of the hero and heroines and the dialogue that ensues between them.

Śuka, in short, states that great and powerful persons, not to mention the Lord, are exempt from the ethical norms of this world. A much more compelling argument that undergirds the complete story, however, may be that Krishna is the most intimate spouse or dearest friend of all living beings because, as the supreme Lord, he is the soul within all souls. In fact, there is at least one expression of this intimate presence of God in each act of the drama. The narrator recognizes Krishna as "the supreme Person who is present internally and externally for all living beings, as heavenly air pervades all beings, within and without" (RL 2.4). He also states that Krishna is "the true companion of all souls" (RL 4.13) and is the one who "dwells within the Gopīs and within their husbands" (RL 5.36). The Gopīs themselves describe their beloved as "the Witness residing in the hearts of all embodied beings" (RL 3.4) and, in conversation with Krishna, acknowledge that he is "the dearest beloved of all living beings, the most intimate relation" (RL 1.32). A natural conclusion, then, is that Krishna, who resides eternally within the heart, is the true spouse of everyone. The cowherd husbands of the Gopīs, on the other hand, are temporary relations in this life, and therefore illusory. From this it could be argued that since Krishna is the intimate and eternal spouse of the maidens, the cowherd husbands are married to another's wife!

Throughout the Bhāgavata Purāṇa, we find that God, being omnipotent, is capable of embracing and transcending *dharma* at the same time. This ethical paradox is observable in the Rāsa Līlā in the apparently duplicitous, teasing words of Krishna to the Gopīs. Such words cleverly demonstrate how Krishna simultaneously supports *dharma* in the everyday world and passionate devotion in the transcendent world. Likewise, the greater Bhāgavata text maintains that normative social roles and identities leading one to the service of God should be preserved. It also promotes, however, a breaking away, an antithetical approach to social convention that is particularly notable with regard to the cowherd maidens of Vraja.

In the Rāsa Līlā, there is no better expression of the supreme Lord both maintaining and transcending *dharma* than in the third scene of Act One, when Krishna greets the Gopīs just after they have left their homes. Commentators delight in the double entendre of Krishna's words in several verses here, allowing him to both uphold and overlook *dharma*. In the following verse, for example, Krishna attempts to "frighten" the Gopīs into doing the "right thing," while ostensibly offering protective words:

> Night has a frightening appearance;
> inhabiting this place are
> fearsome creatures!
> Please return to Vraja—
> women should not remain here,
> O ones with beautiful waists.
>
> (RL 1.19)

But commentators point out that the ways in which the Sanskrit words are combined in the above verse, as well as the varying ways that negatives can be applied to particular words, can produce opposite meanings, which allow Krishna to suggest to the Gopīs that they *should* remain with him in the forest:

> Night is without a frightening appearance (*aghora-rūpa*);
> inhabiting this place are
> creatures that are not fearsome (*aghora-sattva*).
> Please do not return to Vraja (*pratiyata vrajam na*)—
> women should remain here (*iha stheyam*),
> O ones with beautiful waists.

A few verses later, Krishna seems concerned about the proper dharmic behavior for the cowherd maidens, which clearly would be to return to their families. He explicitly encourages them to be faithful to their dharmic duties:

Please go to the village without delay!
O chaste ladies, attend your husbands.
Your calves and children are crying for you—
you must go feed and nurse them.

(RL 1.22)

This verse can also be interpreted, however, as Krishna attempting to persuade the Gopīs that there is no need for them to conform to dharmic obligations and, instead, to stay with him:

Please do not go back right away
to attend your husbands, O chaste ladies.
Your calves and children are crying for others;
you need not feed and nurse them.

Two verses later, Krishna further emphasizes to the Gopīs the importance of following *dharma*, by making a declaration of what their "highest dharmic" obligation (*parodharma*) is:

For every woman the highest *dharma* (*parodharma*)
is to serve her husband without falsity,
Be agreeable toward his family members,
and nourish the children.

(RL 1.24)

Here again, there is a double entendre. Commentators point out that Krishna is also saying to the cowherd maidens:

> For the *dharma* of all other women (*parodharma*)
> is to serve false husbands . . .

In this instance, the word *parodharma*, instead of meaning "the highest *dharma*," is taken as "the *dharma* of other women," whom Krishna claims are serving only "false husbands."[2] By implication, he is proclaiming himself to be the only true husband of the Gopīs. Thus, their highest duty or *parodharma*, which was initially understood in relation to their cowherd husbands, is now to be seen in relation to Krishna, their "true husband." In fact, the word *parodharma* refers to the highest *dharma* of loving devotion to God, or *bhakti*:

> The highest *dharma* (*parodharma*) for all humans is
> certainly devotion (*bhakti*) unto the transcendent Lord;
> It is selfless and unremitting, and it is that
> by which the self is most deeply satisfied.
> (BhP 1.2.6)

Here, the true meaning of *parodharma* is clearly defined by the *Bhāgavata* text itself, supporting the idea that the highest *dharma* is ultimately devotional love for the supreme Lord.

Following Krishna's playful words, the Gopīs, in response to his apparently duplicitous words, cleverly retort using his reversible logic to serve their own desires:

[2] The prefix "*para-*" used with *dharma* in the first instance utilizes the sense of degree, i.e., "the higher," or in the superlative sense, "the highest" (the latter sense of which is used throughout this study as meaning specifically *bhakti*, or devotion). In the second instance commentators also cleverly interpret the prefix in its sense of relation, i.e., "other," "strange," or "different."

O dear one, as you
who knows *dharma*
have stated,
The proper duty for women
is to be loyal to husbands,
children, and close friends.
Let this *dharma* of ours be for you,
O Lord, since you are
the true object of such teachings.
Truly you are the dearest
beloved of all living beings,
the most intimate relation,
for you are the supreme Soul.

(RL 1.32)

It appears from this verse that for the maidens the idea of relinquishing normative social conventions is impossible to resist, since for them Krishna is the most beloved of all beings; therefore, an exclusive relationship with him would be fulfilling the highest *dharma*.

The passionate devotion of the cowherd maidens is clear. They are irresistibly drawn to their Lord, and certainly leaving their husbands along with all worldly dharmic duties is an expression of their passion and utter self-sacrifice for him. The humility of the Gopīs is also clear. They wish to follow their "true" *dharma* and submit themselves to Krishna, who is their "real" husband, thus relinquishing their "false" husbands. In so doing, however, their honorable social status could be destroyed by apparent dharmic transgressions. Traditional commentators interpret the cowherd maidens' apparent abandonment of family and social obligations as dharmic transcendence, and therefore find it to be not only acceptable but even highly desirable; whereas the Bhāgavata text is less willing to see the Gopīs' transgression as a transcendent movement crossing beyond dharmic boundaries. Instead, the Bhāgavata attempts to recover *dharma* and compensate for the subversive behavior of the maidens through Yogamāyā's arrangement of illusory bodies, which preserves their dharmic position in the home and yet allows for their ostensibly transgressive participation in God's *līlā*.

As we have seen, Krishna cleverly pacifies the husbands of the Gopīs while virtually borrowing their wives (RL 5.38), indicating that the Lord regards the upholding of dharmic obligations to be crucial, even if it is toward "false husbands" (RL 1.24). It is interesting that in the *Harivaṁśa* and *Viṣṇu Purāṇa* versions of the story, the cowherd maidens are *not* given duplicate forms by which their husbands at home would be pacified. The Bhāgavata distinguishes itself ethically by insuring that the cowherd husbands remain satisfied, even while their wives are with Krishna for the night. This synthesis of *dharma* with *parodharma* preserves the ethical boundaries of *dharma* while giving full expression to the boundless love of the cowherd maidens.

The key to understanding the Chaitanya school's approach to the *parodharma* of *bhakti* is found in the way it views the subordinate role of women, specifically the women of Vraja, within the ancient Indian social order known as *varṇāśrama dharma*,[3]. The position of women was somewhat removed from the laws of *dharma*, since their social identity was always in relation to a male's, whether it be a father, brother, or husband. That a woman did not possess a status of her own proved to be conducive to the life of devotion. Furthermore, her feminine nature was taken to be that of inherent humility and meekness in service to both the worldly male and the supreme "male," thereby satisfying dharmic obligations as well as transcending them.

[3] The *varṇāśrama* consists of both *varṇa* and *āśrama*. This system has to do with four hierarchically arranged social-vocational strata of society, or *varṇa*, which, in ancient India, consisted of the educational class (*brāhmaṇa*) as the highest, the governmental class (*kṣatriya*), the business or agricultural class (*vaiśya*), and the working class (*śudra*). The four stages of the life-cycle, or *āśrama*, began with the student stage (*brahmacārya*), then moved into the marital stage (*gṛhastha*), then the retired stage (*vanaprastha*), and finally the renounced stage (*sannyāsa*). The divisions of *varṇa* are often mistaken for the "caste system," which has to do with finer subdivisions or distinctions within each of the *varṇas*, known as *jāti* or "class," also translated as "caste," historically a much later development than the overall *varṇāśrama* system.

The subservient, loving role of women is employed by the school as the model for illuminating and exemplifying the highest and most intense form of *bhakti*, demonstrated in the devotion of the Gopīs. Chaitanya, who is Krishna himself, understood by his followers to be the embodiment of the love shared between Rādhā and Krishna, descended in order to experience the nature of the Gopīs' devotion, specifically that of Rādhā. The description of such pure devotion, found in the *Bhakti Sūtra* of Nārada, presents the model of the Gopīs, who embody the humility of an eternal servant (*nitya-dāsa*) and the passion of an eternal lover (*nitya-kānta*).[4] Chaitanya, as the paradigmatic devotee, sets the stage for the school's ethics of devotion by desiring to become the humble servant of the servant of the servant of the lotus feet of the Lord of the Gopīs.[5]

For the Vaishnava, then, the combination of humility and passion in devotion is an essential balance, exhibited by the Gopīs. The intimate deity is emphasized over the cosmic or almighty deity and yet, for the devotee, they are always experienced in dialectical tension with one another. Neither is excluded; rather, the one is implicitly or explicitly experienced while the other is in the background. The intimate deity inspires a passionate devotion, and the cosmic or powerful deity, a devotion of humility. The devotee "knows" the greatness of God, but due to being absorbed in devotional passion, appears to "forget" this dimension. With *parodharma* in the foreground, however, the devoted soul continues to apprehend, in the background, the ethical dimension of *dharma* that flows from the divinity.

Veneration and awe for the greatness of the deity create an atmosphere of deep reverence and humble admiration among followers, whereas intimacy with the divine elevates the devotee

[4] The *Bhakti Sūtra*, text 66: "... devotional love manifests as the self constantly devoted to God as an eternal servant and eternal lover. One should cultivate pure love, *premā*, for God, and pure love alone."

[5] See CC 2.13.80: "I am the servant of the servant of the servant of the lotus feet of the husband of the Gopīs" (*gopī-bhartuḥ pada-kamalayor dāsa-dāsānudāsaḥ*).

into a transethical sphere of love and amorous play with the Lord, as well as affectionate fellowship with other devotees. This intimacy is nowhere else demonstrated more dramatically than in the Rāsa dance itself, in which the Gopīs join hands in fellowship, and simultaneously, as individuals, interact exclusively and amorously with their beloved.

Although the Rāsa dance is the culmination of the drama, the Gopīs experience and express their most intense feelings for Krishna in his absence, specifically in the middle act, "The Song of the Gopīs." The greatest form of intimacy with the deity is understood by this school as *viraha-bhakti*, "devotional love in the experience of the absence of God." The *Bhakti Sūtra* describes *viraha*, out of eleven different types of loving attachment to God, as the highest process: "Devotion in separation from the Beloved is the highest devotion of all."[6] The Chaitanya school not only accepts this statement but indeed models its devotion specifically on "the attainment of service in separation," known as *vipralambha-sevā*.[7] It is especially this type of loving service that balances humility and passion in devotion.

In contrast, the intimacy of union with God, as we have seen in the fifth act, can lead to "forgetfulness" of the knowledge of God's greatness, causing humility to remain in the background of passion. Whereas when the Gopīs either anticipate or actually experience separation from Krishna, they are more conscious of his almighty attributes, which, in turn, stimulates humility. At times though, even in Krishna's presence, the Gopīs, fearing separation, are humbled by his supreme status: "O unattainable one, do not reject us—accept us as your devotees just as you, the Lord, the original Person, accept those who desire liberation" (RL 1.31). Here the maidens, while present before their beloved, fear his rejection; in anticipation

[6] The *Bhakti Sūtra*, text 82.

[7] The literal meaning of *vipralambha-sevā* is "performing service (*sevā*) while having attained (*lambha*) distance (*vipra*)." In the Chaitanya tradition, distance or separation in divine love is a most positive experience of union, paradoxically, and not the negative experience associated with the way lovers of this world agonize when apart.

of Krishna's imminent absence, both their humility in service and passion in devotion are heightened (RL 1.38). Humility, then, intensifies passion, and conversely, passion augments humility.

Thus, the cowherd maidens exhibit the essential dynamic within *bhakti*: the experience of an ever-intensifying dialectical tension between the absence and presence of God exhibited in various phases of separation and union. It is precisely because of this dialectical balance that any concern about an excessive emotionalism on the part of practitioners is unfounded. Passion and humility synergistically combine in the hearts of the devoted followers of the Chaitanya tradition, forming an axiological core of an ethics of devotion that is also embedded in the Rāsa Līlā text. These ethical dimensions have yet to be discovered and further illuminated by scholars both inside and outside the tradition.

The Rāsa Līlā story reveals nine distinct emotional phases of supreme love. These nine divine states are easily perceived in the cowherd maidens' love for Krishna, as it develops in the acts of the drama. The first phase of supreme love begins at the very start of the drama, in Act One, scene 1, when the Gopīs hear the sound of Krishna's flute. The emotions that stir in their hearts as a result constitute the "Awakening" phase. The stage of "Anticipation" follows, when the Gopīs run from their homes into the forest, eager to see Krishna. Upon entering into Krishna's overwhelming presence in scene 3, the Gopīs experience the "Meeting" phase. Scene 4 symbolizes the "Conflict" phase, manifesting as the Gopīs' pride, and Krishna's subsequent disappearance. The painful "Separation" phase follows, marking the start of Act Two, where the whole tenor of the text shifts significantly as the Gopīs search the woods for their beloved. The sixth phase of "Loss" is characterized by deep longing and torment in love, which the Gopīs pour into their songs for the duration of Act Three.

Then, the text swirls back into joyful emotions, in the "Reunion" phase of Act Four, which begins to unfold as soon as Krishna rejoins the cowherd maidens. Divine love then culminates as the phase of "Rejoicing" in the triumph of love, which takes place when Krishna and the Gopis perform the wonderous circle dance of the Rāsa in

Act Five. Finally, the ninth phase of love, titled "Returning" manifests when the Gopīs reluctantly return to their homes. It is clear from these cyclical phases of divine love that the Rāsa dance of Krishna and the Gopīs is hardly an isolated event, away from all other persons. But, instead, as the ultimate symbol of love, the dance of divine love continuously draws to it all souls with eager hearts.

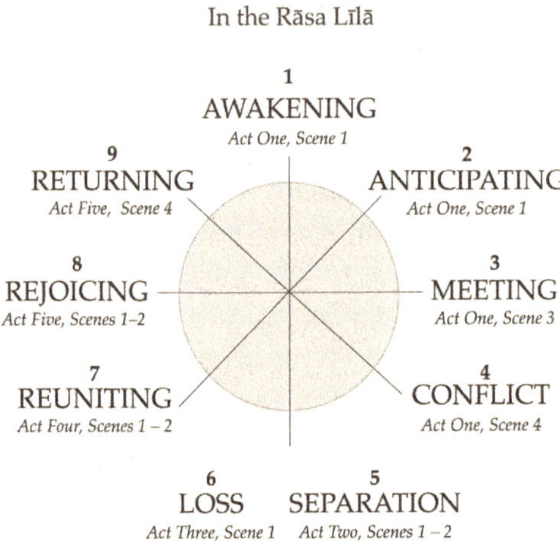

Figure 11. The cyclical nature of divine love, which keeps turning eternally in the *līlā* of the Rāsa's sacred drama.

These nine phases of divine love are cyclical, themselves appearing like a circle, or *maṇḍala,* because these phases turn each night indefinitely within the eternal realm. Moreover, such phases of divine love adorn not just the hearts of yoga practitioners, but of those belonging to other mystical traditions as well, for the way divine love unfolds in human hearts is universal. And, while each phase is a constituent of the boundless love experienced in the divine realm, certain phases may be emphasized by a particular tradition or individual, in accordance with the love sentiments turning within the hearts of those who experience them.

15
The Vision of Devotional Love

Toward the beginning of this study, it was suggested that the Gopīs' love for Krishna could appear to be passionate and selfish in ways that mirror worldly relationships of lust and, perhaps surprisingly, that this is intentional on the part of the author. The Rāsa Līlā displays divine love while distinguishing it from worldly love, since the special nature of *līlā* is both playful and didactic. Although *līlā* is for the pleasure of Krishna and his devotees, and everything that occurs in *līlā* contributes to the delight and celebration of supreme love and beauty, there are aspects that also instruct those who have yet to enter into its esoteric domain. The pure love of the Gopīs in *līlā* is therefore displayed in the drama, and the reader is simultaneously instructed about the impure love found in this world, love that is tainted by selfishness and pride.

The major lesson that the Rāsa Līlā offers, then, is on the nature of love. Krishna instructs the cowherd maidens about various types of pure and impure love, and we learn that he regards the Gopīs' love for him as perfect and unconditional (RL 4.20–22). Krishna's dalliance with the one special Gopī is meant to contrast love of God with the degraded love of this world that is exhibited in adulterous affairs (RL 2.34), and he teaches, through his sudden disappearance from the maidens, that God disappears from those whose love is mixed with pride (RL 1.47–48). In order to appreciate more fully the passionate love of the Gopīs and the difference between worldly and divine passion, we need to become aware of the nuances of words used throughout the drama to express love.

In Sanskrit, there are numerous words for "love," and the author of the Bhāgavata engages many of them in the Rāsa Līlā. The most

The Yoga of Love. Graham M. Schweig, Oxford University Press. © Oxford University Press 2025.
DOI: 10.1093/oso/9780197768426.003.0019

frequently used words are those verbs and nouns derived from four verbal roots that essentially mean "to love": *prī-*, *bhaj-*, *kam-*, and *ram-*.[1] Words derived from the first two, *prī-* and *bhaj-*, carry the sense of a pure love, affection, or adoration—a selfless love untainted by desire or self-concern—resembling the Greek word *agapé*. Some meanings of words derived from the verb root *prī-* are to "love," "please," and "delight."[2] Senses of words coming from the verb root *bhaj-* are to "adore," "worship," and "reciprocate."[3] These words are associated with a nonerotic, giving, and affectionate love that could be applied to a variety of love relations.

On the other hand, words derived from the second two verbal roots, *kam-* and *ram-*, carry the sense of passionate love, including sexual connotations. Meanings of words derived from the verb root *ram-* are to "delight," "please," and "enjoy sensually."[4] Some senses

[1] Other words meaning love also appear in the passage: *bhāvanā*, "love" (RL 1.9), "imitation" (RL 2.16), and "absorbed" (RL 2.44); *manmatha*, "amorous passion," which can also be a name for the god of love (RL 4.2); *anaṅga*, "love" (RL 1.4), another name for the god of love, literally, "the limbless one," *aṅga*, "O dear one," literally, "O limb" (RL 1.32 and 1.40); *anuvṛtti*, "following," "acting suitably to," "having regard or respect," "the act of continuance," and "(true) love" (RL 1.32, 4.20, and 4.21); *sauhṛda*, "devotional affection" (RL 1.15); "endearment," or "endearing" (RL 4.17 and 4.18); and *vallabha*, "beloved" (RL 5.15).

[2] Translations and forms of this root found in the episode are the following: *prīta*, "pleased" (RL 2.28, 5.2); *prīti*, "affection" (RL 2.8 and 4.3); *premā*, "love" (RL 2.5, 3.10, 3.17, 4.6, 5.21 and 5.24); *preṣṭham*, "beloved" (RL 1.10, 1.30 and 4.3) and the superlative form "most dear" (RL 1.32); "darling beloved" RL 2.39); *priya* (masc.) and *priyā* (fem.), "beloved" (This word for "lover," "beloved," or "dear" is the most frequently used among words of affection and love, appearing 26 times throughout the episode: RL 1.2 (2×), 1.13, 1.18, 1.28, 1.30, 1.33, 1.36, 1.43, 2.3 (2×), 2.7, 2.11, 2.12, 2.31.a, 2.32, 2.36, 2.38, 2.40, 3.10, 3.19, 4.21 (2×), 5.6, 5.9, and 5.39.); *vipriya*, "unpleasant" (RL 1.28); *preyas* (the comparative of *priya*, "dearer," "a dear friend," or "lover"), "beloved" (RL 2.31.a and 2.32); and the verbal forms: *prīyatā*, "pleased" (RL 5.10) and *prīyante*, "being dear" (RL 1.23).

[3] Forms and translations appearing in the Rāsa Līlā text are the following: *bhakti*, "devotion" (RL 5.40); *bhakta* (masc.) and *bhaktā* (fem.), "devotee" (RL 1.31) or "devoted one" (RL 5.37); and various verbal forms, *bhajatā*, "love" (RL 4.21); *bhajasva*, "please accept" (RL 1.31); *bhajanti*, "love" (RL 4.16 [2×], 17, 18, 19, 21); *abhajata*, "love" (RL 4.16, 18, 19, 20); and *bhajate*, "accept" (RL 1.31), "honors" (RL 2.36), and "worship" (RL 5.37).

[4] Forms and translations appearing in the Rāsa Līlā text are the following: the infinitive *rantum*, "to enjoy love" (RL 1.1); *rati*, "attraction" (RL 1.33), "love" (RL 1.46), "amorous" (RL 5.9 and 5.21), and "enjoyment" (RL 5.24); *ramaṇa*, "enjoyment" (RL 1.39), "darling one" (RL 2.39), and "charming lover" (RL 3.13); *ramayām*, "enjoying"

of words derived from the verb root *kam-* are to "desire," "long for," and "be enamored of"; and the noun *kāma*, prominent in the Bhāgavata text, means "pleasure," "lust," and "passion."[5] These words describe erotic love, love of passionate desire, and generally refer to the love within amorous relationships, much like the Greek word *eros*.[6]

From the meanings of words derived from these four verbal roots, we can understand that both pure and erotic senses of love are woven together throughout the Rāsa Līlā. The question remains, how does the boundless love of the Gopīs, who are overflowing with romantic desire and amorous affection, express the purity of love that the author of the drama claims they possess, and that many Vaishnava traditions honor and even celebrate? What is the relation of the erotic and passionate to the pure and selfless? In the last verse of the Rāsa Līlā episode, it is stated that *kāma* will be cleansed from the heart of a faithful soul (RL 5.40), yet the emotions and actions of the Gopīs in their love toward Krishna arise from *kāma* (RL 1.38). The Chaitanya school has treated this apparent contradiction extensively.

The tradition's interpretation of the terms *kāma* ("passionate love") and *premā* ("pure love") is crucial for understanding the concept of selfless devotion. Krishnadāsa, in his work *Chaitanya Charitāmṛta*, applies these most widely used terms in order to distinguish between "worldly love" and "divine love." Perhaps the most

(RL 1.46); *rata*, "enjoys" (RL 2.34); *reme*, "enjoying" (RL 5.9, 5.21, 5.17, 5.20, and 5.24); *surata*, "erotic love" (RL 3.2) and "amorous joy" (RL 3.13); and *saurata*, "sexual desire" (RL 5.26).

5 The idea of *kāma* is one of the "four aims of life," *puruṣārthas*, along with *dharma*, *artha*, and *mokṣa*. The word *kāma* can mean "desire or carnal gratification," "lust," "the god of love," or "name of Baladeva, Pradyumna, and the Supreme Being" (VA).

6 The meanings of the verb *kam-* can be to "desire," "long for," and so on. Translations and forms of this root appearing in this passage are *kāma*, "desire" (RL 1.15, 1.38, 2.36, 3.5, and 3.13) and "lustfulness" (RL 5.40); *kānta* (masc.) and *kāntā* (fem.), "beloved" (RL 1.4, 2.31b, 2.33, 3.5, and 3.11), "lover" (RL 5.15), and "desired one" (RL 1.12 and 2.11); *kāmin* (masc.) and *kāminyā* (fem.), "the amorous one" (RL 2.31–32), "one desirous of love" (RL 2.33), and "lustful one" (RL 2.34).

concise explanation of the difference between the two is found in the fourth chapter of the Ādi Līlā:

> The desire to please one's own senses,
> in my opinion, is to be called *kāma.*
> The desire to please the senses of Krishna
> takes the name *premā.*
>
> (CC 1.4.165)

The distinctions between *kāma* and *premā* are even more sharply defined when *kāma* is compared to "blind darkness," and *premā* is compared to the "pure light of the sun" (CC 1.4.171).[7]

Generally speaking, the word *kāma* refers to love in the sense of worldly pleasure, and *premā* to love in the sense of spiritual pleasure. Krishnadāsa describes the Gopīs as the paradigmatic exemplars of *premā*, emphasizing the intention behind their love rather than the form in which the love appears:

> They (the Gopīs) give up everything
> for the sake of Krishna.
> The motive of their pure
> and passionate love
> is the happiness of Krishna.
>
> (CC 1.4.175)

[7] The Chaitanya school has a more limited or strict sense of the word *premā* than what is demonstrated in the Bhāgavata. For the school, *premā* indicates only "spiritual" love. The love in *premā* occurs only between human and divine beings or between one divine personage and another, and therefore cannot be applied to the love between one human and another. In the Bhāgavata, however, the numerous applications of the word would suggest a much broader meaning.

The Bhāgavata applies this word *premā* in the sense of pure love to the conjugal relationships of this world (see BhP 3.23.5, 4.28.43, 6.19.17, 7.11.27, 9.18.20, 10.58.8, and 10.81.26). Paternal *premā* is found (see BhP 1.9.11, 4.9.43, and 4.9.48), and fraternal *premā* is also demonstrated (see BhP 4.20.18). A more carnal type of *premā* can be found (see BhP 4.25.25), which is unusual. A human's love for the earth can be expressed as *premā* (see BhP 4.18.28) and for an animal (BhP 5.8.21 and 10.13.35). However, *premā* is most commonly found in expressions of the soul's love for the deity (see BhP 1.8.45, 1.10.16, 9.10.38, 10.14.49, 10.15.20, 10.17.16, 10.38.36, 10.46.27, 10.55.39, 10.73.35, 10.84.66, and 18.85.38).

This passage clearly indicates that the Gopīs' love is not tainted by any selfish concern. Krishnadāsa is careful to point out that the singular "motive" of the Gopīs is "the happiness of Krishna" (*kṛṣṇa-sukha-hetu*), even while they experience and express their amorous and passionate devotion to him. He finds a radical difference between the soul with selfish motives and the soul with no motive other than the intense desire to please God, and he repeatedly contrasts the theocentric motivation of the Gopīs with the egocentric motivation characteristic of worldly love (CC 2.8.217). He states that the love of the Gopīs is naturally pure, not tainted by the impurities of *kāma*:

> The natural love of the Gopīs
> is without any trace of *kāma*;
> It is without fault,
> and it resembles the beauty
> and purity of molten gold.
>
> (CC 1.4.209)

The Gopīs "have achieved the perfection of loving service," for they have only Krishna as their desired object of love (CC 1.4.212).

The word *kāma* has for its most essential meaning simply "desire." Used in the contra-devotional sense, the word has a selfish or self-serving objective, and thus Krishnadāsa calls it *prākṛta-kāma*, "worldly desire," which can be further understood as "lustfulness." The distinction between desire that is truly loving and the desire of lustfulness is again contrasted by Krishnadāsa:

> Therefore the happiness (of the Gopīs)
> nourishes the happiness of Krishna,
> Because there is no fault of lustfulness (*kāma-doṣe*)
> in the pure love of the Gopīs (*gopī-preme*).
>
> (CC 1.4.195)

The word *kāma* is not restricted, however, to a negative connotation. In fact, as it is applied to the Gopīs in the Rāsa Līlā, *kāma* can mean, paradoxically, "desire" that is "utterly unselfish" or "unself-serving," that is, "selfless." Thus, *kāma* indicates a force within humans that is either the path to worldly bondage and suffering or the path to liberation. It is plainly stated that the Gopīs "discarded all desires for his sake" (RL 1.30). Yet it is also explicitly stated, throughout the Bhāgavata, that the Gopīs attain liberation on account of their desire or *kāma* for Krishna (BhP 7.1.30, 31): "Those women [the Gopīs] who desired me (*mat-kāmā*) knew me as their amorous lover and paramour, although they did not know my true nature" (BhP 11.12.13ab).

It is interesting to observe the first instance of the word *kāma* within the Rāsa Līlā, found in the theological discourse of the narrator to his listener:

> Desire (*kāma*), anger, fear, and
> certainly loving attachment,
> intimacy and affection
> Should always be directed toward Hari;
> by so doing, persons become
> fully absorbed in God.
>
> (RL 1.15)

Here, the positive engagement of *kāma* sharply contrasts with the negative application of the word generally found in the Bhagavad Gītā, where *kāma* designates an unfavorable state of being in which the soul is controlled by the three worldly forces, or *tri-guṇas*. In the twelfth verse of the seventh chapter of the Gītā, however, an exception is found in which Krishna declares, "I am *kāma*" (BG 7.12). This singular positive use of the word in the Gītā anticipates its more favorable usage in the Rāsa Līlā. Although the negative sense of *kāma* is also prevalent in the Bhāgavata text, the theme of directing all desire to God is clearly more prominent, thereby engaging *kāma* in a positive way. This is in contrast with the theme of transcending desire, which engages the unfavorable sense of the term that runs throughout the Gītā.

Favorable usages of *kāma* in relation to both Krishna and the Gopīs occur more frequently in the Rāsa Līlā. It is said that Krishna fulfills all desires, *kāma-dam*, in the following line of a verse: "O beloved, please place on our heads your hand, beautiful as a lotus, that fulfills all wishes" (RL 3.5). And the cowherd maidens, who are burning with desire for their beloved Krishna, have all desires satisfied through serving him: "O jewel among men, please grant unto us whose hearts are burning with intense desire, inspired by your beautiful glances and smiles, the chance to serve you" (RL 1.38). Furthermore, not only do the Gopīs attain liberation by means of *kāma* but the various ways in which *kāma* manifests in their liberated state also becomes, for Vaishnavas, the model of passionate devotional love.

The word *kāma*, then, can mean "desire" in the neutral sense of being innately a part of the human character—desire that can be directed either to worldly pleasures or to the pleasure of the divine. When *kāma* is directed toward satisfying the self, it serves as a means of bondage to worldly existence; whereas when directed toward pleasing the divine object, it serves as a means of liberation—and it can become the very expression of devotion even after one has attained the liberated state.

According to the Chaitanya school, the word *kāma* can be understood as "divine passion" in those *līlās* of Krishna in which the Gopīs display an intensity of *premā*. The love of the Gopīs can appear in the form and image of *kāma* or worldly love, and thus the word can be used to describe certain aspects of *premā*, which, as we have seen, has the sole intention of Krishna's happiness:

> The love (*premā*) of the Gopīs is natural,
>   it is not worldly love (*prākṛta kāma*).
> Because it [appears to be] the same
>   as the activities of worldly love (*kāma-krīḍā*),
>   I will refer to such activities by the term *kāma*.
>
> (CC 2.8.215)

Whatever emotionally charged expressions of love the Gopīs exhibit, must be recognized, according to Krishnadāsa, as existing only for Krishna's pleasure. Indeed, if there is any happiness or pleasure on the part of the maidens, it manifests only to serve the happiness of their beloved. Krishnadāsa provides the principle for understanding what can appear to be excessive emotionalism on the part of the Gopīs:

> So whatever affection we observe
> in the Gopīs' own forms,
> Know for certain that it must be
> for Krishna only.
>
> (CC 1.4.181)

This verse describes Krishnadāsa's hermeneutic for appreciating the heightened emotionalism of the cowherd maidens to be utterly theocentric, and therefore pure and selfless. In such exemplary devotional love, the soul loses itself in the beloved object.

16

Symbolism in the Rāsa Līlā

The Rāsa *maṇḍala* is the circle of the Rāsa, which represents the ultimate, most triumphant phase of supreme love. Contained within the eighth phase of "rejoicing in love," this *maṇḍala*, or circle, is the main symbol in the Rāsa Līlā. As such it has become the focal point of liturgical practices for the Chaitanya School—along with other Vaishnava sects—represented in the worshiped images of Rādhā and Krishna, found at the center of the *maṇḍala*.

The word *maṇḍala* means "circle" or "round," and comes from the verb root *maṇḍ*, which means "to adorn" or "to decorate." The Rāsa Līlā drama is veritably decorated with a *maṇḍala* of maidens. Not just ordinary maidens, but the Gopīs: supreme *yoginīs* who have mastered all nine phases of love, featured prominently at the start of the climactic scene of the drama: "The Rāsa dance and its festival fully blossomed with the perfect turning forth of Vraja Gopikās in a circular movement so beautifully adorned (RL 5.3)." The scene depicting the Rāsa *maṇḍala*, "the wondrous circle of the Rāsa dance," is to this day the most celebrated among all scenes from the story, and is widely presented in various art forms, dramatic performances, and poetic works.

The Yoga of Love. Graham M. Schweig, Oxford University Press. © Oxford University Press 2025.
DOI: 10.1093/oso/9780197768426.003.0020

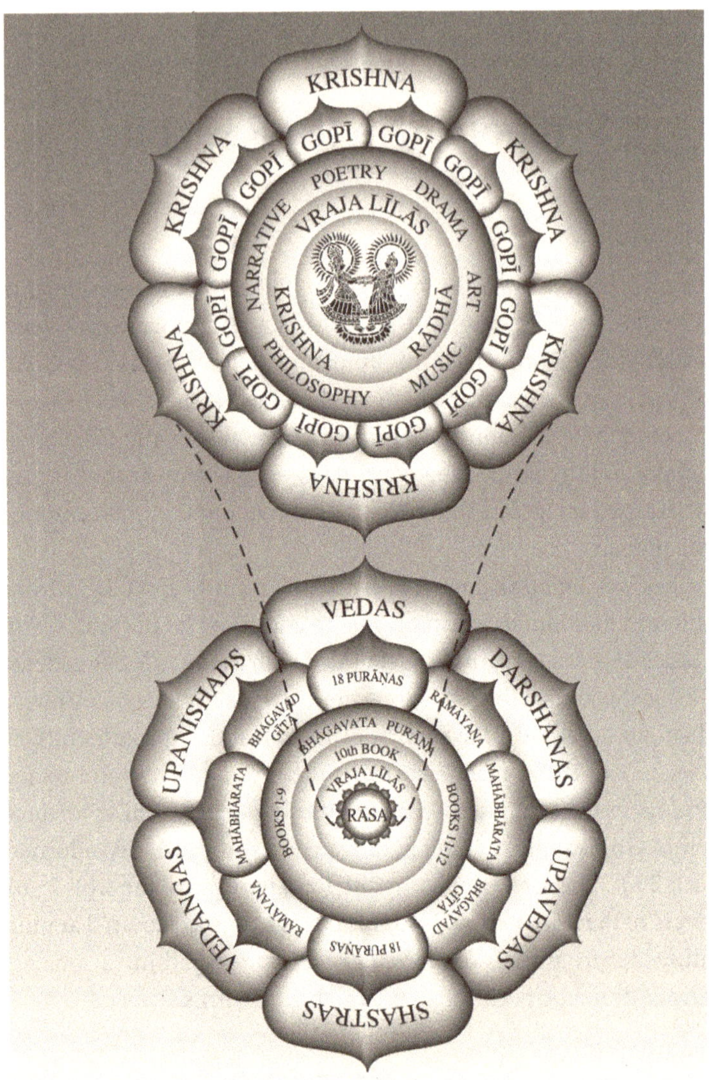

Figure 12. Rāsa Līlā at the heart of all exoteric literature (lower lotus *maṇḍala* whorl) and Rāsa Līlā as the window into esoteric visions (upper lotus *maṇḍala* whorl).

Various *maṇḍala* configurations and designs were also incorporated in ancient architecture and sacrificial rites during the Vedic period because they were thought to be powerfully emblematic of the cosmos. Such configurations also functioned on a more internal level as an aid in various forms of yogic and tantric meditation, stimulating subtle energies within the body.[1] The *maṇḍala* of the Rāsa dance, however, is not merely made up of static or graphic geometric configurations. Rather, it is dynamic and ecstatic, its circle consisting of special souls dancing with the divinity, meditation upon which cultivates the innermost emotions of the heart.

According to Carl G. Jung, the *maṇḍala* is "an archetypal image whose occurrence is attested throughout the ages."[2] The *maṇḍala* is a God-image for Jung, and "signifies the *wholeness of the self*."[3] Additionally, it serves as a threshold into the spiritual—thus Jung characterizes the *maṇḍala* as a "window on eternity."[4] The *maṇḍala* in the Jungian psychical context parallels the *maṇḍala* in the Vaishnava sacred literary context. Psychologically, the *maṇḍala* represents the fulfillment of the self as well as a window into the deeper recesses of the spiritual self. Similarly, the Rāsa *maṇḍala* is the climactic event of the Rāsa Līlā, which in turn is the ultimate fulfillment of all scripture, and the *maṇḍala* also functions canonically as a window into the more esoteric *līlās* of Rādhā and Krishna.

The Rāsa *maṇḍala* functions canonically in two primary ways: first, it is enshrined by other exoteric traditional works; and

[1] See Mircea Eliade's relevant discussion on "Maṇḍala" in his work *Yoga: Immortality and Freedom*, translated from the French by Willard R. Trask (Princeton: Princeton University Press, [1958] 1969), pp. 219–227.

[2] C. G. Jung, *Memories, Dreams, Reflections*, recorded and edited by Aniela Jaffé, translated from the German by Richard and Clara Winston (New York: Vintage Books, 1965 [1961]), pp. 334–335.

[3] *Memories, Dreams, Reflections*, p. 335. Italics are found in original.

[4] *Memories, Dreams, Reflections*, p. 197.

second, the *maṇḍala* itself enshrines even more esoteric works. It is enthroned by the encircling canonical literature as the ultimate revelation of the intimate deity. Imagine all the scriptural texts accepted by the Chaitanya school being placed within the concentric *maṇḍala*-like arrangement of petals forming the whorl of a lotus flower—the outer leaves forming the foundational texts, and the inner circling petals, as they move closer to the center, enshrining the highest revelational text, the Bhāgavata, found in the very center of the flower. In the middle of this center pod are the Vraja *līlās* of the tenth book, at the heart of which is the Rāsa Līlā, the essence of which is the Rāsa *maṇḍala*. This, then, is the exoteric arrangement of the Vaishnava canon.

The Rāsa *maṇḍala*, which is the very center of the lotus and ultimate focal point of all exoteric scriptural texts, also serves to enthrone other more subjective, personal visions in literary works about the intimate deity. The *maṇḍala* becomes the outer petals of another lotus, enthroning esoteric visions of Vraja *līlās*, especially those focusing on intimate *līlās* of the supreme Goddess, Rādhā, and her consort, Krishna. In many ways, the living tradition embodies these visions and develops them in a variety of cultural and literary outpours. Utilizing the Rāsa *maṇḍala* as the threshold into such esoteric expressions, pilgrimage dramas from Vraja introduce every dramatic performance of Krishna's *līlās* with a reenactment of the Rāsa *maṇḍala*. These regularly performed plays are named after the Rāsa Līlā, and are known as "*rās līlās*."[5]

[5] The spelling "*rās līlā*" is Hindi for "Rāsa Līlā" from the Sanskrit.

Figure 13. A *rās līlā* pilgrimage drama with boys dressed as Gopīs. Young boys play the parts of the cowherd maidens dancing in the circular Rāsa dance around Krishna in a Vraja drama troupe performance at the Shri Chaitanya Prem Samsthan, Vrindāvan, Uttar Pradesh, India. Photograph taken by Gerald Carney.

In his study of such dramas, Norvin Hein states that the reenactment of the Rāsa dance is their "most sacred component" and their "recurrent feature."[6] Such performances invoke this most exalted *līlā* in order to usher in a performance of any one of the

[6] Norvin Hein, *The Miracle Plays of Mathurā* (New Haven: Yale University Press, 1972), p 129. Hein states that "The analysis of a rāslīlā performance must begin with notice of its two radically different parts, the rās and the līlā. The rās portion, so named because its principal feature is the set of dances called the rās, is a ritual reenactment of the most sacred of all Kṛishṇaite stories, the incident of Kṛishṇa's dance with the gopīs. . . . Thus we have in the rāslīlā a coupling of an enactment of the moonlight dance of Kṛishṇa with a dramatization of some other deed of his" (142–143). Hein presents ten various segments within the Rāsa dance as "(A) The open circle (B) The closed circle (C) The mimicking of Kṛishṇa (D) The three hops (E) Kṛishṇa's solo dance on his knees (F) The adjusting of Rādhā's ornaments (G) The promenade (H) The whirling of partners (I) The dalliance of Rādhā and Kṛishṇa (J) The clapping circle" (145–147).

numerous divine acts of Krishna.[7] When the Rāsa Līlā story itself is performed as a drama (Figure 13), it is known by the name *mahārās*, or "the great Rāsa dance."[8] Even the stage or the physical platform arena on which the dramas are enacted is often circular, and is called the *rāsmaṇḍal* (as in Rāsa *maṇḍala*), a name, adopted from the story, which describes the circle of dancers in the Rāsa dance.[9]

The pilgrimage performances of Vraja, then, initially invoke images of the Rāsa Līlā, yet go beyond the Bhāgavata by means of dramatic content into more esoteric realms. Hein explains that the literary source of the many dozens of dramatic themes enacted in these productions is indeed the Bhāgavata, though the dramas are often based on the poetry and song of *bhakti* poets, who have derived their inspiration from the Bhāgavata.[10] In addition, there is a large body of literature that retells, embellishes, or reminisces about the specific story or particular themes of the Rāsa Līlā. [11] Like Indian music that begins with a basic melodic formula known as *rāga*, in which the musician expands upon and develops his piece from a single formulaic melody line, so, on the stage, a performance introduced by the Rāsa dance "borrows" its theme from the greater Bhāgavata or the Rāsa story itself and develops the theme in its retelling.

[7] Hein states that "the number of distinct *līlās* which are played by the troupes of Braj probably approaches 150" (*Miracle Plays of Mathurā*, p. 154).

[8] For a transcription of a *mahārās* performance, see chapter 4, "The Great Circle Dance," in *At Play with Krishna: Pilgrimage Dramas from Brindavan*, by John Stratton Hawley in association with Shrivatsa Goswami (Princeton: Princeton University Press, 1981), pp. 155–226.

[9] Hein, *Miracle Plays of Mathurā*, p. 137.

[10] Hein, *Miracle Plays of Mathurā*, p. 157.

[11] To name just a few, the work entitled *Aścarya Rāsa Pravandha* ("The Story of the Marvelous Rāsa Dance"), by Prabodhānanda Sarasvatī, who lived around the time of Chaitanya or perhaps just after him in the sixteenth century, is a work that retells the various scenes of the Rāsa Līlā with great poetic detail. Rāmānanda Rāya, a contemporary of Chaitanya, writes a drama that is his own re-vision of the Rāsa Līlā drama, known as the *Jagannātha Vallabha Nāṭaka*. And in his retelling of key Vraja *līlās* in his *Ānanda Vṛndāvana Campu*, Kavikarṇapūra of the sixteenth century devotes much attention to his own retelling of the Rāsa Līlā toward the end of the work. Krishnadāsa Kavirāja Gosvāmī does the same in his *Govinda Līlāmṛta*, supplying in some cases exquisitely detailed embellishments on the Rāsa story, even a technical discussion on the types of music being sung during the Rāsa dance. There are many others, too numerous to list here. A modern retelling of the tenth book of the Bhāgavata, including the Rāsa Līlā chapters with interwoven commentary is *Kṛṣṇa: The Supreme Personality of Godhead*, by A. C. Bhaktivedanta Swami.

As the *maṇḍala* of the Rāsa dance frames pilgrimage dramas, it also poses as a calendrical *maṇḍala* that introduces the autumn month known as Kārttik, the most sacred month of the Vaishnava lunar calendar. This month is ushered in on a special holy day that commemorates the Rāsa dance, a day when the full moon rises as it does in the Rāsa Līlā story.

Another example of the *maṇḍala* acting in the life of the practitioner is found in the recitation of the divine names in the form of the *mahāmantra*, "the greatest (*mahā*) prayer-formula (*mantra*) for deliverance." This *mantra* is virtually a sonic reenactment of the Rāsa *maṇḍala*, consisting of a series of alternating names of God in the vocative case, both calling out for and praising the presence of the divine. When the *mantra* is recited repeatedly in meditation or song, it worshipfully enthrones the Soul of the soul within the heart of the devotee, forming a sonic *maṇḍala*.

The circuitous arrangement of the words of this *mahāmantra* consists of an alternating pattern between an equal number of feminine (as "*hare*") and masculine (as "*kṛṣṇa*"—the transliterated form of the name "Krishna"—and as "*rāma*") names of the divine. The sacred thirty-two-syllable *mantra* appears as follows: *hare kṛṣṇa / hare kṛṣṇa / kṛṣṇa kṛṣṇa / hare hare / hare rāma / hare rāma / rāma rāma / hare hare.* The patterned movement of eight pairs of feminine and masculine names of the divine can be observed in the mantra. Within four of the pairs (the first, second, fifth, and sixth) the feminine and masculine names appear alternately. In the other four pairs (the third, fourth, seventh, and eighth) two masculine names appear together in one pair, followed by two feminine names in the next pair. Thus, the dance-like movement can be observed both within and between pairs. Additionally, the mantra begins and ends with feminine names, enclosing the masculine names, just as the Gopīs engulf Krishna when they encircle him during the commencement of the Rāsa dance. When practitioners recite the *mantra* over and over, the divine names form a circular pattern imitative of the exchange between the feminine and masculine partners in the Rāsa dance. It can be seen, then, that the presence of the Rāsa *maṇḍala* is archetypal in Vaishnava devotional practices. (See Figure 14.)

Figure 14. The circuitous formation of the divine names in the *mahāmantra* that parallels the *maṇḍala* formation of the divine figures in the circuitous dance of the Rāsa. The author superimposed his circular Sanskrit wording of the *mahāmantra* onto the main composition of the Rāsa Maṇḍala painting by Kim Waters (described in Figure 9 above).

The early twentieth-century theologian and comparativist Rudolf Otto states that the scholar of religion must find a religious tradition's "deepest and most characteristic element, as its peculiar and central idea—or better, as its peculiar gift, the last and highest good which it has to give to humanity."[12] The Rāsa Līlā,

[12] Rudolf Otto, *India's Religion of Grace and Christianity Compared and Contrasted*, translated by Frank Hugh Foster, D.D. (New York: The MacMillan Company, 1930), p. 12.

which carries the special message of supreme love, could easily be considered one of Vaishnavism's greatest gifts to the world. At the center of this gift is the Rāsa *maṇḍala*.

Gifts derive their power by how meaningful an exchange they facilitate between the gift-giver and the gift-receiver. When the gift of the Rāsa *maṇḍala*—as a symbol of supreme love—begins to speak in meaningful ways beyond the boundaries of the tradition from which it sprung, it grows from holding a singularly intrinsic value to taking on a multivalent extrinsic purpose. This is the triumphant point at which a symbol bursts through the boundaries of its own tradition and culture and begins to speak to the greater human community.

The cowherd maidens linking arms in the dance represent the linking of human hearts and the solidarity of the human community of devoted souls. All souls, collectively, are invited to dance together with God, while simultaneously each individual soul is able to dance with God personally and exclusively. The Rāsa dance symbolizes the humility and passion of the devoted soul—the humility of love expressed through linking with other human beings collectively, and the passion of love through souls linking intimately with the supreme exclusively. This linking is the meaning of yoga, of which, as we have seen, the Gopīs are masters.

The concept, therefore, of yoga being practiced alone, in isolation, disconnected from any community—popular in pan-Indian traditions that strive for renunciation either for its own sake or for the sake of achieving liberation—is a grand departure from the message of the Rāsa Līlā text. In *bhakti* yoga, true renunciation can only be the result of pure love, and renunciation is usually forced, entered into prematurely, or artificial if it is not a spontaneous derivative of such devotional love. The joyful solidarity between souls dancing in the Rāsa *maṇḍala* demonstrates that in yoga we don't renounce community, but rather a selfish, prideful stance within the community.

The divine circle of the Rāsa dance then begins to symbolize a genuine religious pluralism in which human beings of different faiths can love God, or the divine, in joyous harmony, and individually, as each soul receives God's singular and superlative attention. Diana L. Eck sees the Rāsa Līlā as presenting a symbol of supreme love when she states that the theological message of the story is essentially "God's infinite capacity to love."[13] Her statement is supported by her observation that "there was plenty of Krishna to go around, an abundance of Krishna's presence."[14] Thus, it is only after devoted souls come together to surround the divinity in a great circle—their arms linked in affectionate fellowship—that the deity agrees to connect personally with each soul—implying that God is indebted toward those who bond with other souls for the purpose of honoring, serving, and loving him.

Ontologically speaking, it is impossible for a finite being to possess the infinite. It is plausible, however, according to Vaishnava teachings, not only for a soul to possess God but also for God to be conquered by a soul with a pure devotional heart. The idea of the soul's love conquering God is presented by the Bhāgavata: although the Lord is unconquerable by anyone in all the three worlds, he is conquered by those who are devoted to him (BhP 10.14.3). Moreover, it is significant that Krishna's bluish complexion appears to change to green, "like a magnificent emerald," as he consorts with the Gopīs in the Rāsa dance (RL 5.7). The Gopīs' love is so powerful that Krishna's color changes, signifying that he is conquered by their love.

Jīva Gosvāmī, in his theological work, presents many verses from the Rāsa Līlā, especially from the second scene of the fifth act, that further demonstrate how the love of devoted souls can control God.[15] Viśvanātha Chakravartin also sees the Rāsa Līlā as expressing this power of the soul's love by stating in his

[13] Diana L. Eck, *Encountering God: A Spiritual Journey from Bozeman to Banaras* (Boston: Beacon Press, 1993), p. 47.

[14] Eck, *Encountering God*, p. 46.

[15] In PrS 130, Jīva quotes RL 1.1 and 42, as well as 5.17, 21, 22, and 24 as examples of how Krishna is controlled by his devotee. See PrS 295–299 for further discussion on how the different types of intimate devotees control the Lord. Jīva also states that the ability to control God by love is also available in other *rasas*, not just the *rasa* of passionate love. See PrS 127–129.

commentary: "the Rāsa Līlā is the loving smile of the intimate devotee of the Lord, the most victorious, praised for the ability to bring Krishna under control" (SD 5.40). What is more, traditional commentators speak about how divine possessiveness is desirable and considered a special form of grace. Possessiveness out of love for the beloved object, completely devoid of worldly pride, jealousy, and self-interest, arises from devotional passion and pure love. But possessiveness tainted with pride and self-concern can lead to destructiveness and take one away from God's love.

In the Rāsa dance, this possessing of God represents one of the greatest miracles of divine love. Eck, however, explains that "the moment the milkmaids became possessive, each thinking that Krishna was dancing with her alone, Krishna disappeared."[16] This statement appears to represent a misreading of the text and perhaps misses the essential message of the Rāsa dance—when the Gopīs experience Krishna's exclusive attention, this is presented by the author of the text as a wonderful achievement. Eck seems to confuse this positive exclusivity or possessiveness of divine love occurring in the beginning of the fifth act with the apparent egocentrism exemplified by the Gopīs found at the end of the first act:

> Thus, those who received honor
> from the Beloved Lord,
> Krishna, the great Soul,
> Thought themselves the best
> among all women in the world—
> they then became filled with pride.
>
> (RL 1.47)

From this verse, it could be understood that at the precise moment one insists on having a relationship with the divinity while

[16] Diana L. Eck, *Encountering God: A Spiritual Journey from Bozeman to Banaras* (Boston: Beacon Press, 1993), p. 46.

excluding other souls, one loses God's favor. Krishna vanishes from the Gopīs only when they feel themselves to be the best women in the world, although, as he explains to the maidens, they were never out of his sight (RL 4.21).

The lesson here is that our vision of God is lost when we become self-interested, though as we are told, we are never lost to God's vision. It is not possessiveness or jealousy that consumes the Gopīs; rather, it is pride, the setting of themselves apart from others and a corresponding lack of humility.[17]

Furthermore, in the Bhāgavata text, Krishna does not leave the Gopīs during the Rāsa dance, as Eck implies. Indeed, it is the Gopīs who return to their homes and take Krishna's leave at the end of this timeless and magical night:

> During the sacred hour before dawn,
> at the end of the night of Brahmā
> and with the consent of Vāsudeva,
> The Gopīs returned to their homes,
> though reluctantly—
> for they so loved the Beloved Lord
> and they were so loved by him.
>
> (RL 5.39)

Thus, the dance lasts an entire "night of Brahmā," which, in cosmic terms, is equivalent to at least 432,000,000 human years!

From the tradition's perspective, however, this dance is eternal. Though, as a story, the Rāsa Līlā has a beginning and an end, as a sacred love story it is the timeless dance in which Divinity and the soul lose themselves forever in the rhythms, melodies, and movements of divine love. The drama of the Rāsa is a celebration

[17] Eck makes the following compelling statement: "The point is one that speaks to us all: The moment we human beings grasp God with jealousy and possessiveness, we lose hold of God. One might add that the religious point here is quite the opposite of God's jealousy, of which we hear so much in the Old Testament; it is God's infinite capacity to love and the problem of *human* jealousy" (*Encountering God*, p. 47).

of souls joining together to glorify the Divine's unlimited power to love, and further, to love each soul intimately.

Attaining such loving intimacy is the goal of *bhakti* yoga. The extraordinary hero and heroines of the Rāsa Līlā thus become master practitioners of yoga, Krishna included! For none is beyond the supreme power of love. Ultimately, all the rich poetry and deep symbolism of the Rāsa Līlā text thus become windows into esoteric visions of the very center of Divinity: the love between the divine couple, Rādhā and Krishna. This sacred love then becomes a song, as well as a dance, and the reader is invited to join the celebration along with the chorus of celestial singers. In fact, Chaitanya himself inquires, "Among all songs, which song is the very essence of the soul?" Rāmānanda replies, "That which is about the loving encounters of Rādhā and Krishna—this is the inmost heart of all songs" (CC 2.8.250). Hence, the Rāsa story can truly be called the Song of Songs of India, prominent among other sacred love stories of the world.

In fact, so celebrated is the love revealed therein that traditions which honor the story claim that all love is but a spark of the archetypal fire of the Rāsa's divine love. For, although the story's text and tenor are quite otherworldly, the messages it contains speak to us in this world, generation after generation. And it is by hearing or reciting the Rāsa story that we too will go beyond the spark to be consumed by this fire of Love.

In the West, the famous words of the Latin poet Virgil resonate with this very vision: "Love conquers all things; we too should surrender unto Love."[18] Viśvanātha Cakravartin, in his final comment on the Rāsa story, seems to answer Virgil's calling when he proclaims, "Indeed, we have thus become conquered by pure love."[19]

Divine love, as we have seen, is a type of eternal dance in which souls continually move toward and apart from God within the various phases of love—love that is ever-increasing in intensity,

[18] *Omnia vincit amor, et nos cedamus amori* (Eclogues X.1.69).
[19] *premnā jitā evābhūmeti*, SD 5.40.

at every moment. The culmination of these phases is the dance itself, the festive exultation of supreme love that is ever beckoning all souls to join in the triumph of divine love. The hearts of those who are already a part of the dance, for whom passionate and exclusive intimacy with God is already attained, melt with compassion for those who have not yet arrived, and yearn for all to delight in the dance of divine love.

PART VI
THE SANSKRIT TEXTS

Note on Translation

I have viewed the translating of the Rāsa Līlā text something like the task of conducting a symphony orchestra. A poem in its original but inaccessible language is like an orchestral score that does not come alive until it is conducted and performed. The conductor must read the score, and the musicians reincarnate the piece of music in performance. Similarly, the translator of poetry must conduct the complex piece, with all its movements and orchestral color, in a new and unique performance according to his or her appreciation and love for the music. Like musicians, the English words play their parts, as they are employed to translate the Rāsa Līlā verse; their instruments of meaning are woven into the orchestral performance of the reincarnated poem.

For many years I have dedicated myself to making audible the dramatic and melodious music of the Sanskrit verse in the Rāsa Līlā text. Sanskrit is a language in which words find, as a rule, an extraordinary spectrum of meanings, taking in much more of the universe than we are accustomed to finding in English. Connotative sense is more important in English than it is in Sanskrit, since the latter casts a much wider lexical net for words, gathering an enormous range of denotative senses containing many shades of meaning. Context, then, for Sanskrit words is especially critical for understanding the specific, even precise, denotative force of words. This is just one reason why it often takes more than one English word to embody the particular sense of a single Sanskrit word.

Furthermore, unlike English, Sanskrit prose does not depend on the ordering of words to form sentences; all syntactical information for sentence structure is embedded in the endings of nouns and

The Yoga of Love. Graham M. Schweig, Oxford University Press. © Oxford University Press 2025.
DOI: 10.1093/oso/9780197768426.003.0021

verbs. That is, Sanskrit is a highly inflected language in which noun stems receive any number of endings that indicate gender, number, and case, whereas verb stems receive endings as to tense, number, and person. For this reason, as well, a Sanskrit word often requires more than one word in English to communicate its sense.

This syntactical flexibility and its lexical treasures make Sanskrit an ideal language for poetic expression—each verse offers a special melody, a unique picture. Conveying even a modicum of these poetic qualities in the Sanskrit through translation would be an achievement. Even more challenging, the epic verse of the Rāsa Līlā contains a blend of deep theological content woven together with subtle eloquent poetic or dramatic elements.

As the theology of the Rāsa Līlā drama illuminates sacred love, I gave special attention to the great array of Sanskrit words and phrases that appear in this epic drama to convey the many nuances of love. Attempting to translate such words and phrases into English is problematic, since there are no comparable English words that relate the specific experience of love described by such Sanskrit terms. On the other hand, the English word "love" must be utilized in translating Sanskrit words pertaining to "love" precisely because there is no one word in Sanskrit that is uniquely as indispensible in the ultimate expression of the human heart. This way the English reader's own heart is not deprived of love's absolute sense intended by the more specific Sanskrit words and can begin to harmonize with the sacred love song imbedded in the original text.

When our heart begins to awaken to love, we suddenly become aware of its rhythmic beats. One of the ways that this sacred love story beckons the reader into such beats is through the ancient art of repetition, which, in turn, creates a rhythm mimicking the skipping of a heartbeat. In Sanskrit, repetition of words and meanings is a powerful way of inducing a love-struck, meditative-like state in the reader. Repetition conveys the depth and pursuit of a sacred vision. While other translations simply avoid this common repetitive element by using synonyms, this translation honors the tradition's original vision by not eliminating any of the original instruments of repetition from this work.

Further percussion is layered into a faithful translation of Rāsa Līlā drama through the use of highly structured form and meter. Each of the many types of epic verse throughout the text is a quatrain, consisting of rhythmic long and short syllabic patterns within measured verse lines. End-rhyme is not strict, nor is it particularly emphasized, as we often find in English; rather, verse rhythms and patterns of assonance and consonance are a more prominent feature. Furthermore, Sanskrit is especially beautiful, in part because of its rules governing euphonic combination or *sandhi*, whereby endings of words coalesce with the beginnings of following words, creating conjunctions between words that produce a sonorous flow. Sanskrit, then, becomes a particularly enticing language to hear.

It would be impossible in the English language to imitate the tremendous poetic palette found in the Sanskrit. I believe, however, that there are certain epiphanic qualities of the text that can emerge in the process of translation, even while remaining faithful to the original text. I have endeavored to produce a very accurate reading of the Rāsa Līlā, while striving to convey mimetically some of the flow and cadence in the phraseology of the English rendition. Often this phraseology occurs naturally in compound word phrases in the Sanskrit, even phrases consisting of one or more compounds appearing as a unit, that is, a complex compound. This phenomenon that pervades the language is known as *samāsa,* in which words in related phrases merge without inflection, except for the last word of the simple or complex compound.

In addition to phraseologies, I also have attempted to respect the order of words in verses. As mentioned above, Sanskrit word order is not important syntactically. But this freedom of word order makes the ordering of words in poetic verse even more crucial, as it allows such ordering to be all the more deliberate and purposeful. Thus, the particular revelational quality of each verse depends upon the ordering of its words and, further, the corresponding phrases that they form.

In my translation of verse, utilizing what I call "dedicated free verse translation" form, I have attempted, whenever possible, to remain at least roughly faithful to the original ordering of words and phrases. Furthermore, for the purpose of conveying the phraseologies of the original, I have endeavored to emulate an appearance of the original verse form: the quarter- or half-verse breaks found in the Sanskrit are indicated by, first, a single leading line beginning a verse, under which slightly indented phrases continuing that line appear, many times one on top of another, until the verse arrives at the next quarter line (in the case of all longer verse meters) or the half verse line (in the case of the *anuṣṭubh* meter, which consists of eight-syllable quarter-verse lines). The indentation and line breaks in the English translation attempt to follow or mirror the four-quarter line structure of the Sanskrit verse.

The most widely employed purāṇic meter in the Rāsa Līlā text is the *śloka* or *anuṣṭubh* meter. Throughout the translation, verses of this meter type are indicated by only two leading lines, with their respective sets of following indented line or lines. An example of this shortest verse is the following transliterated verse (with quarter-verse divisions marked by commas), and its corresponding format in English translation:

dṛṣṭaṁ vanaṁ kusumitaṁ, rākeśa-kara-rañjitam
yamunānila-līlaijat, taru-pallava-śobhitam

You have seen the forest
  filled with flowers,
  glowing with the rays
  of the full moon;
Made beautiful by leaves of trees,
  playfully shimmering
  from the gentle breeze
  off the river Yamunā.

All other verses that are of one of several longer varieties found in the Rāsa Līlā, are placed in four sets of leading lines along with their indentations, as I demonstrate in the following verse:

Seeing lotus flowers bloom, *(dṛṣṭvā kumudvantam)*
  and the perfect circle of the moon *(akhaṇḍa-maṇḍalaṁ)*
Beaming like the face of Ramā, *(ramānanābhaṁ)*
  reddish as fresh *kuṅkuma*; *(nava-kuṅkumāruṇam)*
Seeing the forest colored *(vanaṁ ca . . . rañjitaṁ)*
  by the moon's gentle rays, *(tat-komala-gobhī)*
He began to make sweet music, *(jagau kalaṁ)*
  melting the hearts of *(manoharam)*
  fair maidens with beautiful eyes. *(vāma-dṛśām)*

The above is an especially good example of the order of words in the translation closely paralleling that of the original word order. In the transliteration of the verse, I have underlined the repeated assonances and consonances that give the verse its rhyme and rhythm:

dṛṣṭvā kumudvantam akhaṇḍa-maṇḍalaṁ
  ramānanābhaṁ nava-kuṅkumāruṇam
vanaṁ ca tat-komala-gobhī rañjitaṁ
  jagau kalaṁ vāma-dṛṣāṁ manoharam

It can be seen, then, that the verse lineation and structure in translation is informed by the ordering and rhythms of words, phrases, and ideas within the original source text.

Other approaches I engage include the following: personal or proper names are duplicated as they appear in the transliteration, unaltered; meanings or identifications are provided in footnotes to the translation; and the precise wording of the original is respected, as there is a certain precision to its poetry. Pronouns, therefore, are not substituted for their antecedent personal names or ideas. My conviction is that the poet of the original text places in each verse exactly what the reader needs to know before the narrative and poetic imagery are revealed in the successive verses. Additionally, in the service of the general reader, only a minimal number of Sanskrit words and terms have been retained in the translation. Some more commonly known Sanskrit words are anglicized and not italicized.

Capitalization as we know it in English does not exist in Sanskrit. Although initial letters of proper names and beginnings of sentences are capitalized in the translation of Sanskrit, personal pronouns for the deity are not. Certain words, however, that are associated with the divinity are capitalized, in order to distinguish these superlative senses from their typical usages. For example, in the translation of the phrase *ādi-puruṣa,* which means "original (*ādi-*) person (*-puruṣa*)," I capitalize the initial letter of the word "person" to express the powerful sense of divinity that this word has for the Vaishnava tradition. The word *ātman* I translate as "Soul" in order to indicate that the soul spoken of here is different from a mortal soul. This use of capitalization for expressing divine personification can be seen in other instances as well; thus, I have an initial capital for the word "love" when it is directly associated with Krishna as the personification of the original, supreme Cupid.

In short, it is my hope that this translation will do everything it can to give readers a sense that their own hearts have been struck by the original Cupid's divine bow. While most translations of the Rāsa Līlā story appear somewhat muffled within larger translations of the greater Bhāgavata text, this translation stands alone to amplify the sacred love song and bring out the meditative richness of each Sanskrit verse. This emphasis is drawn directly from the Chaitanya school's vision of the text, which promises to transport readers beyond the ordinary, and into the orchestral chambers of the soul.

English Transliteration of the Texts

Introduction

The English transliteration of the original Sanskrit text is provided in this section of the book. I have consulted several Sanskrit texts and have found that alternate wordings of the Rāsa Līlā verses are few and negligible. (I have not provided variant readings for either the Veṇu Gīta nor the Bhramara Gīta.) Such variant readings as exist do not change the dramatic content and theological concepts of the Rāsa Līlā. In the service of scholarship, however, I have provided these variations of particular verses in footnotes to the original text that I used for my English translation. The italicized words in footnotes to verses indicate the variant readings of such verses.[1]

The transliterated text as it appears here has been formatted for the nonspecialist reader to gain a visual sense of the versification of the original Sanskrit. The eight-syllable quarter lined metered verses, or *anuṣṭubh*, appear as two-line couplets of Sanskrit text, the quarter lines indicated by an inserted comma in each line. The other five types of longer metered verse forms appear as quatrains, easily distinguishable from the common two-lined *anuṣṭubh* verses by the four lines of elaborate and embellished metered verses. The English translation also imitates this visual distinction between the couplet appearance of *anuṣṭubh* verses and the quatrain formation of longer verses. This is accomplished in the *anuṣṭubh* verses by presenting two "leading lines," or nonindented lines of text, under each of which one or several indented lines appear; likewise, for the more complex metered verses, I have presented four leading lines, each followed by one or more indented lines.

[1] The various source texts I utilized for presenting and translating the verses of the Rāsa Līlā, Veṇu Gīta, and Bhramara Gīta, and other select verse translations from the Bhāgavata Purāṇa presented throughout this work are listed in the Select Bibliography.

In some editions of the text there are differences in verse divisions and therefore their numbering, particularly in the second and fifth chapters of the episode. This lack of consistency does not pose a challenge, however, since it was the habit of medieval commentators to identify verses by the first several words of the first line, without reference to any sequential numeration. Any confusion in attempting to identify my translation with other original texts containing differing verse divisions is avoided by presenting each verse in its English transliteration.

The Sanskrit Text of the Rāsa Līlā

Act One

Bhāgavata Purāṇa, Book 10, Chapter 29

śrī-bādarāyaṇir uvāca

1 bhagavān api tā rātrīḥ, śāradotphulla-mallikāḥ
vīkṣya rantuṁ manaś-cakre, yoga-māyām upāśritaḥ *
2 tadoḍurājaḥ kakubhaḥ karair mukhaṁ
prācyā vilimpann aruṇena śantamaiḥ
sa carṣaṇīnām udagāc chuco mṛjan
priyaḥ priyāyā iva dīrgha-darśanaḥ
3 dṛṣṭvā kumudvantam akhaṇḍa-maṇḍalaṁ
ramānanābhaṁ nava-kuṅkumāruṇam
vanaṁ ca tat-komala-gobhī rañjitaṁ
jagau kalaṁ vāma-dṛśāṁ manoharam

*1 śrī *śuka* uvāca

4 niśamya gītaṁ tad anaṅga-vardhanaṁ
vraja-striyaḥ kṛṣṇa-gṛhīta-mānasāḥ
ājagmur anyonyam alakṣitodyamāḥ
sa yatra kānto java-lola-kuṇḍalāḥ
5 duhantyo 'bhiyayuḥ kāścid, doham hitvā samutsukāḥ
payo 'dhiśritya saṁyāvam, anudvāsyāparā yayuḥ
6 pariveṣayantyas tad dhitvā, pāyayantyaḥ śiśūn payaḥ
śuśrūṣantyaḥ patīn kāścid, aśnantyo 'pāsya bhojanam
7 limpantyaḥ pramṛjantyo 'nyā, añjantyaḥ kāśca locane
vyatyasta-vastrābharaṇāḥ, kāścit kṛṣṇāntikaṁ yayuḥ
8 tā vāryamāṇāḥ patibhiḥ, pitṛbhir bhrātṛ-bandhubhiḥ
govindāpahṛtātmāno, na nyavartanta mohitāḥ
9 antar-gṛha-gatāḥ kāścid, gopyo 'labdha-vinirgamāḥ
kṛṣṇaṁ tad-bhāvanā-yuktā, dadhyur mīlita-locanāḥ
10 duḥsaha-preṣṭha-viraha-, tīvra-tāpa-dhutāśubhāḥ
dhyāna-prāptācyutāśleṣa-, nirvṛtyā kṣīṇa-maṅgalāḥ
11 tam eva paramātmānaṁ, jāra-buddhyāpi saṅgatāḥ
jahur guṇa-mayaṁ dehaṁ, sadyaḥ prakṣīṇa-bandhanāḥ

śrī-parīkṣid uvāca

12 kṛṣṇaṁ viduḥ paraṁ kāntaṁ, na tu brahmatayā mune
guṇa-pravāhoparamas, tāsāṁ guṇa-dhiyāṁ katham

śrī śuka uvāca

13 uktaṁ purastād etat te, caidyaḥ siddhiṁ yathā gataḥ
dviṣann api hṛṣīkeśaṁ, kim utādhokṣaja-priyāḥ
14 nṛṇāṁ niḥśreyasārthāya, vyaktir bhagavato nṛpa
avyayasyāprameyasya, nirguṇasya guṇātmanaḥ
15 kāmaṁ krodhaṁ bhayaṁ sneham, aikyaṁ sauhṛdam eva ca
nityaṁ harau vidadhato, yānti tan-mayatāṁ hi te
16 na caivaṁ vismayaḥ kāryo, bhavatā bhagavaty aje
yogeśvareśvare kṛṣṇe, yata etad vimucyate
17 tā dṛṣṭvāntikam āyātā, bhagavān vraja-yoṣitaḥ
avadad vadatāṁ śreṣṭho, vācaḥ peśair vimohayan

śrī-bhagavān uvāca

18 svāgataṁ vo mahā-bhāgāḥ, priyaṁ kiṁ karavāṇi vaḥ
vrajasyānāmayaṁ kaccid, brūtāgamana-kāraṇam
19 rajany eṣā ghora-rūpā, ghora-sattva-niṣevitā
pratiyāta vrajaṁ neha, stheyaṁ strībhiḥ su-madhyamāḥ
20 mātaraḥ pitaraḥ putrā, bhrātaraḥ patayaś ca vaḥ
vicinvanti hy apaśyanto, mā kṛḍhvaṁ bandhu-sādhvasam
21 dṛṣṭaṁ vanaṁ kusumitaṁ, rākeśa-kara-rañjitam
yamunānila-līlaijat, taru-pallava-śobhitam *
22 tad yāta mā ciraṁ goṣṭhaṁ, śuśrūṣadhvaṁ patīn satīḥ*
krandanti vatsā bālāś ca, tān pāyayata duhyata
23 atha vā mad-abhisnehād, bhavatyo yantritāśayāḥ
āgatā hy upapannaṁ vaḥ, prīyante mayi jantavaḥ
24 bhartuḥ śuśrūṣaṇaṁ strīṇāṁ, paro dharmo hy amāyayā
tad-bandhūnāṁ ca kalyāṇaḥ, prajānāṁ cānupoṣaṇam
25 duḥśīlo durbhago vṛddho, jaḍo rogy adhano 'pi vā
patiḥ strībhir na hātavyo, lokepsubhir apātakī
26 asvargyam ayaśasyaṁ ca, phalgu kṛcchraṁ bhayāvaham
jugupsitaṁ ca sarvatra, hy aupapatyaṁ kula-striyaḥ
27 śravaṇād darśanād dhyānān, mayi bhāvo 'nukīrtanāt
na tathā sannikarṣeṇa, pratiyāta tato gṛhān

śrī-śuka uvāca

28 iti vipriyam ākarṇya, gopyo govinda-bhāṣitam
viṣaṇṇā bhagna-saṅkalpāś, cintām āpur duratyayām
29 kṛtvā mukhāny ava śucaḥ śvasanena śuṣyad
  bimbādharāṇi caraṇena bhuvaḥ likhantyaḥ |
asrair upātta-masibhiḥ kuca-kuṅkumāni
  tasthur mṛjantya uru-duḥkha-bharāḥ sma tūṣṇīm

*21a dṛṣṭaṁ vanaṁ *kumuditaṁ*
*22a tad yāta mā ciraṁ *ghoṣaṁ*

30 preṣṭhaṁ priyetaram iva pratibhāṣamāṇaṁ
kṛṣṇaṁ tad-artha-vinivartita-sarva-kāmāḥ
netre vimṛjya ruditopahate sma kiñcit
saṁrambha-gadgada-giro 'bruvatānuraktāḥ

śrī-gopya ūcuḥ

31 maivaṁ vibho 'rhati bhavān gadituṁ nṛ-śaṁsaṁ
santyajya sarva-viṣayāṁs tava pāda-mūlam
bhaktā bhajasva duravagraha mā tyajāsmān
devo yathādi-puruṣo bhajate mumukṣūn *
32 yat paty-apatya-suhṛdām anuvṛttir aṅga
strīṇāṁ sva-dharma iti dharma-vidā tvayoktam
astv evam etad upadeśa-pade tvayīśe
preṣṭho bhavāṁs tanu-bhṛtāṁ kila bandhur ātmā
33 kurvanti hi trayi ratiṁ kuśalāḥ sva ātman
nitya-priye pati-sutādibhir ārti-daiḥ kim
tan naḥ prasīda parameśvara mā sma chindyā
āśāṁ dhṛtāṁ tvayi cirād aravinda-netra*
34 cittaṁ sukhena bhavatāpahṛtaṁ gṛheṣu
yan nirviśaty uta karāv api gṛhya-kṛtye
pādau padaṁ na calatas tava pāda-mūlād
yāmaḥ kathaṁ vrajam atho karavāma kiṁ vā*
35 siñcāṅga nas tvad-adharāmṛta-pūrakeṇa
hāsāvaloka-kala-gīta-ja-hṛc-chayāgnim
no ced vayaṁ virahajāgny-upayukta-dehā
dhyānena yāma padayoḥ padavīṁ sakhe te
36 yarhy ambujākṣa tava pāda-talaṁ ramāyā
datta-kṣaṇaṁ kvacid araṇya-jana-priyasya
asprākṣma tat-prabhṛti nānya-samakṣam añjaḥ
sthātuṁs tvayābhiramitā bata pārayāmaḥ

*31d devo yathādi-puruṣo *bhajato* mumukṣūn
*33c tan naḥ prasīda *varadeśvara* mā sma chindyā
*34d yāmaḥ kathaṁ vrajam *maho* karavāma kiṁ vā

37 śrīr yat padāmbuja-rajaś cakame tulasyā
labdhvāpi vakṣasi padaṁ kila bhṛtya-juṣṭam
yasyāḥ sva-vīkṣaṇa utānya-sura-prayāsas
tadvad vayaṁ ca tava pāda-rajaḥ prapannāḥ
38 tan naḥ prasīda vṛjinārdana te 'ṅghri-mūlaṁ
prāptā visṛjya vasatīs tvad-upāsanāśāḥ
tvat-sundara-smita-nirīkṣaṇa-tīvra-kāma-
taptātmanāṁ puruṣa-bhūṣaṇa dehi dāsyam
39 vīkṣyālakāvṛta-mukhaṁ tava kuṇḍala-śrī-
gaṇḍa-sthalādhara-sudhaṁ hasitāvalokam
dattābhayaṁ ca bhuja-daṇḍa-yugaṁ vilokya
vakṣaḥ śriyaika-ramaṇaṁ ca bhavāma dāsyaḥ
40 kā stry aṅga te kala-padāyata-veṇu-gīta-
sammohitārya-caritān na calet tri-lokyām
trailokya-saubhagam idaṁ ca nirīkṣya rūpaṁ
yad go-dvija-druma-mṛgāḥ pulakāny abibhran*
41 vyaktaṁ bhavān vraja-bhayārti-haro 'bhijāto
devo yathādi-puruṣaḥ sura-loka-goptā
tan no nidhehi kara-paṅkajam ārta-bandho
tapta-staneṣu ca śiraḥsu ca kiṅkarīṇām *

śrī-śuka uvāca

42 iti viklavitaṁ tāsāṁ, śrutvā yogeśvareśvaraḥ
prahasya sa-dayaṁ gopīr, ātmārāmo 'py arīramat
43 tābhiḥ sametābhir udāra-ceṣṭitaḥ
priyekṣaṇotphulla-mukhībhir acyutaḥ
udāra-hāsa-dvija-kunda-dīdhatir
vyarocataiṇāṅka ivoḍubhir vṛtaḥ
44 upagīyamāna udgāyan, vanitā-śata-yūthapaḥ
mālāṁ bibhrad vaijayantīṁ, vyacaran maṇḍayan vanam*

*40a kā stry aṅga te kala-padāyata-*mūrcchitena* OR
kā stry aṅga te kala-*padāmṛta*-veṇu-gīta-
*41a vyaktaṁ bhavān vraja-*janārti*-haro 'bhijāto
*44d *vyacarat savanād danam*

45 nadyāḥ pulinam āviśya, gopībhir hima-vālukam
juṣṭaṁ tat-taralānandi-, kumudāmoda-vāyunā *
46 bāhu-prasāra-parirambha-karālakoru-
nīvī-stanālabhana-narma-nakhāgra-pātaiḥ
kṣvelyāvaloka-hasitair vraja-sundarīṇām
uttambhayan rati-patiṁ ramayāṁ cakāra
47 evaṁ bhagavataḥ kṛṣṇāl, labdha-mānā mahātmanaḥ
ātmānaṁ menire strīṇāṁ, māninyo hy adhikaṁ bhuvi
48 tāsāṁ tat-saubhaga-madaṁ, vīkṣya mānaṁ ca keśavaḥ
praśamāya prasādāya, tatraivāntaradhīyata

Act Two

Bhāgavata Purāṇa, Book 10, Chapter 30

śrī-śuka uvāca

1 antarhite bhagavati, sahasaiva vrajāṅganāḥ
atapyaṁs tam acakṣāṇāḥ, kariṇya iva yūthapam
2 gatyānurāga-smita-vibhramekṣitair
mano-ramālāpa-vihāra-vibhramaiḥ
ākṣipta-cittāḥ pramadā ramā-pates
tās tā viceṣṭā jagṛhus tad-ātmikāḥ
3 gati smita prekṣaṇa-bhāṣaṇādiṣu
priyāḥ priyasya pratirūḍha-mūrtayaḥ
asāv ahaṁ tv ity abalās tad-atmikā
nyavediṣuḥ kṛṣṇa-vihāra-vibhramāḥ
4 gāyantya uccair amum eva saṁhatā
vicikyur unmattaka-vad vanād vanam
papracchur ākāśa-vad antaraṁ bahir
bhūteṣu santaṁ puruṣaṁ vanaspatīn

*45c *reme* tat-taralānandi-

5 dṛṣṭo vaḥ kaccid aśvattha, plakṣa nyagrodha no manaḥ
nanda-sūnur gato hṛtvā, prema-hāsāvalokanaiḥ
6 kaccit kurabakāśoka-, nāga-punnāga-campakāḥ
rāmānujo māninīnām, ito darpa-hara smitaḥ
7 kaccit tulasi kalyāṇi, govinda-caraṇa-priye
saha tvāli-kulair bibhrad, dṛṣṭas te 'ti-priyo 'cyutaḥ
8 mālaty adarśi vaḥ kaccin, mallike jāti-yūthike
prītiṁ vo janayan yātaḥ, kara-sparśena mādhavaḥ
9 cūta-piyāla-panasāsana-kovidāra-
jambv-arka-bilva-bakulāmra-kadamba-nīpāḥ
ye 'nye parārtha-bhavakā yamunopakūlāḥ
śaṁsantu kṛṣṇa-padavīṁ rahitātmanāṁ naḥ *
10 kiṁ te kṛtaṁ kṣiti tapo bata keśavāṅghri-
sparśotsavotpulakitāṅga-ruhair vibhāsi
apy aṅghri-sambhava urukrama-vikramād vā
āho varāha-vapuṣaḥ parirambhaṇena
11 apy eṇa-patny upagataḥ priyayeha gātrais
tanvan dṛśāṁ sakhi su-nirvṛtim acyuto vaḥ
kāntāṅga-saṅga-kuca-kuṅkuma-rañjitāyāḥ
kunda-srajaḥ kula-pater iha vāti gandhaḥ
12 bāhuṁ priyāṁsa upadhāya gṛhīta-padmo
rāmānujas tulasikāli-kulair madāndhaiḥ
anvīyamāna iha vas taravaḥ praṇāmaṁ
kiṁ vābhinandati caran praṇayāvalokaiḥ
13 pṛcchatemā latā bāhūn, apy āśliṣṭā vanaspateḥ
nūnaṁ tat-karaja-spṛṣṭā, bibhraty utpulakāny aho
14 ity unmatta-vaco gopyaḥ, kṛṣṇānveṣaṇa-kātarāḥ
līlā bhagavatas tās tā, hy anucakrus tad-ātmikāḥ
15 kasyācit pūtanāyantyāḥ, kṛṣṇāyanty apibat stanam
tokayitvā rudaty anyā, padāhan śakaṭāyatīm *
16 daityāyitvā jahārānyām, eko kṛṣṇārbha-bhāvanām
riṅgayām āsa kāpy aṅghrī, karṣantī ghoṣa-niḥsvanaiḥ

*9b *jambīra*-bilva-bakulāmra-kadamba-nīpāḥ
*15c *tokāyitvā* rudaty anyā

17 kṛṣṇa-rāmāyite dve tu, gopāyantyaś ca kāścana
vatsāyatīṁ hanti cānyā, tatraikā tu bakāyatīm *
18 āhūya dūra-gā yadvat, kṛṣṇas tam anuvartatīm
veṇuṁ kvaṇantīṁ krīḍantīm, anyāḥ śaṁsanti sādhv iti
19 kasyāñcit sva-bhujaṁ nyasya, calanty āhāparā nanu
kṛṣṇo 'haṁ paśyata gatiṁ, lalitām iti tan-manāḥ
20 mā bhaiṣṭa vāta-varṣābhyāṁ, tat-trāṇaṁ vihitaṁ mayā
ity uktvaikena hastena, yatanty unnidadhe 'mbaram
21 āruhyaikā padākramya, śirasy āhāparāṁ nṛpa
duṣṭāhe gaccha jāto 'haṁ, khalānāṁ nanu daṇḍa-kṛt
22 tatraikovāca he gopā, dāvāgniṁ paśyatolbaṇam
cakṣūṁṣy āśv apidadhvaṁ vo, vidhāsye kṣemam añjasā
23 baddhānyayā srajā kācit, tanvī tatra ulūkhale
badhnāmi bhāṇḍa bhettāraṁ, haiyaṅgava-muṣaṁ tv iti
bhītā su-dṛk pidhāyāsyaṁ, bheje bhīti-viḍambanam *
24 evaṁ kṛṣṇaṁ pṛcchamānā, vṛndāvana-latās tarūn
vyacakṣata vanoddeśe, padāni paramātmanaḥ
25 padāni vyaktam etāni, nanda-sūnor mahātmanaḥ
lakṣyante hi dhvajāmbhoja-, vajrāṅkuśa-yavādibhiḥ *
26 tais taiḥ padais tat-padavīm, anvicchantyo 'grato 'balāḥ
vadhvāḥ padaiḥ su-pṛktāni, vilokyārtāḥ samabruvan
27 kasyāḥ padāni caitāni, yātāyā nanda-sūnunā
aṁsa-nyasta-prakoṣṭhāyāḥ, kareṇoḥ kariṇā yathā
28 anayārādhito nūnaṁ, bhagavān harir īśvaraḥ
yan no vihāya govindaḥ, prīto yām anayad rahaḥ
29 dhanyā aho amī ālyo, govindāṅghry-abja-reṇavaḥ
yān brahmeśau ramā devī, dadhur mūrdhny agha-nuttaye
30 tasyā amūni naḥ kṣobhaṁ, kurvanty uccaiḥ padāni yat
yaikāpahṛtya gopīnāṁ, raho bhuṅkte 'cyutādharam
31[1] na lakṣyante padāny atra, tasyā nūnaṁ tṛṇāṅkuraiḥ
khidyat-sujātāṅghri-talām, unninye preyasīṁ priyaḥ

*17b *gopāvatsāyitāḥ parāḥ*
17 *vatsāyitān gṛhītvānyān bhrāmayitvā nyapāthat* ¶
kṛṣṇāyitān jaghānānyāntatrekāṁ tu bakāyitām
*23ab *baghnantyanyāṁ srajaikāha tvāmayolūkhale hare*
Some editions of BhP do not include the third line (23ef).
*25cd lakṣyante hi *yadambhojdhvajavajrāṅkuśādibhiḥ*

31[2] imāny adhika-magnāni, padāni vahato vadhūm
gopyaḥ paśyata kṛṣṇasya, bhārākrāntasya kāminaḥ
atrāvaropitā kāntā, puṣpa-hetor mahātmanā*
32 atra prasūnāvacayaḥ, priyārthe preyasā kṛtaḥ
prapadākramaṇa ete, paśyatāsakale pade
33 keśa-prasādhanaṁ tv atra, kāminyāḥ kāminā kṛtam
tāni cūḍayatā kāntām, upaviṣṭam iha dhruvam
34 reme tayā cātma-rata, ātmārāmo 'py akhaṇḍitaḥ
kāmināṁ darśayan dainyaṁ, strīṇāṁ caiva durātmatām
35 ity evaṁ darśayantyas tāś, cerur gopyo vicetasaḥ
yāṁ gopīm anayat kṛṣṇo, vihāyānyāḥ striyo vane
36 sā ca mene tadātmānaṁ, variṣṭhaṁ sarva-yoṣitām
hitvā gopīḥ kāma-yānā, mām asau bhajate priyaḥ
37 tato gatvā vanoddeśaṁ, dṛptā keśavam abravīt
na pāraye 'haṁ calituṁ, naya māṁ yatra te manaḥ
38 evam uktaḥ priyām āha, skandha āruhyatām iti
tataś cāntardadhe kṛṣṇaḥ, sā vadhūr anvatapyata
39 hā nātha ramaṇa preṣṭha, kvāsi kvāsi mahā-bhuja
dāsyās te kṛpaṇāyā me, sakhe darśaya sannidhim

śrī-śuka-uvāca

40 anvicchantyo bhagavato, mārgaṁ gopyo 'vidūritaḥ
dadṛśuḥ priya-viśleṣān, mohitāṁ duḥkhitāṁ sakhīm
41 tayā kathitam ākarṇya, māna-prāptiṁ ca mādhavāt
avamānaṁ ca daurātmyād, vismayaṁ paramaṁ yayuḥ
42 tato 'viśan vanaṁ candra-, jyotsnā yāvad vibhāvyate
tamaḥ praviṣṭam ālakṣya, tato nivavṛtuḥ striyaḥ
43 tan-manaskās tad-ālāpās, tad-viceṣṭās tad-ātmikāḥ
tad-guṇān eva gāyantyo, nātmāgārāṇi sasmaruḥ
44 punaḥ pulinam āgatya, kālindyāḥ kṛṣṇa-bhāvanāḥ
samavetā jaguḥ kṛṣṇaṁ, tad-āgamana-kāṅkṣitāḥ

*31[2] This verse is not found in some editions of the BhP.
The third line (31[2]e–f) of this verse is not included in some editions that present the first two lines of this verse (31[2]a–d).
31[2]d bhārākrāntasya *gāminaḥ*

Act Three

Bhāgavata Purāṇa, Book 10, Chapter 31

gopya ūcuḥ

1 jayati te 'dhikaṁ janmanā vrajaḥ
śrayata indirā śaśvad atra hi
dayita dṛśyatāṁ dikṣu tāvakās
tvayi dhṛtāsavas tvāṁ vicinvate
2 śarad-udāśaye sādhu-jāta-sat-
sarasijodara-śrī-muṣā dṛśā
surata-nātha te'śulka-dāsikā
vara-da nighnato neha kiṁ vadhaḥ
3 viṣa-jalāpyayād vyāla-rākṣasād
varṣa-mārutād vaidyutānalāt
vṛṣa-mayātmajād viśvato bhayād
ṛṣabha te vayaṁ rakṣitā muhuḥ*
4 na khalu gopikā-nandano bhavān
akhila-dehinām antarātma-dṛk
vikhanasārthito viśva-guptaye
sakha udeyivān sātvatāṁ kule
5 viracitābhayaṁ vṛṣṇi-dhūrya te
caraṇam īyuṣāṁ saṁsṛter bhayāt
kara-saroruhaṁ kānta kāma-daṁ
śirasi dhehi naḥ śrī-kara-graham
6 vraja-janārti-han vīra yoṣitāṁ
nija-jana-smaya-dhvaṁsana-smita
bhaja sakhe bhavat-kiṅkarīḥ sma no
jalaruhānanaṁ cāru darśaya

*3a viṣa-*jalāśayā* vyāla-rākṣasād

7 praṇata-dehināṁ pāpa-karṣaṇaṁ
tṛṇa-carānugaṁ śrī-niketanam
phaṇi-phaṇārpitaṁ te padāmbujaṁ
kṛṇu kuceṣu naḥ kṛndhi hṛc-chayam
8 madhurayā girā valgu-vākyayā
budha-manojñayā puṣkarekṣaṇa
vidhi-karīr imā vīra muhyatīr
adhara-sīdhunāpyāyayasva naḥ
9 tava kathāmṛtaṁ tapta-jīvanaṁ
kavibhir īḍitaṁ kalmaṣāpaham
śravaṇa-maṅgalaṁ śrīmad ātataṁ
bhuvi gṛṇanti ye bhūri-dā janāḥ
10 prahasitaṁ priya-prema-vīkṣaṇaṁ
viharaṇaṁ ca te dhyāna-maṅgalam
rahasi saṁvido yā hṛdi spṛśaḥ
kuhaka no manaḥ kṣobhayanti hi
11 calasi yad vrajāc cārayan paśūn
nalina-sundaraṁ nātha te padam
śila-tṛṇāṅkuraiḥ sīdatīti naḥ
kalilatāṁ manaḥ kānta gacchati
12 dina-parikṣaye nīla-kuntalair
vana-ruhānanaṁ bibhrad āvṛtam
ghana-rajasvalaṁ darśayan muhur
manasi naḥ smaraṁ vīra yacchasi
13 praṇata-kāma-daṁ padmajārcitaṁ
dharaṇi-maṇḍanaṁ dhyeyam āpadi
caraṇa-paṅkajaṁ śantamaṁ ca te
ramaṇa naḥ staneṣv arpayādhi-han
14 surata-vardhanaṁ śoka-nāśanaṁ
svarita-veṇunā suṣṭhu cumbitam
itara-rāga-vismāraṇaṁ nṛṇāṁ
vitara vīra nas te 'dharāmṛtam

15 aṭati yad bhavān ahni kānanaṁ
truṭi yugāyate tvām apśyatām
kuṭila-kuntalaṁ śrī-mukhaṁ ca te
jaḍa udīkṣatāṁ pakṣma-kṛd dṛśām
16 pati-sutānvaya-bhrātṛ-bāndhavān
ativilaṅghya te 'nty acyutāgatāḥ
gati-vidas tavodgīta-mohitāḥ
kitava yoṣitaḥ kas tyajen niśi
17 rahasi saṁvidaṁ hṛc-chayodayaṁ
prahasitānanaṁ prema-vīkṣaṇam
bṛhad-uraḥ śriyo vīkṣya dhāma te
muhur ati-spṛhā muhyate manaḥ
18 vraja-vanaukasāṁ vyaktir aṅga te
vṛjina-hantry alaṁ viśva-maṅgalam
tyaja manāk ca nas tvat-spṛhātmanāṁ
sva-jana-hṛd-rujāṁ yan niṣūdanam
19 yat te sujāta-caraṇāmburuhaṁ staneṣu
bhītāḥ śanaiḥ priya dadhīmahi karkaśeṣu
tenāṭavīm aṭasi tad vyathate na kiṁ svit
kūrpādibhir bhramati dhīr bhavad-āyuṣāṁ naḥ

Act Four

Bhāgavata Purāṇa, Book 10, Chapter 32

śrī-śuka uvāca

1 iti gopyaḥ pragāyantyaḥ, pralapantyaś ca citradhā
ruruduḥ su-svaraṁ rājan, kṛṣṇa-darśana-lālasāḥ
2 tāsām āvirabhūc chauriḥ, smayamāna-mukhāmbujaḥ
pītāmbara-dharaḥ sragvī, sākṣān manmatha-manmathaḥ

3 taṁ vilokyāgataṁ preṣṭhaṁ, prīty-utphulla-dṛśo 'balāḥ
uttasthur yugapat sarvās, tanvaḥ prāṇam ivāgatam[*]
4 kācit karāmbujaṁ śaurer, jagṛhe 'ñjalinā mudā
kācid dadhāra tad-bāhum, aṁse candana-bhūṣitam
5 kācid añjalināgṛhṇāt, tanvī tāmbūla-carvitam
ekā tad-aṅghri-kamalaṁ, santaptā stanayor adhāt
6 ekā bhru-kuṭim ābadhya, prema-saṁrambha-vihvalā
ghnantīvaikṣat kaṭākṣepaiḥ, sandaṣṭa-darśana-cchadā
7 aparānimiṣad-dṛgbhyāṁ, juṣāṇā tan-mukhāmbhujam
āpītam api nātṛpyat, santas tac-caraṇaṁ yathā
8 taṁ kācin netra-randhreṇa, hṛdi kṛtvā nimīlya ca
pulakāṅgy upaguhyāste, yogīvānanda-samplutā[*]
9 sarvās tāḥ keśavāloka-, paramotsava-nirvṛtāḥ
jahur viraha-jaṁ tāpaṁ, prājñaṁ prāpya yathā janāḥ
10 tābhir vidhūta-śokābhir, bhagavān acyuto vṛtaḥ
vyarocatādhikaṁ tāta, puruṣaḥ śaktibhir yathā
11 tāḥ samādāya kālindyā, nirviśya pulinaṁ vibhuḥ
vikasat-kunda-mandāra-, surabhy-anila-ṣaṭpadam
12 śarac-candrāṁśu-sandoha-, dhvasta-doṣā-tamaḥ śivam
kṛṣṇāyā hasta-taralā-, cita-komala-vālukam
13 tad-darśanāhlāda-vidhūta-hṛd-rujo
manorathāntaṁ śrutayo yathā yayuḥ
svair uttarīyaiḥ kuca-kuṅkumāṅkitair
acīkḷpann āsanam ātma-bandave
14 tatropaviṣṭo bhagavān sa īśvaro
yogeśvarāntar-hṛdi kalpitāsanaḥ
cakāsa gopī-pariṣad-gato 'rcitas
trailokya-lakṣmy-eka-padaṁ vapur dadhat
15 sabhājayitvā tam anaṅga-dīpanaṁ
sahāsa-līlekṣaṇa-vibhrama-bhruvā
saṁsparśanenāṅka-kṛtāṅghri-hastayoḥ
saṁstutya īṣat kupitā babhāṣire

[*]3a taṁ vilokyāgataṁ *kṛṣṇaṁ*
[*]8d yogīvānanda-*nirbharā*

śrī-gopya ūcuḥ

16 bhajato 'nubhajanty eka, eka etad-viparyayam |
nobhayāṁś ca bhajanty eka, etan no brūhi sādhu bhoḥ

śrī-bhagavān uvāca

17 mitho bhajanti ye sakhyaḥ, svārthaikāntodyamā hi te
na tatra sauhṛdaṁ dharmaḥ, svārthārthaṁ tad dhi nānyathā
18 bhajanty abhajato ye vai, karuṇāḥ pitarau yathā
dharmo nirapavādo 'tra, sauhṛdaṁ ca su-madhyamāḥ
19 bhajato 'pi na vai kecid, bhajanty abhajataḥ kutaḥ
ātmārāmā hy āpta-kāmā, akṛta-jñā guru-druhaḥ
20 nāhaṁ tu sakhyo bhajato 'pi jantūn
bhajāmy amīṣām anuvṛtti-vṛttaye
yathādhano labdha-dhane vinaṣṭe
tac-cintayānyan nibhṛto na veda
21 evaṁ mad-arthojjhita-loka-veda-
svānāṁ hi vo mayy anuvṛttaye 'balāḥ
mayāparokṣaṁ bhajatā tirohitaṁ
māsūyituṁ mārhatha tat priyaṁ priyāḥ

Act Five

Bhāgavata Purāṇa, Book 10, Chapter 33

śrī-śuka uvāca

1 itthaṁ bhagavato gopyaḥ, śrutvā vācaḥ su-peśalāḥ
jahur viraha-jaṁ tāpaṁ, tad-aṅgopacitāśiṣaḥ
2 tatrārabhata govindo, rāsa-krīḍām anuvrataiḥ
strī-ratnair anvitaḥ prītair, anyonyābaddha-bāhubhiḥ
3 rāsotsavaḥ sampravṛtto, gopī-maṇḍala-maṇḍitaḥ
yogeśvareṇa kṛṣṇena, tāsāṁ madhye dvayor dvayoḥ
praviṣṭena gṛhītānāṁ, kaṇṭhe sva-nikaṭaṁ striyaḥ

4 yaṁ manyeran nabhas tāvad, vimāna-śata-saṅkulam
divaukasāṁ sa-dārāṇām, autsukyāpahṛtātmanām [*]
5 tato dundubhayo nedur, nipetuḥ puṣpa-vṛṣṭayaḥ
jagur gandharva-patayaḥ, sa-strīkās tad-yaśo 'malam
6 valayānāṁ nūpurāṇāṁ, kiṅkiṇīnāṁ ca yoṣitām
sa-priyāṇām abhūc chabdas, tumulo rāsa-maṇḍale
7 tatrātiśuśubhe tābhir, bhagavān devakī-sutaḥ
madhye maṇīnāṁ haimānāṁ, mahā-marakato yathā
8 pāda-nyāsair bhuja-vidhutibhiḥ sa-smitair bhrū-vilāsair
bhajyan madhyaiś cala-kuca-paṭaiḥ kuṇḍalair gaṇḍa-lolaiḥ
svidyan-mukhyaḥ kavara-rasanāgranthayaḥ kṛṣṇa-vadhvo
gāyantyas taṁ taḍita iva tā megha-cakre virejuḥ
9 uccair jagur nṛtyamānā, rakta-kaṇṭhyo rati-priyāḥ
kṛṣṇābhimarśa-muditā, yad-gītenedam āvṛtam
10 kācit samaṁ mukundena, svara-jātīr amiśritāḥ
unninye pūjitā tena, prīyatā sādhu sādhv iti
tad eva dhruvam unninye, tasyai mānaṁ ca bahv adāt[*]
11 kācid rāsa-pariśrāntā, pārśva-sthasya gadā-bhṛtaḥ
jagrāha bāhunā skandhaṁ, ślathad-valaya-mallikā
12 tatraikāṁsa-gataṁ bāhuṁ, kṛṣṇasyotpala-saurabham
candanāliptam āghrāya, hṛṣṭa-romā cucumba ha
13 kasyāścin nāṭya-vikṣipta-, kuṇḍala-tviṣa-maṇḍitam
gaṇḍaṁ gaṇḍe sandadhatyāḥ, prādāt tāmbūla-carvitam
14 nṛtyatī gāyatī kācit, kūjan nūpura-mekhalā
pārśva-sthācyuta-hastābjaṁ, śrāntādhāt stanayoḥ śivam
15 gopyo labdhvācyutaṁ kāntaṁ, śriya ekānta-vallabham
gṛhīta-kaṇṭhyas tad-dorbhyāṁ, gāyantyas taṁ vijahrire
16 karṇotpalālaka-viṭaṅka-kapola-gharma-
vaktra-śriyo valaya-nūpura-ghoṣa-vādyaiḥ
gopyaḥ samaṁ bhagavatā nanṛtuḥ sva-keśa-
srasta-srajo bhramara-gāyaka-rāsa-goṣṭhyām

[*]4d autsuky*anibhṛtā*tmanām
[*]10d *prīyamāṇena* sādhv iti

17 evaṁ pariṣvaṅga-karābhimarśa-
snigdhekṣaṇoddāma-vilāsa-hāsaiḥ
reme rameśo vraja-sundarībhir
yathārbhakaḥ sva-pratibimba-vibhramaḥ
18 tad-aṅga-saṅga-pramudākulendriyāḥ
keśān dukūlaṁ kuca-paṭṭikāṁ vā
nāñjaḥ prativyoḍhum alaṁ vraja-striyo
visrasta-mālābharaṇāḥ kurūdvaha
19 kṛṣṇa-vikrīḍitaṁ vīkṣya, mumuhuḥ khe-cara-striyaḥ
kāmārdhitāḥ śaśāṅkaś ca, sa-gaṇo vismito 'bhavat
20 kṛtvā tāvantam ātmānaṁ, yāvatīr gopa-yoṣitaḥ
reme sa bhagavāṁs tābhir, ātmārāmo 'pi līlayā
21 tāsām rati-vihāreṇa, śrāntānāṁ vadanāni saḥ
prāmṛjat karuṇaḥ premṇā, śantamenāṅga pāṇinā
22 gopyaḥ sphurat-puraṭa-kuṇḍala-kuntala-tviḍ-
gaṇḍa-śriyā sudhita-hāsa-nirīkṣaṇena
mānaṁ dadhatya ṛṣabhasya jaguḥ kṛtāni
puṇyāni tat-kara-ruha-sparśa-pramodāḥ
23 tābhir yutaḥ śramam apohitum aṅga-saṅga-
ghṛṣṭa-srajaḥ sa kuca-kuṅkuma-rañjitāyāḥ
gandharva-pālibhir anudruta āviśad vāḥ
śrānto gajībhir ibha-rāḍ iva bhinna-setuḥ
24 so 'mbhasy alaṁ yuvatibhiḥ pariṣicyamānaḥ
premṇekṣitaḥ prahasatībhir itas tato 'ṅga
vaimānikaiḥ kusuma-varṣibhir īḍyamāno
reme svayaṁ sva-ratir atra gajendra-līlaḥ
25 tataś ca kṛṣṇopavane jala-sthala-
prasūna-gandhānila-juṣṭa-dik-taṭe
cacāra bhṛṅga-pramadā-gaṇāvṛto
yathā mada-cyud dviradaḥ kareṇubhiḥ *

*25d yathā *madādho* dviradaḥ kareṇubhiḥ

26 evaṁ śaśāṅkāṁśu-virājitā niśāḥ
sa satya-kāmo 'nuratābalā-gaṇaḥ
siṣeva ātmany avaruddha-saurataḥ
sarvāḥ śarat-kāvya-kathā-rasāśrayāḥ

śrī-parīkṣid uvāca

27 saṁsthāpanāya dharmasya, praśamāyetarasya ca
avatīrṇo hi bhagavān, aṁśena jagad-īśvaraḥ
28 sa kathaṁ dharma-setūnāṁ, vaktā kartābhirakṣitā
pratīpam ācarad brahman, para-dārābhimarśanam
29 āpta-kāmo yadu-patiḥ, kṛtavān vai jugupsitam
kim-abhiprāya etan naḥ, śaṁśayaṁ chindhi su-vrata

śrī-śuka uvāca

30 dharma-vyatikramo dṛṣṭa, īśvarāṇāṁ ca sāhasam
tejīyasāṁ na doṣāya, vahneḥ sarva-bhujo yathā
31 naitat samācarej jātu, manasāpi hy anīśvaraḥ
vinaśyaty ācaran mauḍhyād, yathārudro 'bdhi-jaṁ viṣam
32 īśvarāṇāṁ vacaḥ satyaṁ, tathaivācarituṁ kvacit
teṣāṁ yat sva-vaco-yuktaṁ, buddhimāṁs tat samācaret
33 kuśalācaritenaiṣām, iha svārtho na vidyate
viparyayeṇa vānartho, nirahaṅkāriṇāṁ prabho
34 kim utākhila-sattvānāṁ, tiryaṅ-martya-divaukasām
īśituś ceśitavyānāṁ, kuśalākuśalānvayaḥ
35 yat-pāda-paṅkaja-parāga-niṣeva-tṛptā
yoga-prabhāva-vidhutākhila-karma-bandhāḥ
svairaṁ caranti munayo 'pi na nahyamānās
tasyecchayātta-vapuṣaḥ kuta eva bandhaḥ
36 gopīnāṁ tat-patīnāṁ ca, sarveṣām eva dehinām
yo 'ntaś carati so 'dhyakṣaḥ, krīḍaneneha deha-bhāk*
37 anugrahāya bhaktānāṁ, mānuṣaṁ deham āsthitaḥ
bhajate tādṛśīḥ krīḍā, yāḥ śrutvā tat-paro bhavet

*36d *eṣa* krīḍana-dehabhāk

38 nāsūyan khalu kṛṣṇāya, mohitās tasya māyayā
manyamānāḥ sva-pārśva-stān, svān svān dārān vrajaukasaḥ
39 brahma-rātra upāvṛtte, vāsudevānumoditāḥ
anicchantyo yayur gopyaḥ, sva-gṛhān bhagavat-priyāḥ
40 vikrīḍitaṁ vraja-vadhūbhir idaṁ ca viṣṇoḥ
śraddhānvito 'nuśṛṇuyād atha varṇayed yaḥ
bhaktiṁ parāṁ bhagavati pratilabhya kāmaṁ
hṛd-rogam āśv apahinoty acireṇa dhīraḥ*

The Sanskrit Text of the Veṇu Gīta

Bhāgavata Purāṇa, Book 10, Chapter 21

śrī-śuka uvāca

1 itthaṁ śarat-svaccha-jalaṁ, padmākara-sugandhinā
nyaviśad vāyunā vātaṁ, sa-go-gopālako 'cyutaḥ
2 kusumita-vanarāji-śuṣmi-bhṛṅga
dvija-kula-ghuṣṭa-saraḥ-sarin-mahīdhram
madhupatir avagāhya cārayan gāḥ
saha-paśu-pāla-balaś cukūja veṇum
3 tad vraja-striya āśrutya, veṇu-gītaṁ smarodayam
kāścit parokṣaṁ kṛṣṇasya, sva-sakhībhyo 'nvavarṇayan
4 tad varṇayitum ārabdhāḥ, smarantyaḥ kṛṣṇa-ceṣṭitam
nāśakan smara-vegena, vikṣipta-manaso nṛpa
5 barhāpīḍaṁ naṭa-vara-vapuḥ karṇayoḥ karṇikāraṁ
bibhrad vāsaḥ kanaka-kapiśaṁ vaijayantīṁ ca mālām
randhrān veṇor adhara-sudhayāpūrayan gopa-vṛndair
vṛndāraṇyaṁ sva-pada-ramaṇaṁ prāviśad gīta-kīrtiḥ
6 iti veṇu-ravaṁ rājan, sarva-bhūta-manoharam
śrutvā vraja-striyaḥ sarvā, varṇayantyo 'bhirebhire

* 40c bhaktiṁ *harau* bhagavati pratilabhya kāmaṁ

śrī-gopya ūcuḥ

7 akṣaṇvatāṁ phalam idaṁ na paraṁ vidāmaḥ
sakhyaḥ paśūn anuviveśayator vayasyaiḥ
vaktraṁ vrajeśa-sutayor anaveṇu-juṣṭaṁ
yair vā nipītam anurakta-kaṭākṣa-mokṣam
8 cūta-pravāla-barha-stabakotpalābja
mālānupṛkta-paridhāna-vicitra-veśau
madhye virejatur alaṁ paśu-pāla-goṣṭhyāṁ
raṅge yathā naṭa-varau kvaca gāyamānau
9 gopyaḥ kim ācarad ayaṁ kuśalaṁ sma veṇur
dāmodarādhara-sudhām api gopikānām
bhuṅkte svayaṁ yad avaśiṣṭa-rasaṁ hradinyo
hṛṣyat-tvaco 'śru mumucus taravo yathāryaḥ
10 vṛndāvanaṁ sakhi bhuvo vitanoti kīrtiṁ
yad devakī-suta-padāmbuja-labdha-lakṣmi
govinda-veṇum anu matta-mayūra-nṛtyaṁ
prekṣyādri-sānv-avaratānya-samasta-sattvam
11 dhanyāḥ sma mūḍha-gatayo 'pi hariṇya etā
yā nanda-nandanam upātta-vicitra-veśam
ākarṇya veṇu-raṇitaṁ saha-kṛṣṇa-sārāḥ
pūjāṁ dadhur viracitāṁ praṇayāvalokaiḥ
12 kṛṣṇaṁ nirīkṣya vanitotsava-rūpa-śīlaṁ
śrutvā ca tat-kvaṇita-veṇu-vivikta-gītam
devyo vimāna-gatayaḥ smara-nunna-sārā
bhraśyat-prasūna-kabarā mumuhur vinīvyaḥ
13 gāvaś ca kṛṣṇa-mukha-nirgata-veṇu-gīta
pīyūṣam uttabhita-karṇa-puṭaiḥ pibantyaḥ
śāvāḥ snuta-stana-payaḥ-kavalāḥ sma tasthur
govindam ātmani dṛśāśru-kalāḥ spṛśantyaḥ
14 prāyo batāmba vihagā munayo vane 'smin
kṛṣṇekṣitaṁ tad-uditaṁ kala-veṇu-gītam
āruhya ye druma-bhujān rucira-pravālān
śṛṇvanti mīlita-dṛśo vigatānya-vācaḥ

15 nadyas tadā tad upadhārya mukunda-gītam
āvarta-lakṣita-manobhava-bhagna-vegāḥ
āliṅgana-sthagitam ūrmi-bhujair murārer
gṛhṇanti pāda-yugalaṁ kamalopahārāḥ
16 dṛṣṭvātape vraja-paśūn saha rāma-gopaiḥ
sañcārayantam anu veṇum udīrayantam
prema-pravṛddha uditaḥ kusumāvalībhiḥ
sakhyur vyadhāt sva-vapuṣāmbuda ātapatram
17 pūrṇāḥ pulindya urugāya-padābja-rāga
śrī-kuṅkumena dayitā-stana-maṇḍitena
tad-darśana-smara-rujas tṛṇa-rūṣitena
limpantya ānana-kuceṣu jahus tad-ādhim
18 hantāyam adrir abalā hari-dāsa-varyo
yad rāma-kṛṣṇa-caraṇa-sparaśa-pramodaḥ
mānaṁ tanoti saha-go-gaṇayos tayor yat
pānīya-sūyavasa-kandara-kandamūlaiḥ
19 gā gopakair anu-vanaṁ nayator udāra
veṇu-svanaiḥ kala-padais tanu-bhṛtsu sakhyaḥ
aspandanaṁ gati-matāṁ pulakas taruṇāṁ
niryoga-pāśa-kṛta-lakṣaṇayor vicitram
20 evaṁ-vidhā bhagavato, yā vṛndāvana-cāriṇaḥ
varṇayantyo mitho gopyaḥ, krīḍās tan-mayatāṁ yayuḥ

The Sanskrit Text of the Bhramara Gīta

Bhāgavata Purāṇa, Book 10, Chapter 47, Verses 1–21

śrī-śuka uvāca

1 taṁ vīkṣya kṛṣānucaraṁ vraja-striyaḥ
pralamba-bāhuṁ nava-kañja-locanam
pītāmbaraṁ puṣkara-mālinaṁ lasan-
mukhāravindaṁ parimṛṣṭa-kuṇḍalam

2 su-vismitāḥ ko 'yam apīvya-darśanaḥ
kutaś ca kasyācyuta-veṣa-bhūṣaṇaḥ
iti sma sarvāḥ parivavrur utsukās
tam uttamaḥ-śloka-padāmbujāśrayam
3 taṁ praśrayeṇāvanatāḥ su-sat-kṛtaṁ
sa-vrīḍa-hāsekṣaṇa-sūnṛtādibhiḥ
rahasy apṛcchann upaviṣṭam āsane
vijñāya sandeśa-haraṁ ramā-pateḥ
4 jānīmas tvāṁ yadu-pateḥ, pārṣadaṁ samupāgatam
bhartreha preṣitaḥ pitror, bhavān priya-cikīrṣayā
5 anyathā go-vraje tasya, smaraṇīyaṁ na cakṣmahe
snehānubandho bandhūnāṁ, muner api su-dustyajaḥ
6 anyeṣv artha-kṛtā maitrī, yāvad-artha-viḍambanam
pumbhiḥ strīṣu kṛtā yadvat, sumanaḥsv iva ṣaṭpadaiḥ
7 niḥsvaṁ tyajanti gaṇikā, akalpaṁ nṛpatiṁ prajāḥ
adhīta-vidyā ācāryam, ṛtvijo datta-dakṣiṇam
8 khagā vīta-phalaṁ vṛkṣaṁ, bhuktvā cātithayo gṛham
dagdhaṁ mṛgās tathāraṇyaṁ, jārā bhuktvā ratāṁ striyam
9 iti gopyo hi govinde, gata-vāk-kāya-mānasāḥ
kṛṣṇa-dūte samāyāte, uddhave tyakta-laukikāḥ
10 gāyantyaḥ prīya-karmāṇi, rudantyaś ca gata-hriyaḥ
tasya saṁsmṛtya saṁsmṛtya, yāni kaiśora-bālyayoḥ
11 kācin madhukaraṁ dṛṣṭvā, dhyāyantī kṛṣṇa-saṅgamam
priya-prasthāpitaṁ dūtaṁ, kalpayitvedam abravīt

gopy uvāca

12 madhupa kitava-bandho mā spṛśaṅghriṁ sapatnyāḥ
kuca-vilulita-mālā-kuṅkuma-śmaśrubhir naḥ
vahatu madhu-patis tan-māninīnāṁ prasādaṁ
yadu-sadasi viḍambyaṁ yasya dūtas tvam īdṛk
13 sakṛd adhara-sudhāṁ svāṁ mohinīṁ pāyayitvā
sumanasa iva sadyas tatyaje 'smān bhavādṛk
paricarati kathaṁ tat-pāda-padmaṁ nu padmā
hy api bata hṛta-cetā hy uttamaḥ-śloka-jalpaiḥ

Four *short vowels*: a | i | u | ṛ

Eight *long vowels*: ā | ī | ū | ṝ | e | ai | o | au

Consonants (in English alphabetical order)

b like "b" in "bee"

bh sounds like the "b" when added to the word "hug" as in subheading

c like "ch" in "chart" (never pronounced like the English "k" or "s")

ch sounds like the "ch" in the word combination of "ch" plus the word "heart" as in "ch-heart" (the word "challenge")

d like "d" in "double"*

dh sounds like the aspirated "d" in "down"

ḍ like "d" in "red"; in the West, we do not hear the subtle distinctions between the two "d's" and are not used to making these distinctive sounds with the tongue in English.

ḍh like the aspirated "d" in "down"

[f] [The letter "f" is not used in the English transliteration of Sanskrit letters; there is no phonetic sound of "f" in Sanskrit, and thus the phonetic combination of ph produces the phonetic sound of "f"—only an aspirated p (see "ph" below).]

g like "g" in "gate" (the soft "g" as pronounced in the word "germane" is never represented by this consonant but is found only in the Sanskrit letter "j")

gh like the aspirated "g" in "Ghent"

h like "h" in "hot" (standing alone or followed by a vowel, without following a consonant)

_+h any consonant followed by "h" is merely aspirated, like the subtle aspirated breath sound naturally occurring after the letter "p" in the word "pot" (whereas aspiration is naturally absent after the letter "d" in the word "dot"); thus "ph" sounds like these letters in the word "loophole" (not an "f" sound); and the "th" in Sanskrit sounds like the "th" in "Thomas" and not a "th" sound as in "thorn," as is typically the case in English.

ḥ the silent consonant often found at the end of words; this is known in Sanskrit as the *visarga*; when located at the end of a word at the end of a sentence, it reduplicates the last syllable: for example, the "ḥ" in "rāmaḥ" sounds like "rāmaha," and "śaktiḥ" sounds like "śaktihee."

j like "j" in "joy"

jh like "j" and "h" in Jehovah

jñ like "gy" for the word jñāna, which is pronounced like gyāna; or "jn" as in ājñā; the combination "jñ" as found in the word jñāna is often pronounced like the "gy" in the name of a Hungarian tribe, "Magyar."

k like "k" in "kit"

kh like the aspirated "k" in "kind"

l like "l" in "lake"

m like "m" in "mark"

ṁ/ṃ like "ng" in the French word "long"; this nasal is known in Sanskrit as the *anusvāra*; the earlier established transliteration (as is the practice according to the International Alphabet of Sanskrit Transliteration) utilizing the overdot—as in ṁ—is utilized in this work for representing the *anusvāra*.

n like "n" in "soon"; the other following n's listed below are only the subtlest variations without a diacritic mark

ṅ like "n" in "song"

ñ like "n" in "staunch"

ṇ like "n" in "sand"

p like "p" in "pan"

ph like "p" in "part" with aspirated breath (it never makes the sound of "f" as it often does in English, as in the "ph" in the word "phase")

[q] [There is no consonantal equivalent for the English letter q in the Sanskrit. Therefore, "q" is not used in the English transliteration of Sanskrit letters.]

r like "r" in "rain"

ṛ (is a vowel; see "ṛ" in "Vowels," above)

s like "s" in "suit"

ś like "sh" in "shoot" (this sibilant and the following are commonly pronounced by English speakers without any discernable distinction)

ṣ like "sh" in "shout"

t like "t" in "tool" (with tip of tongue near the place where the teeth meet the roof of the mouth)*

ṭ like "t" in "shout" (with tip of tongue toward the middle of the roof of the mouth)

th like "t" in "Thomas" (with aspirated breath; the phonetic sounding of *th* does not exist in any Sanskrit, and it never makes the sound of "th" as it mostly does in English, such as the "th" in the word "thought")

ṭh similar to "th" above, but sounds like the "t(h)" in "tarnish"

v like "v" in "value" (when the letter "v" follows a consonant, it is often softened tothe sound of a "w," e.g., *sattva* will often be sounded as sattwa and *svāhā* sounded as swāhā)

[w] [The letter "w" is not used in the English transliteration of Sanskrit letters. However, the letter "w" is at times used in the phonetic spelling of Sanskrit words when the letter "v" is softened—see pronunciation of "v" above.]

[x] [There is no transliteration that utilizes this English letter, nor does the phonetic sounding of this letter exist in any Sanskrit consonants.]

y like "y" in "yarn"

[z] [The letter "z" is not used in the English transliteration of Sanskrit letters.]

Good recitation: Syllables containing short vowels are sounded for half the length of time as syllables containing long vowels. However, when a short vowel syllable is followed by more than one consonant within a word or between words, then the short syllable is sounded for the length of time a long syllable is. More specifically, when a short vowel in a syllable is followed by more than one consonant within a word or the last syllable of a word containing a short vowel is followed by a single consonant beginning in the next word of the sentence, then the short vowel is sounded for twice the length it would be normally. These are instances in which the short vowel syllable becomes sounded for the same length of time as a long syllable.

Sanskrit Alphabetical Order and Linguistic Designations of Transliterated Letters

(sequence: first read across, then down, then across, etc.)

Vowels

short	*long*
a (ʻ)	ā
i	ī
u	ū
ṛ	ṝ
	e
	ai
	o
	au

Vowel Modifiers

ṁ/ṃ	*anusvāra*
ḥ	*visarga*

Consonants

k	kh	g	gh	ṅ	*gutturals*
c	ch	j	jh	ñ	*palatals*
ṭ	ṭh	ḍ	ḍh	ṇ	*linguals*
t	th	d	dh	n	*dentals*
p	ph	b	bh	m	*labials*
y	r	l	v		*semivowels*
ś	ṣ	s			*sibilants*
h					*aspirate*

Glossary of Words and Names

Names and Key Terms in Sanskrit and English Found in the Rāsa Līlā and Related Texts

Acyuta "The infallible one." A name for Krishna.

Adhokṣaja "The Lord who is beyond the perception of the senses." A name for Krishna.

ādi-puruṣa "The original Person." An epithet for Krishna. See *puruṣa.*

aguru A fragrant paste consisting of aloe-tree wood. Also known as *alguru.*

Arjuna One of five righteous Pāndava brothers; the great general in the *Mahābhārata* war who was counseled on the battlefield by Krishna in their dialogue of the Bhagavad Gītā.

arka A very insignificant plant among all the botanicals of the forest.

ātman "Soul," "self," "mind"; referring to Krishna as "[supreme] Soul." (Also spelled *ātmā.*) See *ātmārāma, mahātma, paramātman.*

ātmārāma "One who possesses pleasure (*rāma*) within the self (*ātmā*)." This phrase often refers to Krishna or saintly persons.

avatāra "The crossing over and descent of the divine," especially to this world. Krishna is known as the original *avatāra* from whom all other *avatāras* come.

Badarayaṇa The father of the sage Śuka, the narrator of the Rasa Lila story, and most of the Bhāgavata text. Bādarāyaṇa, who is also known as Vyāsa, is the compiler of the most ancient Indian sacred texts known as the Vedas. With the exception of the first verse, throughout the story, the narrator is referred to by the simple name Śuka. In some editions of the Bhāgavata, the RL story begins with the epithet "son of Bādarāyaṇa," invoking the narrator's authoritative status, in order to specially honor the greatest of divine stories.

Balarāma The brother of Krishna.

Bhagavān "The Beloved Lord," or the "one who possesses all supreme excellences in full." The word means generally "God" or "the divine," or more literally "one who possesses (*-vān*) all excellences (*bhaga-*)." Refers to Krishna throughout the episode, meaning the powerful yet intimate and personal "supreme Lord."

bhakti "Devotional love," "loving devotion to God," "worship of the divinity," "honor," "the offering of the whole heart to the divine," etc.

Brahmā The "deity of creation" (to be distinguished from Brahman). Often associated with the other primary cosmic divinities of sustenance, Vishnu, and destruction, Śiva. In this episode, Brahmā is also called Vikhanas (see Vikhanas).

Brahman "Supreme spirit," "God," or "ultimate reality." The totality of supreme reality, or the non-dual dimension of the supreme reality.

Cedi, king of Śiśupāla, the king who insulted Krishna in the assembly of great personalities and elders attending the *rājasūya* sacrifice. Krishna granted liberation to him by beheading him with his *cakra*.

Damodara A name for Krishna, meaning "one whose waist has been bound." Krishna's mother, Yaśodā, attempts to bind him with a rope to keep him from stealing butter (see BhP 10.9).

Devakī The name of Krishna's original birth mother, the wife of Vasudeva.

Devī The Goddess.

dharma "Duty," "religion," "the laws of goodness," "essential nature," etc. See *sva-dharma*.

dhīra A person who is "peaceful and wise."

Gandharvas Plural for Gandharva. The name of a group of celestial singers who produce the most exquisitely divine music with instruments.

Goddess See Indirā, Lakṣmī, Ramā, Śrī.

Gopa "One who protects the cows." A cowherd boy or man. More specifically, a husband of a Gopī.

Gopī A married or unmarried cowherdess or milkmaiden. In the RLP, the word is used mostly in the plural to refer to Krishna's beloveds. See Gopīs. For literal meaning, see Gopa.

Gopīs Plural form of Gopī. The specific group of cowherd maidens from rural the area of Vraja who are viewed as the divine goddess consorts of Krishna. The collective heroines of the RLP drama.

Govinda "One who tends the cows." A proper name for Krishna. Viśvanātha explains that the name Govinda can be used to convey the sense of someone "who utilizes (*vindate*) playful speech (*gāḥ*)."

guṇa "Underlying forces of worldly nature," the three constituent "qualities" of the natural world as well as the consciousness of the conditioned self, consisting of *sattva*, *rajas*, and *tamas* (clarity or light, haziness, and darkness of spirit, respectively). See *nirguṇa*.

Hari "One who steals one's heart," or "one who takes away suffering." A name for Krishna.

Hṛṣīkeśa "The Lord of the senses." A name for Krishna.

Indirā A name for the goddess Lakṣmī, the consort of Nārāyaṇa.

Īśa "Cosmic controller." In the RLP, refers to the deity Śiva. The word can refer to Krishna or Vishnu as "the Lord." See Rudra.

īśvara "The supreme cosmic controller." A word for the divine or an epithet of Krishna.

kajjala A blackish substance, sometimes considered a collyrium, applied to the eyelashes or eyelids as decorative makeup.

Kālindī Another name for the river Yamunā.

kāma "Love," "worldly love," "passion" (worldly, or divine). The word is typically referring to worldly love. Teachers of the Chaitanya school have a special application of this word to indicate the intensity of pure love or *premā*.

Karnikāra Golden yellow flowers that hang in bunches growing from the branches of the Indian Laburnum (*cassia fistula*) tree. The flowers consist of beautiful delicate blossoms that are primarily ornamental, since they do not produce a scent.

Keśava "The long-haired one." A name for Krishna.

Krishna (Kṛṣṇa) The "dark" one, or "blackish," indicating Krishna's dark "sapphire-like" color. The most prominent personal name for Bhagavān, or the Supreme Lord, throughout the Rāsa Līlā episode. Krishna as a name of God denotes particularly, for the Chaitanya school and other Vaishnava lineages, the original form of God from whom all other divine forms and manifestations come.

Kṛṣṇa The diacritic spelling for the name Krishna. See Krishna.

Kṛṣṇā Another name for the river Yamunā (not to be confused with the diacritic spelling of Krishna's name as Kṛṣṇa, the former having the long vowel "ā", i.e, a macron diacritic mark over the letter "a").

kuṅkuma A brilliant or deep reddish powder, often translated as "saffron." A powdered substance that is often described as saffron or vermilion. It is produced from the plant and pollen of the flowers of the botanical crocus sativus. This substance is often placed above the forehead in the area of the parted hair by married Indian women.

Lakṣmī The supreme Goddess, divine consort of Vishnu or Nārāyaṇa.

līlā "Play" or "divine play." The word can have the sense of "playfulness" as well as the different sense of "drama." It refers to the revelational displays or dramatic manifestations of the various divine events in the divine life of Krishna.

Mādhava A name for Krishna, derived from the word *madhu*, which means "honey" or "sweet."

Madhu The name of the dynasty into which Krishna was born.

Madhupati "Lord of the Madhu dynasty." An epithet of Krishna.

mahātman "The great Soul." An epithet of Krishna.

Mālatī A type of jasmine flower. See Mallikā.

Mallikā Jasmine flowers. Exotically fragrant small star-shaped white or pink blossoms.

Mathurā The biggest city in the Vraja region, located within about ten miles of Vrindāvana village.

Maya, son of The personality whose son is the demon Vyomāsura. The episode of Krishna slaying Vyomāsaura is found in BhP 10.37.28–33. Maya should be distinguished from the similar word "*māyā*," meaning "energy," or "illusion," etc.

māyā "Power," "energy," "illusion." Māyā often appears as the shortened form of "Yogamāyā" (see Yogamāyā).

Mukunda "One who grants liberation (*mukti*)." An epithet of Krishna.

Murāri "Enemy of the Mura demon." An epithet of Krishna.

Nanda The name of Krishna's foster father, the husband of Yaśodā.

nirguṇa "Without *guṇa*," or "without being bound by the underlying forces of nature." See *guṇa*.

paramātman "Supreme Soul" or "supreme Self." Krishna's special expansive form located in the heart of all beings and at the core of all existences.

parameśvara "Supreme controller" or "supreme Lord." An epithet of Krishna.

Parikṣit The king to whom the Rāsa Līlā and the other stories of the Bhāgavata Purāṇa are narrated.

premā "Love" or "affection." It can mean "pure love" and specifically "love of God."

Pulinda Aboriginal women spoken of in the Venu Gīta (BhP 10.21.17).

puruṣa "Person," either referring to divinity or a human. This word has many senses. It can mean "spirit" in contra-distinction to *prakṛti* or "the physical world." The word can also mean "person," as in a human, or as a divine person, God, as in the phrase "the original supreme person." See *ādi-puruṣa*.

Pūtanā The demoness who tried to kill Krishna as a baby by nursing from her poisoned breast. The Pūtanā story is found in the BhP 10.6.1–44.

Ramā Name for Lakṣmī, the divine consort of Krishna when he is in his more majestic and powerful form known as Lord Nārāyaṇa. To be distinguished from the incarnation of Vishnu, Rāma (the macron diacritic over the first "a" rather than the second). See Śrī.

Rāma The shortened name for Krishna's brother, Balarāma. (To be distinguished from Nārāyaṇa's consort Ramā—the macron diacritic over the second "a" rather than the first). Context will usually reveal the personage to whom this name refers. This abbreviated name, though not applicable in this text, can also refer to Krishna's incarnation of Rāmacandra, found in the *Rāmāyana* by Valmiki. Finally, this name can refer to Krishna himself, as "the one who experiences supreme pleasure" (which is possible meaning intended for the name Rāma in the *mahāmantra*).

rasa "Taste." The word can be understood as "the intimate experiences or relationships with God," and more broadly, a deep aesthetic appreciation or experience. In order to distinguish *rasa* from *rāsa* (see Rāsa), I have presented the latter in non-italic letters and with initial upper case "r": Rāsa.

Rāsa "The Rāsa dance." Specifically, a special ancient, sophisticated dance form of India, in which a circle of women are formed with interlocking arms, each of whom has a male partner who places his arm around the neck of each female. The dance also involves singing as well. Viśvanātha points out that Rāsa also refers to the sum of all *rasas* or all intimate experiences with the supreme.

Rāsa-*goṣṭhī* The "assembly" or "gathering" of the Rāsa dance. Another way of referring to the Rāsa Līlā story.

Rāsa-*krīḍā* The "play" of the Rāsa dance. Another way of referring to the Rāsa Līlā story. The related word *vikrīḍitam* appears in RLP 5.40. See the synonymn *līlā*.

Rāsa *maṇḍala* The actual "circle" (*maṇḍala*) of the "*rāsa*" dance. Another way of referring to the Rāsa Līlā episode, but more specifically to the *rāsa* dance.

Rāsa Līlā The "play (*līlā*) of the dance (*rāsa*)," or as I have more broadly translated it, "Dance of Divine Love." The most commonly used name to refer to the specific episode within the tenth book of the Bhāgavata Purāṇa (versions of which are also found in the *Harivaṁśa* and *Vishnu Purāṇa*) which tells the story of how Krishna attracts the cowherd maidens away from their homes and to the forest where all of them, in the final fifth chapter, dance and sing together lovingly in the Rāsa dance. This phrase, however, does not appear in the episode or the whole of the Bhāgavata text itself.

rās līlā Name of the pilgrimage dramas performed in Vraja that always commence with a reenactment of the Rāsa dance.

rāsotsava "Festival (-*utsava*) of the Rāsa dance."

Rātrī "Night." The Goddess presiding over the Night presented in the Ṛg Veda.

Rudra A name for the powerful cosmic deity Śiva, the deity of cosmic dissolution. See Īśa.

Sātvatas Sacred to the Satvats or those who worship Krishna; name for the Yādava dynasty, the Yadus who worship Krishna.

Śauri The name of Krishna as the one who appears in the dynasty of Śūra. This name conveys the heroic character of Krishna.

Śrī A name for the Goddess Lakṣmī, the divine consort of Nārāyaṇa. See Ramā.

Śrutis The plural form of the word *Śruti*, which refers to the revelational scriptures of the Vedas and other closely associated literatures, like the Upanishads.

Śiva See Rudra.

Śuka The narrator of the Bhāgavata text to the king Parīkṣit. He is the son of Vyāsa, the compiler of the Vedas.

sva-dharma "One's own *dharma*." See *dharma*.

tad-ātmika "The self completely absorbed in that [beloved object, viz., Krishna]." A phrase descriptive of the Gopīs' state of mind.

tan-maya "One who is filled with that [beloved object, viz., Krishna]." A phrase descriptive of the Gopīs' state of mind.

tat-parā "One who is fully dedicated to that [beloved object, viz., Krishna]." A phrase descriptive of the Gopīs state of mind.

tulasī The most sacred plant to Krishna. The green leaves and delicate green and purple blossoms of the plant are offered to Krishna's feet and are used in his garlands as well. This plant produces delicate purplish flowerets with its own distinct scent. Also personified as the Goddess Tulasī.

Udhava The messenger of Krishna to the Gopīs, who possesses a bodily likeness of Krishna. The passage in which Uddhava appears is BhP 10.47, in which the famous Bhramara Gīta appears.

Urukrama "The wide striding one." A name for Krishna referring to Krishna's incarnation as Vāmana.

Uttamaśloka Epithetical name for Krishna or Vishnu translated in the Bhramara Gīta as, "the most excellent and famous one," or more literally meaning, "the one whose hymns of praise (*śloka*) are the greatest or highest (*uttama*)." This name for Krishna is used throughout the Bhāgavata text but is not found in the Rāsa Līlā story.

Vaijayantī "Victory." The name of Krishna's garland of five different colored flowers strung together.

Varāha The name of Krishna's incarnation in the form of a divine boar.

Vāsudeva "Son of Vasudeva (Krishna's father)." A name for Krishna.

Vedas The Vedas (or Veda) are the foundational sacred Sanskrit texts of India, seen by many Hindu traditions as the basis for and symbol of all knowledge. Acceptance of the authority of the Veda, on some level, is necessary for validating religious orthodoxy or identity.

Vikhanas Name for the god of creation, known most often as Brahmā (to be distinguished from the word Brahman, "the supreme spirit").

Vishnu (Viṣṇu) "The all-pervading one." A name for Krishna in his divine manifestation of power and cosmic majesty.

Vraja The rural village, synonymous with Vrindāvana, or the greater region in North India in which Krishna and his consorts reside.

Vrindāvana "The forest (*-vana*) of Tulasī (*vrindā-*)." The name of the specific village where Krishna resides, within the Vraja region. See *tulasī*.

Vṛṣṇis The people of the Vṛṣṇi dynasty, the dynasty from which Krishna comes.

Yadus Another name of the dynasty from which Krishna comes.

Yamunā The sacred river that runs through Vraja, famous for being so dear to Krishna and the Gopīs. Also known as the Kalindī and the Kṛṣṇā in this episode. See Kalindī and Kṛṣṇā.

yoga "Union" or "connection," connoting the soul's intimate relationship with the divine. The physical and meditation discipline by which mystics can attain perfection as well as many supernatural powers.

Yogamāyā "Illusive power of *yoga*." The Goddess, or Devī, the feminine embodiment of "illusive power" who makes arrangements for God's pleasure. This term more connotatively means "the illusive power of God (*māyā*), which creates arrangements for loving union (*yoga*)." This idea is often abbreviated simply with the word "*māyā*." See *māyā*.

yogeśvara "Supreme Lord of yoga." A name for Krishna. This name can be associated with the power of Yogamāyā, implied by the presence of the word "*yoga*" in the name.

yogī One who practices yoga, the powerful discipline which leads to the mastery over the mind and body, leading to blissful states of consciousness in direct relation to the Supreme.

yoginī The female counterpart of the *yogī*. described above.

About the Author-Translator

Graham M. Schweig is a widely published scholar of comparative religion specializing in the religions of India, yoga philosophy, mysticism, interreligious dialogue, and theology. As a translator of ancient Sanskrit texts, Schweig's published books include *Bhagavad Gītā: The Beloved Lord's Secret Love Song* (Harper Collins, 2010) and *Dance of Divine Love: India's Classic Sacred Love Story* (Princeton University Press, 2005). He also recently produced the world's first *Bhagavad Gītā Concordance: A Comprehensive Word Reference with English and Sanskrit Indexes* (Columbia University Press, 2024), and forthcoming with Yale University Press is his own translation of and commentary on Patañjali's Yoga Sūtra.

With a doctoral degree from Harvard University, Schweig is a Professor at Christopher Newport University as well as Distinguished Research and Teaching Faculty at the Center for Dharma Studies of the Graduate Theological Union in Berkeley. Schweig has also maintained an active yoga and meditation practice under the guidance of traditional teachers for well over fifty years and is a recognized advanced teacher by Yoga Alliance. He was born in New York City, raised in Washington, DC, and currently lives in Virginia where he and his wife together mentor serious students from around the world on the yogic life. For more information about the author visit: www.grahamschweig.com.

Select Bibliography

Bhāgavata Purāṇa: Sanskrit Editions and Translations

Bhāgavata Purana. Sanskrit text; multi-commentary edition, including commentaries by Śrīdhara Svāmin, Sanātana Gosvāmin, Jīva Gosvāmin, Viśvanātha Cakravartin. Allahabad, n.d.

Bhāgavata Purāṇa of Kṛṣṇa Dvaipāyana Vyāsa (with Sanskrit Commentary *Bhāvāthabodhinī* of Śrīdhara Svāmin). Edited by J. L. Shastri. Delhi: Motilal Banarsidass, 1983.

Bhaktivedanta Swami Prabhupāda, A. C. *Śrīmad Bhāgavatam*. Original Sanskrit Text. Cantos 1–12 in 18 vols. Sanskrit text, translation, and commentary (Cantos 1 through 10 Part 1). Los Angeles: Bhaktivedanta Book Trust, 1993.

———. *Kṛṣṇa, The Supreme Personality of Godhead: A Summary Study of Śrīla Vyāsadeva's Śrīmad-Bhāgavata*, Tenth Canto. Vols. 1–3. New York: Bhaktivedanta Book Trust, 1970.

Bryant, Edwin F. *Krishna: Srimad Bhagavata Purana, Book X. The Beautiful Legend of God (With Chapters 1, 6, and 29–31 from Book XI)*. New York: Penguin Books, 2003.

Goodall, Dominic. "Bhāgavata-Purāṇa Book X" (Chapters 29–33). In *Hindu Scriptures*, 373–393. Berkeley: University of California Press, 1996.

Goswami, C. L. *Śrīmad Bhāgavata Mahāpurāṇa*. Sanskrit text and English translation. 3rd edition, Vols. Part I and II. Gorakhpur: Gita Press, [1971] 1995.

Mukerjee, Radhakamal. *Lord of the Autumn Moons*, with an introduction and commentary. Bombay: Asia Publishing House, 1957.

Redington, S. J., James D. *Vallabhācārya on the Love Games of Kṛṣṇa*. Delhi: Motilal Banarsidass, 1983.

Sanyal, J. M. *The Srimad-Bhagavatam of Krishna-Dwaipayana Vyasa*. Vols. 1 and 2. English. New Delhi: Munshiram Manoharlal Publishers Pvt. Ltd., 1970.

Schweig, Graham M. *Dance of Divine Love: India's Classic Sacred Love Story: The Rāsa Līlā of Krishna*. Princeton, NJ, and Oxford: Princeton University Press, 2005.

Śrīmad-Bhāgavata-Mahāpurāṇam. With the commentaries of various teachers. Ahmedabhad: Śrī Bhāgavata Vidyāpīṭh Nyāsīpariṣad, n.d.

Śrīmad Bhāgavatam. Volumes I and II. Sanskrit edition. Madras: V. Ramaswamy Sastrulu & Sons, 1937.

Śrīmad Bhāgavatam. Tenth Book with Viśvanātha Cakravartī commentary in Sanskrit text in Bengali transliteration. Śrī Māyāpura: Śrī Caitanya Math, n.d.

Tagare, Ganesh Vasudeo. *The Bhāgavata-Purāna*. Parts 1–5. Introduction, translation, and annotation. Ancient Indian Tradition & Mythology, vols. 7–11. J. L. Shastri, Series Editor. Delhi: Motilal Banarsidass, 1976–1978.

Related Sacred Primary Textual Sources

Baladeva Vidyābhūṣana. *Govinda Bhāṣya.* English translation by Major B. D. Basu. Found in *Vedānta-Sūtras of Bādarāyaṇa with the Commentary of Baladeva.* Sacred Books of the Hindus. New York: AMS Press, 1974.

Harivaṁśaḥ. Critical edition by Parashuram Lakshman Vaidya. 2 vols. Poona: Bhandarkar Oriental Research Institute, 1969–1971.

Jīva Gosvāmin. *Bhāgavata-sandarbha: Tattva, Bhagavata, Paramātma, Kṛṣṇa Sandarbhas.* Sanskrit text in Bengali script. Critical notes by Haridās Śarman. Vrindaban: Pūrīdās, Gaurābda 464 (1950).

———. *Bhāgavata-sandarbha: Bhakti-Prīti Sandarbhas.* Sanskrit text in Bengali script. Critical notes by Haridās Śarman. Vrindaban: Pūrīdās, Gaurābda 465 (1951).

———. *Krama-sandarbha.* Sanskrit text in Bengali script. Critical notes by Haridās Śarman. Vrindaban: Pūrīdās, Gaurābda 466 (1952).

Kṛṣṇadāsa Kavirāja Gosvāmī. *Śrī Caitanya-caritāmṛta.* 9 vols. Original Sanskrit and Bengali text. Translated and commentary by A. C. Bhaktivedanta Swami Prabhupāda. Los Angeles: Bhaktivedanta Book Trust, [1975], 1996.

———. *Śrī Śrī Caitanya Caritāmṛta. Amṛta Pravāha-bhaṣya* Commentary by Bhaktivinoda Thakura. Calcutta: Gaudiya Mission, Caitanyābda 471 (1957).

Līlāśuka Bilvamaṅgala. *The Love of Krishna: The Kṛṣṇakarṇāmṛta of Līlāśuka Bilvamaṅgala.* Edited and translated by Frances Wilson. Philadelphia: University of Pennsylvania Press, 1975.

Schweig, Graham M. *Bhagavad Gītā: The Beloved Lord's Secret Love Song.* New York: Harper Collins Publishers, 2010.

———. *The Bhakti Sūtra: Concise Teaching of Nārada on the Divine Love.* Introduced and translated. Translations from the Asian Classics. New York: Columbia University Press, forthcoming.

———. *The Yoga Sūtra: Patañjali's Concise Teaching on Perfect Union.* New Haven, CT: Yale University Press, forthcoming.

Shri Brahma-Samhita. Sanskrit text and translation by Bhakti Siddhanta Saraswati Goswami. *Brahma-saṁhitā-ṭīkā* commentary of Jīva Gosvāmin (Sanskrit text). 2nd edition. Madras: Sree Gaudiya Math, 1958.

Viśvanātha Cakravartin. *Bhakti-rasāmṛta-sindhu-bindu.* "The Bhaktirasāmṛtasindhubindu of ViŚvanātha Cakravartin," trans. and introduction by Klaus Klostermaier. *Journal of the American Oriental Society.* Volume 94, Number 1, 96–107, January-March 1974.

———. *Śrī-Bhakti-rasāmṛta-sindhu-binduḥ.* Sanskrit text. Vṛndāvana: Śrī-Harināma, n.d.

Related Scholarship and References

Apte, Vaman Shivaram. *The Practical Sanskrit-English Dictionary.* Revised & enlarged edition. Kyoto: Rinsen Book Company, [1957] 1978.

Dasgupta, S. N. *Hindu Mysticism.* New York: Frederick Ungar Publishing Co., [1927] 1977.

De, S. K. *Early History of the Vaiṣṇava Faith and Movement in Bengal.* Calcutta: Firma K. L. Mukhopadhyay, 1961.

Eck, Diana L. *Encountering God: A Spiritual Journey from Bozeman to Banaras.* Boston: Beacon Press, 1993.

Eliade, Mircea. *Yoga: Immortality and Freedom.* Princeton, NJ: Princeton University Press, 1958.

Haberman, David L. *Acting as a Way of Salvation: A Study of Rāgānugā Bhakti Sādhana.* New York: Oxford University Press, 1988.

Hawley, John Stratton, in association with Shrivatsa Goswami. *At Play with Krishna: Pilgrimage Dramas from Brindavan.* Princeton, NJ: Princeton University Press, 1981.

Hein, Norvin J. "Caitanya's Ecstasies and the Theology of the Name." In *Hinduism: New Essays in the History of Religions*, edited by Bardwell L. Smith, 15–32. Leiden: E.J. Brill, 1976.

———. "Comments: Rādhā and Erotic Community." In *The Divine Consort: Rādhā and the Goddesses of India.* Edited by John Stratton Hawley and Donna M. Wulff, 116–124. Berkeley: Berkeley Religious Studies Series, 1982.

———. *The Miracle Plays of Mathurā.* New Haven, CT: Yale University Press, 1972.

Jung, C. G. *Mandala Symbolism.* Translated by R. F. C. Hull. The Collected Works of C. G. Jung, Vol. 9, Part 1. Princeton, NJ: Princeton University Press, 1959.

Kapoor, O. B. L. *The Philosophy and Religion of Śrī Caitanya.* Delhi: Munshiram Manoharlal Publishers Pvt. Ltd., 1976.

Klostermaier, Klaus K. "Criteria of Authenticity of Mystical Experience." *Indian Philosophical Annual*, vol. 17. University of Madras: Radhakrishnan Institute for Advanced Study in Philosophy, 1984–1985.

———. "Hṛdayavidyā: A Sketch of a Hindu-Christian Theology of Love." *Journal of Ecumenical Studies*, 765. Temple University, 1972.

Miller, Barbara Stoler. "The Divine Duality of Rādhā and Krishna" in *The Divine Consort: Rādhā and the Goddesses of India.* Edited by John Stratton Hawley and Donna M. Wulff, 13–26. Berkeley: Berkeley Religious Studies Series, 1982.

Monier-Williams, Monier. *Sanskṛit-English Dictionary.* Oxford: Oxford University Press, [1956] 1974.

Oxford American English Dictionary.

Schweig, Graham M. *Bhagavad Gītā Concordance: A Comprehensive Word Reference with English and Sanskrit Indexes.* New York: Columbia University Press, 2024.

———. "Humility and Passion: A Caitanya Vaishnava Ethics of Devotion." *Journal of Religious Ethics* 30.3, 421–444 (Fall 2002).

Sheth, S. J., Noel. *The Divinity of Krishna.* Delhi: Munshiram Manoharlal Publishers Pvt. Ltd., 1984.

Siegel, Lee. *Sacred and Profane Dimensions of Love in Indian Traditions as Exemplified in the Gītagovinda of Jayadeva.* Delhi: Oxford University Press, 1974.

Smith, Wilfred Cantwell. *What Is Scripture? A Comparative Approach.* Minneapolis: Fortress Press, 1993.

Thielemen, Selina. *Rāsalīlā: A Musical Study of Religious Drama in Vraja.* New Delhi: APH Pub. Corp., 1998.

Webster's Third New International Dictionary.

Index

For the benefit of digital users, indexed terms that span two or more pages (e.g., 52–53) may, on occasion, appear on only one of those pages.

Bolded numbers in this index indicate pages in the translations of the Rāsa Līlā, Song of the Black Bee, and Song of the Flute.

Figures are indicated by an italic f following the page number.